ENGLISH-ESPERANTO DICTIONARY • HAYES, CHARLES FREDERIC

Publisher's Note

Purchase of this book entitles you to a free trial membership in the publisher's book club at www.rarebooksclub.com. (Time limited offer.) Simply enter the barcode number from the back cover onto the membership form on our home page. The book club entitles you to select from millions of books at no additional charge. You can also download a digital copy of this and related books to read on the go. Simply enter the title or subject onto the search form to find them.

Note: This is an historic book. Pages numbers, where present in the text, refer to the first edition of the book and may also be in indexes.

If you have any questions, could you please be so kind as to consult our Frequently Asked Questions page at www.rarebooksclub.com/faqs.cfm? You are also welcome to contact us there.

Publisher: General Books LLC™, Memphis, TN, USA, 2012. ISBN: 9781153604321.

Proofreading: pgdp.net

※ ※ ※ ※ ※ ※ ※ ※

ENGLISH-ESPERANTO
DICTIONARY
BY
J. C. O'CONNOR, Ph.Dr., M.A.
AND
C. F. HAYES
COPYRIGHT
"REVIEW OF REVIEWS" OFFICE, LONDON
1906
AL
SINJORO FELIX MOSCHELES, PREZIDANTO
DE NIA SOCIETO
LA AŬTOROJ DEDIĈAS TIUN ĈI MODESTAN LIBRETON KIEL ES-

PRIMETON
DE DANKEGECO.
PREFACE.

In response to numerous requests from almost every country in which English is spoken, we have much pleasure in presenting to the public this the first English-Esperanto Dictionary. The demands for such a work became so pressing that it was absolutely necessary to issue it as quickly as possible. Were it not for this urgency we would have waited until the larger Dictionary was ready, but the knowledge that the progress of Esperanto would be materially checked or retarded decided us to issue this smaller one. The compiling of a Dictionary is always a difficult task, but the difficulty is increased in a very great degree when an initial and original work is undertaken. Such a work demands careful and thorough research, absolute precision, and much patient labour The labour, however, has been lightened by the good wishes of Esperantists all the world over. Not from England alone, but from that Greater Britain beyond the seas, kindly help has been offered, and gratefully accepted. We have spared no pains in the endeavour to make this Dictionary (within its limits) perfect, and we hope we have succeeded. The busy Briton, who has not time for word-building, will find within the following pages every ordinary English word, with its Esperanto equivalent. It has been said, and with truth, that with a perfect knowledge of one or two thousand words anyone can adequately express oneself—conversationally—on any of the ordinary topics of everyday life, and for this reason we have taken special pains to select those words which are most in use. The student who possesses a knowledge of the process of word-building can from the material within these pages extend such material to an almost unlimited extent. (For an example of this see pages 10-15).

The larger Dictionary is in course of preparation, though some time must necessarily elapse before its publication. For this the collaboration and counsel of the most eminent continental Esperantists have been secured. We shall be extremely grateful to those who use the present work for any suggestions that may render it more useful, in the event of a second edition being required, and also that the larger Dictionary may receive the benefit of such suggestions. (Any such suggestions may be sent to J. C. O'Connor, B.A., Esperanto House, St. Stephen's Square, Bayswater, W.; or to C. F. Hayes, Fairlight, 48, Swanage Road, Wandsworth, S.W.) It is to the interest of all loyal Esperantists to do what they can in anything that may help to extend the scope of this marvellous language, which our revered master has so generously given to the world.

We take this opportunity of tendering our very sincere thanks to Dr. Zamenhof for the invaluable assistance he has given us during the preparation of this little work, as well as for his *aprobita* of it; and at the same time we acknowledge our indebtedness to M. A. Motteau (Author of the Esperanto-English Dictionary) for his careful revision of the proof sheets, and for the many useful suggestions which his thorough knowledge of Esperanto enabled him to give.

Particular attention must be given to the fact that it is to the *root* of a word that the prefixes and suffixes are added. When it is stated that the final letter "i" indicates the infinitive, the letter "o" the noun, the letter "a" the adjective, the letter "e" the adverb, the letter "j" added to form the plural, etc., the pronouns "mi", "li", "vi", etc., do not interfere with the statement, for they are complete words; the letters "m", "l", and "v" are not *roots*. The word "do" is not a noun, because "d" is not a root. The word "plej" is not a plural, because "ple" is not a root. The word "meti", to put, has nothing to do with the diminutive suffix "et", because "m" is not the *root*.

The reader of this Dictionary will see to which part of speech the English word belongs, by looking at the ending of the Esperanto translation of the word.

The Authors.

QUICK LINKS

A 3
B 7
C 11
D 17
E 21
F 23
G 26
H 28
I 30
J 33
K 33
L 34
M 36
N 39
O 41
P 42
Q 49
R 49
S 53
T 61
U 64
V 66
W 67
Y 70
Z 70

PREFIXES.

bo'—denotes relationship resulting from marriage:

patro, father, *bo'patro*, father-in-law.
patrino, mother, *bo'patrino*, mother-in-law.

dis'—denotes division, separation, dissemination:

semi, to sow, *dis'semi*, to scatter.
ŝiri, to tear, *dis'ŝiri*, to tear in pieces.

ek'—denotes an action just begun, also short duration of an action:

kanti, to sing, *ek'kanti*, to begin to sing.
ridi, to laugh, *ek'ridi*, to burst out laughing.

ge'—denotes persons of both sexes taken together:

mastro, master, *ge'mastroj*, master and mistress.
edzo, husband, *ge'edzoj*, husband and wife.

mal'—denotes contraries, opposition of idea:

estimi, to esteem, *mal'estimi*, to despise.
varma, warm, *mal'varma*, cold.
amiko, friend, *mal'amiko*, enemy.

re'—denotes the repetition of an act; it corresponds to the English "re," *back* or *again*:

doni, to give, *re'doni*, to give back; *iri*, to go, *re'iri*, to go again.
diri, to say, *re'diri*, to repeat; *veni*, to come, *re'veni*, to return.

SUFFIXES.

'ad'—denotes duration or continuation of an action:

spiri, to breathe, *spir'ad'o*, breathing.
pafi, to fire (a gun, etc.), *paf'ad'o*, a fusilade.

'aĵ'—denotes a thing having a certain quality, something made from a certain matter:

mola, soft, *mol'aĵ'o*, a soft thing or substance.
ovo, egg, *ov'aĵ'o*, omelet; *bovo*, ox, *bov'aĵ'o*, beef.

'an'—denotes an inhabitant, partisan, member of:

Londono, London, *London'an'o*, a Londoner.
Kristo, Christ, *Krist'an'o*, a Christian.

'ar'—denotes a collection or reunion of certain things:

vorto, a word, *vort'ar'o*, a dictionary.
homo, a man, *hom'ar'o*, mankind.

'ĉj'—inserted between 1-5 letters of a masculine name denotes a term of endearment:

Johano, John, *Jo'ĉj'o*, Jack, Johnnie.
Ernesto, Ernest, *Erne'ĉj'o*, Ernie.

'ebl'—denotes possibility, something likely to happen:

legi, to read, *leg'ebl'a*, legible.
kredi, to believe, *kred'ebl'a*, credible.

'ec'—denotes an abstract quality (similar to the English suffix *ness*):

bona, good, *bon'ec'o*, goodness.
pura, clean, *pur'ec'o*, cleanliness.

'eg'—denotes augmentation, intensity of degree:

granda, great, *grand'eg'a*, enormous.
pafilo, gun, *pafil'eg'o*, cannon.

'ej'—denotes the place specially used for or allotted to:

dormi, to sleep, *dorm'ej'o*, a dormitory.
lerni, to learn, *lern'ej'o*, a school.

'em'—denotes propensity, inclination, disposition:

timi, to fear, *tim'em'a*, timorous.
amo, love, *am'em'a*, lovable.

'er'—denotes one of many objects of the same kind, the smallest fragment:

sablo, sand, *sabl'er'o*, a grain of sand.
mono, money, *mon'er'o*, a coin.

'estr'—denotes a chief, a leader, a ruler, the head of:

imperio, an empire, *imperi'estr'o*, an emperor.
ŝipo, a ship, *ŝip'estr'o*, captain (of a ship).

'et'—denotes diminution of degree:

ridi, to laugh, *rid'et'i*, to smile.
monto, a mountain, *mont'et'o*, a hill.

'id'—denotes the young of, offspring, descendant:

kato, a cat, *kat'id'o*, a kitten.
Izraelo, Israel, *Izrael'id'o*, an Israelite.

'ig'—denotes causing to be in a certain state or condition:

morti, to die, *mort'ig'i*, to kill (to *cause* to die).
pura, clean, *pur'ig'i*, to clean (to make clean).

'iĝ'—denotes to become, to be made to:

ruĝa, red, *ruĝ'iĝ'i*, to become red (to blush).
riĉa, rich, *riĉ'iĝ'i*, to become (or to grow) rich.

'il'—denotes an instrument or tool:

kombi, to comb, *komb'il'o*, a comb.
razi, to shave, *raz'il'o*, a razor.

'in'—denotes feminines:

frato, brother, *frat'in'o*, sister.
leono, lion, *leon'in'o*, lioness.

'ind'—denotes worthiness, to be "worthy of," "deserving of":

laŭdi, to praise, *laŭd'ind'a*, praiseworthy, worthy of praise.
estimi, to esteem, *estim'ind'a*, estimable, worthy of esteem.

'ing'—denotes a holder (thing), that which is used for holding *one* object:

cigaro, a cigar, *cigar'ing'o*, a cigar holder.
kandelo, a candle, *kandel'ing'o*, a candlestick.

'ist'—denotes profession, trade, occupation, etc.:

drogo, a drug, *drog'ist'o*, druggist.

maro, the sea, *mar'ist'o*, a sailor.

'nj'—has the same force as the suffix *ĉj*, but is used for feminine names only.

'uj'—denotes that which contains, produces, encloses or bears:

pomo, apple, *pom'uj'o*, apple-tree; *mono*, money, *mon'uj'o*, a purse. *Anglo*, Englishman, *Angl'uj'o*, England; *cigaro*, a cigar, *cigar'uj'o*, a cigar-case.

"Tree" may also be expressed by *arbo*, *pomarbo*, an apple tree. Names of countries may also be denoted by *lando*, as *Anglolando*, England, *Francolando*, France, *Irlando*, Ireland.

'ul'—denotes a person or being characterised by the idea contained in a root-word:

timo, fear, *tim'ul'o*, a coward, a poltroon.
avara, miserly, *avar'ul'o*, a miserly person (a miser).

moŝto—this word denotes a general title of respect or politeness:

reĝo, a king, *via reĝa moŝto*, your Majesty.
via moŝto, your highness, your eminence, your worship.

HOW TO USE THE PREFIXES AND SUFFIXES.

	Esperanto.	Free Translation.
	Lern'	root word.
i	Lerni	to learn.
ad	Lernadi	" study.
eg	Lernegi	" cram.
ig	Lernigi	" cause to learn.
iĝ	Lerniĝi	" learn intuitively.
et	Lerneti	" dabble in learning.
dis	Dislerni	" learn in a desultory manner.
ek	Eklerni	" begin to learn.
el	Ellerni	" learn thoroughly.
mal	Mallerni	" unlearn.
re	Relerni	" learn again.
ant	Lernanto	a pupil, a learner (mas.).
"	Lernantino	a pupil, a learner (fem.).
an	Lernejano	a schoolboy.
"	Lernejanino	a schoolgirl.
ge	Gelernantoj	pupils (mas. and fem.).
ist	Lernejisto	a school teacher.
estr	Lernejestro	a school master (head teacher). [Error in book: Lernjestro]
ant	Lernantaro	a class.
ej	Lernejo	a school.
et	Lernejeto	an elementary school.
ar	Lernejaro	an university.
ul	Lernulc	a learned man, a savant.
"	Lernulino	a learned woman, a "blue stocking."
aĵ	Lernaĵc	knowledge.
il	Lernilo	intelligence (the).
ind	Lerninda	worth learning.
o	Lerno	act or action of learning.
ebl	Lernebla	learnable.
ec	Lerneco	learnedness.
em	Lernema	studious.
er	Lernero	a subject of a curriculum.
ar	Lernaro	a curriculum.
a	Lerna	learned.
e	Lerne	learnedly.

ABBREVIATIONS.

Adj.	Adjective.	Math.	Math.
Adv.	Adverb.	Med.	Med.
Anat.	Anatomy.	Milit.	Milit.
Arith.	Arithmetic.	Mus.	Mus.
Bot.	Botany.	N.	Nou.
Conj.	Conjunction.	Phil.	Phil.
Fem. F.	Feminine.	Plur.	Plu.
Fig.	Figurative.	Polit.	Pol.
Geog.	Geography.	Prep.	Pre.
Gram.	Grammar.	Prof.	Pro.
Inter.	Interjection.	Relig.	Rel.
Intrans.	Intransitive.	Sing. S.	Sin.
Jud.	Judicial.	Trans.	Tra.
Lit.	Literary.	V.	Ve.
Mas. M.	Masculine.	Zool.	Zo.

ENGLISH-ESPERANTO.

A USEFUL DICTIONARY FOR STUDENTS OF ESPERANTO.

The attention of the reader is particularly called to paragraph 2, page ix., of Preface.

A

A, indefinite article, not used in Esperanto.
Aback, to take, surprizi.
Abaft, posta parto.
Abandon, forlasi.
Abase, humiligi. [Error in book: humilgi]
Abash, hontigi.
Abate (lower), mallevi.
Abate (speed), malakceli.
Abbey, abatejo.
Abbot, abato.
Abbreviate, mallongigi.
Abdicate, demeti la reĝecon.
Abdomen, ventro.
Abduct, forrabi.
Abduction, forrabo.
Abed, lite.
Aberration, spiritvagado.
Abet, kunhelpi.
Abhor, malamegi.
Abhorrence, malamego.
Abide, loĝi (resti).
Ability, lerteco.
Ability, talento.
Abject, humilega.
Abjure, malkonfesi, forĵuri.
Ablative, ablativo.
Able, to be, povi.
Able (skilful), lerta.
Abnegation, memforgeso.
Aboard, en ŝipo.
Angel, anĝelo.
Angelic, anĝela.
Anger, kolero.
Anger, kolerigi.
Angle (corner), angulo.
Angling, fiŝkaptado.
Angle (fish), fiŝkapti.
Angler, fiŝkaptisto.
Angry, to be, koleri.
Anguish, dolorego.
Angular, angula.
Animal, besto.
Animate, vivigi.
Animated, vivigita.
Animating, viviga.
Animation, viveco.
Animosity, malamikeco.
Aniseed, anizo.
Anisette, anizlikvoro.
Ankle, maleolo.
Annals, historio.
Annex, kunigi.
Annexation, kunigo.
Annihilate, neniigi.
Anniversary, datreveno.
Annotate, noti.
Announce, anonci.
Announcement, anonco.
Annoy, ĉagreni.

Abode, loĝejo.
Abolish, neniigi.
Abominable, abomena.
Abomination, abomeno.
Abound, sufiĉegi.
About (prep.), ĉirkaŭ.
About (adv.), ĉirkaŭe.
Above (prep.), super.
Above (adv.), supre.
Above all, precipe.
Abreast, flanko ĉe flanko.
Abridge, mallongigi.
Abridgement, resumo.
Abroad, eksterlande.
Abrupt, subita.
Abscess, absceso.
Abscond, sin forkaŝi.
Absent, to be, foresti.
Absence, foresto—ado.
Absolute, absoluta.
Absolutely, absolute.
Absolution, senkulpigo.
Absolution (from sin), senpekigo.
Absolve, senkulpigi.
Absolve (from sin), senpekigi.
Absorb, sorbi.
Absorption, sorbo.
Abstain, deteni sin.
Abstemious, sobrema.
Abstinence, deteno.
Abstinent, detene-
Annoyance, ĉagreno, enuo.
Annual (publication), jarlibro.
Annual (yearly), ĉiujara.
Annuity, jarpago.
Annul, nuligi.
Annular, ringforma.
Annunciation, anunciacio.
Anoint, ŝmiri.
Anointing, ŝmiro, ado.
Anomaly, anomalio.
Anonymous, anonima.
Answer, respondi.
Answer (affirmatively), jesi.
Answerable for, to be, respondi pri.
Ant, formiko.
Antagonist, kontraŭulo.
Antarctic, antarktika.
Antecedents, antaŭaĵo.
Antechamber, antaŭĉambro.
Antedate, antaŭdatumi.
Antelope, antilopo.
Anterior, antaŭa.
Anteroom, antaŭĉambro.
Anthem, antemo, himnego.
Ant-hill, formikejo.
Anthropology, antropologio.
Antichrist, antikristo.
Anticipate, antaŭvidi.
Antidote, kontraŭveneno.
Antimony, antimono.
Antipathy, antipa-
ma.
Abstract (abridgement), resumo.
Abstract, abstrakti.
Abstracted, abstrakta.
Abstruse, tre malklara.
Absurd, absurda.
Absurdity, absurdo.
Abundance, sufiĉego.
Abuse, trouzi.
Abuse, trouzo.
Abyss, profundegaĵo.
Acacia, akacio.
Academic, akademia.
Academy, akademio.
Accede, konsenti.
Accelerate, akceli.
Accent (sign, mark), signo.
Accent, akcenti.
Accent, akcento.
Accentuate, akcentegi.
Accept, akcepti.
Acceptable, akceptebla.
Acceptance, akceptaĵo.
Acceptation, akcepto.
Access, aliro.
Accession, plimultigo.
Accessory, kunhelpanto.
Accident (chance), okazo.
Accident (injury), malfeliĉo.
Acclamation, aplaŭdego.
Acclimatize, alklimatigi.
Acclivity, supreniro.
Accommodate, al-
tio.
Antipodes, antipodoj.
Antiquary, antikvisto.
Antiquated, antikva.
Antique, antikva.
Antique (noun), antikvaĵo.
Antiquity, antikveco.
Antler, kornbranĉo.
Anvil, amboso.
Anxiety, maltrankvileco.
Anxious, maltrankvila.
Any, ia.
Anybody, iu.
Anyhow, iel.
Anyone, iu.
Anyone's, ies.
Any quantity, iom.
Anything, io.
Anywhere, ie.
Aorta, aorto.
Apace, rapide.
Apart, aparte.
Apartment, ĉambro.
Apathetic, apatia.
Apathy, apatio.
Ape, simio.
Ape (verb), imiti.
Aperient, laksileto.
Aperture, malfermaĵo.
Apex, pinto, suprapinto.
Apiary, abelejo.
Apish, simia.
Apocryphal, apokrifa.
Apogee, apogeo.
Apologise, pardonon peti.
Apologue, apologo.
Apology, apologio.
Apoplexy,
fari.
Accompany, akompani.
Accomplice, kunkulpulo.
Accomplish, plenumi.
Accomplished (of things), elfarita.
Accomplishment, talento.
Accord (music), akordo.
Accord, konsento.
According to, laŭ.
Accouchement, akuŝo.
Account (bill), kalkulo.
Account, rakonto.
Accountable, to be, respondi pri.
Accountant (profn.), kalkulisto.
Account (current), konto kuranta.
Accounts, kalkularo.
Account (rendered), raporto.
Accoutre (milit.), armi.
Accrue, kreskiĝi.
Accumulate, amasigi.
Accumulation, amaso.
Accuracy, akurateco.
Accurate, akurata.
Accursed, malbena.
Accusation, kulpigo.
Accusative, akuzativo.
Accuse, kulpigi.
Accustomed, to be, kutimi.
Ace, aso.
Acerbity, acideco.
Acetous, acida.
Ache, doloro.
Achieve, plenumi.
apopleksio.
Apostle, apostolo.
Apostolic, apostola.
Apostrophe, apostrofo.
Apostrophize, alparoli.
Apothecary, apotekisto.
Apothecary's, apoteko.
Apotheosis, apoteozo.
Appal, terurigi.
Apparatus, aparato.
Apparel, vesto.
Apparent, videbla.
Apparition, apero.
Apparitor (beadle), pedelo.
Appeal, alvoki.
Appear (come in sight), aperi.
Appear, ŝajni.
Appearance (aspect), vidiĝo, mieno.
Appearance, to put in an, ĉeesti.
Appease, pacigi.
Append, aldoni.
Appendage, aldonaĵo.
Appendix, aldono.
Appetising, apetitdona.
Appetite, apetito.
Applaud, aplaŭdi.
Applause, aplaŭdo—ado.
Apple, pomo.
Apple tree, pomarbo, pomujo.
Appliance, aparato.
Application, atento.
Apply (to put on), almeti.
Apply to, sin turni (al).
Appoint (nominate), nomi.

Achievement, elfaro.
Acid, acida.
Acid, acido.
Acidity, acideco.
Acidulous, acideta.
Acknowledge, konfesi.
Acknowledge (letters, etc.), avizi.
Acknowledgement (letters, etc.), avizo.
Acknowledgment, konfeso.
Aconite, akonito.
Acorn, glano.
Acoustics, akustiko.
Acquaint, sciigi.
Acquaintance, konato.
Acquainted, to be, konatiĝi.
Acquiesce, konsenti.
Acquire, akiri.
Acquirement, akiro.
Acquisition, akiraĵo.
Acquit (debt), kvitanci.
Acquit (blame), senkulpigi.
Acrid, acida.
Acrimonious, akretema.
Acrobat, ekvilibristo.
Across, trans.
Act, agi.
Act (statute), regulo, leĝo.
Act (drama), akto.
Action, to bring an, procesi.
Active, aktiva.
[Error in book: activa]
Activity, aktiveco.
Actor, aktoro.
Actor (drama), komediisto.

Appointment, elekto.
Apportion, lotumi, dividi.
Appraise, taksi.
Appreciate, ŝati.
Apprehend (seize), ekkapti.
Apprehend (understand), kompreni.
Apprehension (fear), timo.
Apprentice, lernanto.
Apprenticeship, lernado.
Apprise, sciigi, informi.
Approach, proksimiĝi.
Approaching (time), baldaŭa.
Approbation, aprobo.
Appropriate, to be, difinita por.
Appropriate (take, keep), proprigi.
Approval, aprobo.
Approve, aprobi.
Approximate (time), baldaŭa.
Apricot, abrikoto.
April, Aprilo.
Apron, antaŭtuko.
Apt, kapabla.
Aptitude, kapableco.
Aptly, kapable.
Aquatic, akva.
Aqueduct, akvokonduko.
Aqueous, akva.
Arab, Arabo.
Arable, plugebla.
Arbitrary, arbitra.
Arbitrate, arbitracii.
Arbitration, arbitracio.
Arbitrator (profn.), arbitraciisto.
Arbour, laŭbo.
Arc, arko.

Actual (time), nuna.
Actual, reala.
Actuality, nuneco, realeco.
Actuated, incitita.
Acumen, sagaceco.
Acute, akra.
Acuteness, sagaceco.
Adage, proverbo.
Adapt, alfari.
Adaptation, alfarado.
Add up, sumigi.
Add together, kunmeti.
Add to, aldoni.
Addendum, aldono.
Adder, kolubro.
Addicted, to be, kutimi.
Addition, aldono.
Additional, aldona.
Addled, senfrukta.
Address, adresi.
Adduce, prezenti.
Adept, adepto.
Adequate, sufiĉa.
Adhere, aliĝi.
Adherent, aliĝulo.
Adhesion, aliĝo.
Adhesive, glua.
Adieu, adiaŭ.
Adjacent, apuda.
Adjective, adjektivo.
Adjoining, apuda.
Adjourn, prokrasti.
Adjudge, aljuĝi.
Adjure, petegi.
Adjust, aranĝi, almezuri.
Administer, administri.
Administration, administracio.
Admirable, admirinda.
Admiral, admiralo.

Arcade, arkado.
Arch, arko.
Arch, arkefleksi.
Archangel, ĉefanĝelo.
Archæology, arheologio.
Archbishop, ĉefepiskopo.
Archduke, arĥiduko.
Archer, pafarkisto.
Archipelago, insularo.
Architect, arĥitekturisto.
Architecture, arĥitekturo.
Archives, arĥivo.
Arctic, arktika.
Ardent, fervora.
Ardour, fervoro.
Arduous, laborega.
Arena, areno.
Areopagus, Aeropago.
Argue, argumenti.
Argument, argumento.
Arid, seka.
Aright, bone.
Arise, leviĝi.
Aristocracy, aristokrataro.
Aristocrat, aristokrato.
Arithmetic, aritmetiko.
Ark, ŝipego.
Arm (milit.), armi.
Arm (of the body), brako.
Armament, armilaro.
Armchair, seĝego.
Armistice, interpaco.
Armlet, ĉirkaŭbrako.
Armorials, insigno.
Armour, armaĵo.
Armourer, armil-

Admiration, admiro.
Admire, admiri.
Admission, allaso.
Admissible, permesebla.
Admit, allasi.
Admonish, admoni.
Admonition, admono.
Adolescence, juneco.
Adolescent, junulo.
Adopt, alpreni.
Adopt (child), filigi.
Adore, adori.
Adorn, ornami.
Adroit, lerta.
Adroitness, lerteco.
Adulation, adulacio. flato.
Adult, plenkreskulo.
Adult, plenkreska.
Adulterate, falsi.
Adultery, adulto.
Adultery, to commit, adulti.
Advance, antaŭeniri.
Advancement, progreso.
Advantage, utilo, profito.
Advantageous, utila, profita.
Advent, advento.
Adverb, adverbo.
Adversary, kontraŭulo.
Adverse, kontraŭa.
Adversity, kontraŭeco.
Advert to (to), aluci (al).
Advertise, anonci.
Advertisement, anonco.
Advice, konsilo.
Advise, konsili.

faristo.
Armoury, armilejo.
Armpit, subbrako.
Arms (weapons), armiloj, bataliloj.
Army (military), militistaro.
Army (non-military), armeo.
Army-corps, korpuso.
Arnica, arniko.
Aroma, aromo.
Aromatic, aroma.
Around (prep.), ĉirkaŭ.
Around (adv.), ĉirkaŭe.
Arouse, veki.
Arpeggio, arpeĝo.
Arraign, kulpigi.
Arrange, aranĝi.
Arrant, fama.
Array (deck out), ornami.
Arrears, in, malantaŭe.
Arrest, aresti.
Arrival, alveno.
Arrive (on foot), alveni.
Arrive (by vehicle), alveturi.
Arrogance, aroganteco.
Arrogant, aroganta.
Arrow, sago.
Arsenal, armilejo.
Arsenic, arseniko.
Arson, brulkrimo.
Art, arto.
Artery, arterio.
Artful, ruza.
Arthritic, artritulo.
Artichoke, artiŝoko.
Article, artikolo.
Article (commerce), komercaĵo.
Articulate, elparoli.
Articulation (anat.

Advocate, defendi.
Aerial, aera.
Aerolite, aerolito.
Aeronaut, aerveturanto.
Afar, malproksime.
Affable, afabla.
Affability, afableco.
Affair, afero.
Affected (manner), afekta.
Affected, to be, afekti.
Affecting (touching), kortuŝanta.
Affection, afekteco.
Affection (love), amo.
Affectionate, aminda.
Affectionately, aminde.
Affinity (relationship), parenceco.
Affiliate, aligi, anigi.
Affiliated, to become, aliĝi, aniĝi.
Affirm (attest), atesti.
Affirm (assure), certigi.
Affirmation, atesto.
Affirmation, certigo, jeso.
Affirmative, jesa.
Affix, afikso.
Afflict, malĝojigi.
Affluence, riĉeco.
Affluent, riĉega.
Afford, to give, doni.
Affray, batiĝo.
Affright, timigi.
Affront, insulto.
Afloat, flose, naĝe.
Afraid, timigita.
Aft, posta parto.
After, post.

), artiko.
Artifice, artifiko.
Artificial, artefarita.
Artillery, artilerio.
Artisan, metiisto.
Artist, artisto.
Artless, simplanima, naiva.
Artlessness, naiveco.
As, kiel.
As—as, tiel—kiel.
Ascend, supreniri.
Ascension (feast of), Ĉieliro.
Ascension, suprenirado.
Ascent, supreniro.
Ascertain, certiĝi.
Ascribe, aligi al.
Ashamed, to be, honti.
Ashes, cindro.
Ashpan, cindrujo.
Asia, Azio.
Asiatic, Aziano.
Aside, aparte.
As if, kvazaŭ.
Ask, demandi.
Ask (beg), peti.
Asleep, dormanta (adj.), dormante (adv.).
As long as, tiel longe kiel.
As many, tiom.
As much, tiom.
As many as, tiom, kiom.
As much as, tiom, kiom.
Asp, aspido.
Asparagus, asparago.
Aspect, vidiĝo.
Aspect (phase), fazo.
Aspen, tremolo.
Asperse, kalumnii.
Asphalte, asfalto.
Asphyxia, asfiksio.
Aspirate, elspiri.

Aftermath, postfojno.
Afternoon, posttagmezo.
Afterwards, poste.
Again, ree.
Against, kontraŭ.
Agate, agato.
Age, aĝo.
Aged, maljuna.
Agency, agenteco.
Agenda, memorlibro.
Agent, agento.
Aggrandize, pligrandigi.
Aggrandisement, pligrandigo.
Aggravate, plimalbonigi.
Aggression, atako.
Aggressor, atakanto.
Aghast, terurega.
Agile, facilmova.
Agitate, agiti.
Ago, antaŭ.
Agonize, agonii.
Agony, agonio.
Agree, konsenti.
Agreeable, agrabla.
Agreement (deed), kontrakto.
Agreement, interkonsento.
Agriculture, terkulturo.
Agriculturist, terkulturisto.
Agronomy, agronomio.
Ague, febreto.
Ah! ha!
Ahead, antaŭe.
Aid, helpo.
Aide-de-Camp, adjutanto.
Ail, malsani.
Ailment, malsano.
Aim (purpose), celo.
Air (appearance), mieno.
Air (music), ario.

Aspirant, aspiranto.
Aspiration (breathing), elspiro—ado.
Aspiration (aim, intention), celo.
Aspire, celi.
Ass, azeno.
Assail, ataki.
Assailant, atakanto.
Assassin, mortiganto.
Assault, atako.
Assay, provo.
Assemble, kunveni, kunvoki.
Assembly, kunveno, aŭditorio.
Assent, konsenti, jesi.
Assert, certigi.
Assess, taksi.
Assessment, takso.
Assiduous, diligenta.
Assign, asigni.
Assignment, asigno.
Assimilate, similigi.
Assist, helpi.
Assist (at), ĉeesti (ĉe).
Assistance, helpo.
Assistant, helpanto.
Assistant-master, submajstro.
Associate, kunulo.
Association, societo.
Assort, dece kunmeti.
Assuage, dolĉigi.
Assume, supozi.
Assurance, self, memfido.
Assure, certigi.
Assure (life etc.), asekuri.
Asterisk, steleto.
Asthma, malfacila

Air, aerumi.
Air (atmosphere), aero.
Airball (toy), pilkego.
Airballoon, aerostato.
Airhole, fenestreto.
Airpump, aeroumpilo. [Error in book: aeropompilo]
Aisle, flankaĵo.
Ajar, duonfermita.
Akin, parenca.
Alabaster, alabastro.
Alacrity, rapideco.
Alarm, maltrankviligi.
Alarum (clock), vekhorloĝo.
Alas! ho ve!
Albeit, kvankam.
Album, albumo.
Albumen, albumeno.
Alchemy, alĥemio.
Alcohol, alkoholo.
Alcoholic, alkohola.
Alcoholism, alkoholismo.
Alcove, alkovo.
Alder (tree), alno.
Ale, biero.
Alert, vigla.
Algebra, algebro.
Alias, alie.
Alien, alilandulo.
Alike, simila.
Aliment, manĝaĵo.
Alimony, nutramono.
Alive, viva.
Alkali, alkalio.
All (every one), ĉiu, ĉiuj (plur.).
Allay, trankviligi, kvietigi.
Allege, pretendi.

spirado.
Astonish, mirigi.
Astonished, to be, miri.
Astonishing, mira.
Astonishment, miro.
Astound, miregi.
Astral, astra.
Astray, to go, erariĝi.
Astringent, kuntira.
Astrologer, astrologiisto.
Astrology, astrologio.
Astronomer, astronomiisto.
Astronomy, astronomio.
Astute, ruza.
Asunder, aparte.
Asylum, rifuĝejo.
At, ĉe, je.
At (house of), ĉe.
At all events, kio ajn okazos.
At any time, iam.
Atheist, ateisto.
Atheism, ateismo.
Athletic, atleta.
Athlete, atleto.
Atlas, landkartaro.
Atmosphere, atmosfero.
Atom, atomo.
Atomism, atomismo.
At once, tuj.
Atone, rebonigi.
Atonement, rebonigo.
Atrocious, kruelega.
Atrocity, kruelego.
Atrophy, atrofio.
Attach, alligi.
Attachment, alligo.
Attack, atako.
Attack, ataki.
Attain, atingi.
Attain (to), trafi,

Allegiance, fideleco.
Allegory, alegorio.
Alleviate, dolĉigi.
Alley, aleo, strateto.
Alliance, interligo.
Allocution, paroladeto.
Allot, lotumi.
Allotment, lotaĵo.
Allow, permesi.
Allowance (a/c), dekalkulo.
Allowance (share), porcio.
All-powerful, ĉiopova.
Allude, aludi.
Allure, logi.
Allurement, logo.
Allusion, aludo.
Alluvial, akvemetita.
Ally, interligi.
Almanac, almanako.
Almighty, ĉiopova.
Almost, preskaŭ.
Almond, migdalo.
Alms, almozo.
Almshouse, maljunulejo.
Aloes, aloo.
Aloft, supre.
Alone, sola (adj.), sole (adv.).
Along with, kune kun.
Aloof, to keep, eviti.
Aloud, laŭte.
Alphabet, alfabeto.
Alps, Alpoj.
Already, jam.
Also, ankaŭ.
Altar, altaro.
Alter, aliigi.
Alteration, aliigo.
Altercation, malpaco.

Alternate, alterni.
Alternative, elekteco.
Althea, alteo.
Although, kvankam.
Altitude, alto.
Alto, aldo.
Altogether, tute.
Alum, aluno.
Always, ĉiam.
Amalgam, amalgamo.
Amalgamate, unuigi.
Amalgamation, unuigo.
Amanuensis, skribisto.
Amass, amasigi.
Amateur, nemetiisto.
Amaze, miregigi.
Amazed, to be, miregiĝi.
Amazement, mirego.
Amazing, miriga.
Amazon, rajdantino.
Ambassador, ambasadoro.
Amber, sukceno.
Ambiguous, dusenca.
Ambition, ambicio.
Ambitious, ambicia.
Amble, troteti.
Ambrosia, ambrozio.
Ambulance (place), malsanulejo.
Ambuscade, embusko.
Ambush, embuski.
Ameliorate, plibonigi.
Amend, reformi.
Amends, to make, rekompenci.
America, Ameriko.

August (month), Aŭgusto.
August, nobla.
Aunt, onklino.
Aureola, aŭreolo.
Au revoir, ĝis revido.
Auriferous, orhava.
Auscultate, subaŭskulti.
Auspices, aŭspicioj.
Auspicious, favora.
Austere, severmora.
Austerely, severmore.
Austerity, severmoreco.
Australia, Aŭstralio.
Austrian, Aŭstro.
Authentic, vera, verega.
Authenticate, verigi.
Author, aŭtoro.
Authorise (permit), permesi.
Authorities (of town, etc.), estraro.
Authority, aŭtoritato.
Autocrat, aŭtokrato.
Automatic, aŭtomata.
Automobile, aŭtomobilo.
Autumn, aŭtuno.
Auxiliary, helpanto (noun), helpa (adj.).
Avalanche, lavango.
Avarice, avareco.
Avaricious, avara.
Avaunt, for de tie ĉi!
Avenge, venĝi.
Avenue, aleo.
Average (n.),

American, Amerikano.
Amiability, amindeco.
Amiable, afabla, aminda.
Amicably, pace.
Amid, meze.
Amidst, meze.
Amity, amikeco.
Ammonia, amoniako.
Among, inter.
Amongst, inter.
Amorous, amema.
Amount, sumo.
Amphibious, amfibia.
Amphitheatre, amfiteatro.
Amphora, amforo.
Ample, sufiĉa.
Amplify, grandigi.
Amplitude, amplekso.
Amputate, detranĉi.
Amulet, talismano.
Amuse, amuzi.
Anagram, anagramo.
Analogy, analogio.
Analysis, analizo.
Analyze, analizi.
Anarchy, anarĥio.
Anatomy, anatomio.
Ancestors, praavoj, prapatroj.
Anchor, ankro.
Anchorite, dezertulo.
Ancient, antikva.
And, kaj.
Anecdote, rakonteto.
Anew, ankoraŭ, ree

B

Babble, babili.
Babe, infaneto.
Baboon, paviano.
Baby, infaneto.

mezonombro.
meza kvanto.
Averse, antipatia, kontraŭa.
Aversion, antipatio, kontraŭo.
Avert, deturni.
Avidity, avideco.
Avid, avida.
Avoid, eviti.
Avow, konfesi.
Avowal, konfeso.
Await, atendi.
Awake, veki.
Awake (intrans.), vekiĝi.
Awaken, veki.
Award, aljuĝi.
Aware, to be, scii.
Away!, for!
Away, malproksime.
Awe, teruro, timego.
Awful, terura.
Awkward, mallerta, malgracia.
Awl, borileto.
Awning, sunŝirmilego.
Awry, malrekta.
Axe, hakilo.
Axis, akso.
Axle, akso.
Axle-tree, akso.
Axiom, aksiomo.
Ay (yes), jes.
Aye (always), ĉiam.
Azote, azoto.
Azure, lazuro.

Blanch, paliĝi.
Bland, afabla.
Blanket, lankovrilo.

Bachelor, fraŭlo.
Back (of body), dorso.
Back (reverse side), posta flanko.
Back (behind), poste.
Backbite, kalumnii.
Backbone, spino.
Backslider, rekulpulo.
Backward (slow), mallerta.
Bacon, lardo.
Bad, ly, malbona, e.
Badge, simbolo.
Badger, melo.
Bag, sako.
Bagatelle (trifle), bagatelo.
Baggage, pakaĵo.
Bail, garantiaĵo.
Bailiff (legal), juĝa persekutisto.
Bait, allogaĵo.
Bake, baki.
Baker, panisto, bakisto.
Balance (scales), pesilo.
Balance (poise), balanci.
Balance of a/c, restaĵo.
Balance-sheet, bilanco.
Balcony, balkono.
Bald, senhara.
Baldness, senhareco.
Bale, pakego.
Baleful, pereiga.
Balk, malhelpi.
Ball (globe), globo.
Ball (playing), pilko.
Ball (party), balo.
Ball (bullet), kuglo.
Ballad, balado.
Ballast, balasto.

Blaspheme, blasfemi.
Blast, blovego.
Blaze, flamegi.
Bleach, blankigi.
Bleat, bleki.
Bleed (trans.), sangeltiri.
Bleed (intrans.), sangadi.
Blemish, makulo.
Blend, miksi.
Bless, beni.
Blessing, beno—ado.
Blight, velkigi.
Blind, blinda.
Blind, window, rulkurteno.
Blindness, blindeco.
Blind-alley, senelirejo.
Bliss, feliĉegeco.
Blister, veziko.
Blister (plaster), vezikigilo.
Blithe, gaja.
Bloat, ŝveli.
Block (pulley), rulbloko.
Block (log), ŝtipo.
Blockade, blokado.
Blockhead, malsaĝulo.
Blond, blonda.
Blood, sango.
Bloodshed, sangverŝo—ado.
Bloodvessel, sangvejno.
Bloom, flori.
Blossom, flori.
Blot, makulo.
Blotch, skabio.
Blotting paper, sorba papero.
Blow (stroke), bato.
Blow, blovi.
Blouse, kitelo.
Blow (of flowers), ekflori.
Bludgeon, bas-

Ballet, baleto.
Balloon, aerostato.
Balloon (plaything), aerpilkego.
Ballot, voĉdoni.
Balm, balzamo.
Balm-mint, meliso.
Balsam, balzamo.
Balustrade, balustrado.
Bamboo, bambuo.
Banana, banano.
Band (strap), ligilo.
Band (gang, troop), bando.
Bandage, bandaĝi.
Bandit, malbonulo, rabulo.
Bane, pereigo.
Baneful, pereiga.
Banish (exile), ekzili.
Banish (send away), forpeli.
Bank (money), banko.
Bank (river), bordo.
Bank (sand), sablaĵo.
Bank (note), banka bileto.
Banker, bankiero.
Bankrupt, bankroto.
Bankrupt, to become, bankroti.
Banner, flago, standardo.
Banns, edziĝanonco.
Banquet, festeno.
Banter, moki.
Baptism, bapto.
Baptize, bapti.
Bar, bari.
Barbarian, barbaro.
Barbarism, barbarismo.
Barber, barbiro.

tonego.
Blue, blua.
Bluish, dubeblua.
Blunder, erarego.
Blunt, malakra.
Blunt (mannered), malafabla.
Blur, malpurigi.
Blush, ruĝiĝi.
Bluster, fanfaroni.
Boa, boao.
Boar, porkviro.
Board (food), nutrado—aĵo.
Board (plank), tabulo.
Board, loĝi.
Boarder (house), loĝanto.
Boarder (school), edukato.
Boarding school, edukejo.
Boarding-house, loĝantejo.
Boast, fanfaroni.
Boast, fanfarono.
Boaster, fanfaronulo.
Boat, boato.
Boatman, boatisto.
Boat-hook, hokstango.
Boat-race, ŝipkurado.
Boat (rowing), remboato.
Bobbin, bobeno.
Body, korpo.
Bog, marĉego.
Bohemian, Bohemo.
Boil (blain), furunko.
Boil, boli.
Boiler (saucepan), bolpoto.
Boiler, bolegilo.
Boisterous, perforta.
Bold, maltima.
Boldness, maltimo.
Bolster, kap-

Bard, bardo.
Bare, nuda.
Barefoot, nudpiede.
Bargain, marĉandi.
Barge, ŝarĝbarko.
Bark (ship), barko.
Bark (of dog), hundobleko, bojo.
Bark (of tree), ŝelo.
Bark (a tree), senŝeligi.
Barley, hordeo.
Barm, feĉo.
Barn, garbejo.
Barometer, barometro.
Baron, barono.
Barrack, soldatejo.
Barrel, barelo.
Barrel-organ, gurdo.
Barren, senfrukta.
Barrenness, senfrukteco.
Barricade, barikado.
Barrier, barilo.
Barrister, advokato.
Barrow, puŝveturilo.
Barter, interŝanĝi.
Barytone, baritono.
Basalt, bazalto.
Base, fundamento.
Base (mean), malnobla.
Basely, perfide.
Baseless, senfundamenta.
Basement, subetaĝo.
Baseness, perfideco.
Bashful, modesta.
Basin, pelvo.
Basis, fundamento.

kuseno.
Bolt, rigli.
Bolt, riglilo.
Bomb, bombo.
Bombard, bombardi.
Bonbon, bombono.
Bond (finance), obligacio.
Bondage, servuto.
Bondman, vasalo.
Bondservant, servutulo.
Bondsman (surety), garantianto.
Bone, osto.
Bonnet, ĉapo.
Bonny, beleta.
Bonus, liberdonaco.
Booby, simplanimulo.
Book, libro.
Book-keeper, librotenisto.
Book (copybook), kajero.
Bookseller, libristo.
Boom, soni.
Booming, sonado.
Boon, bonfaro, gajno.
Boorish, maldelikata.
Boot, boto.
Booth, budo.
Bootless, neprofita.
Bootmaker, botisto.
Booty, akiraĵo.
Borax, borakso.
Border (edge), randaĵo.
Border, to put a, borderi.
Bore (a hole), bori.
Bore (of a gun), kalibro.
Borer (tool), borilo.
Born, to be, nask-

Basket, korbo.
Bass (music), baso.
Bastard, bastardo.
Baste, surverŝi.
Bastion, bastiono.
Bat (animal), vesperto.
Bath, banilo.
Bathe, bani sin.
Baths (place), banejo.
Battalion, bataliono.
Battery (milit.), baterio.
Battle, batalo.
Battle, fight a, batali.
Battledore, pilkraketo.
Bauble, bagatelo.
Bawl, kriegi.
Bay (geog.), golfeto.
Bay (bark), hundobleki, boji.
Bay, to keep at, repuŝi.
Bayonet, bajoneto.
Bazaar, bazaro.
Be, esti.
Be, able to, povi.
Be, obliged to, devi.
Be, willing to, voli.
Beach, marbordo.
Beacon, lumturo.
Bead, globeto.
Beadle, pedelo.
Beak, beko.
Beam (timber), trabo.
Beam (light), radio.
Beam (of scales), vekto.
Bean, fabo.
Bear (animal), urso.
Bear, give birth to, naski.
Bear with, suferi.
iĝi.
Born again, renaskiĝi.
Borne, portita.
Borough, urba distrikto.
Borrow, prunto preni.
Bosom, brusto.
Botany, botaniko.
Botch (spoil), malbonigi.
Both, ambaŭ.
Bother, enui.
Bottle, botelo.
Bottom, fundo.
Bottom, malsupro.
Bough, branĉo.
Bouillon, buljono.
Boulder, ŝtonego.
Bounce, salti.
Bound, salti.
Bound, salto.
Boundary, limo.
Bounden, deviga.
Bountiful, malavara.
Bounty, helpa mono.
Bouquet, bukedo.
Bourn, limo.
Bout (contest), konkurso.
Bow, saluti.
Bow, saluto.
Bow, pafarko.
Bow (violin), arĉo.
Bow (ribbons), banto.
Bowels, internaĵo.
Bower, laŭbo.
Bowl, pelvo.
Box (small), skatolo.
Box, kesto.
Box, money, monoskatoleto.
Box (shrub), bukso.
Box (theatre), loĝio.
Box, pugnebati.
Boy, knabo.
Brace, paro.
Bearable, tolerebla.
Beard, barbo.
Beardless, senbarba.
Bearer, alportanto.
Beast (animal), besto.
Beast (brute), bruto.
Beastly, bruta.
Beat, bati.
Beat (with a rod), vergi.
Beatitude, feliĉegeco.
Beau, koketulo.
Beautiful, bela.
Beauty, beleco.
Bearer, kastoro.
Because, ĉar, tial ke.
Beckon, signodoni.
Become, iĝi, fariĝi.
Becoming, konvena, deca.
Bed, lito.
Bed (horse), paĵlaĵo.
Bed (garden), bedo.
Bed (river), kuŝujo.
Bedding, litaĵo.
Bedroom, dormoĉambro.
Bedstead, kuŝejo.
Bee, abelo.
Beehive, abelujo.
Beech-tree, fago.
Beef, bovaĵo.
Beer, biero.
Beet (root), beto.
Beetle, skarabo.
Befall, okazi.
Befitting, deca.
Before (prep.), antaŭ.
Before (adv.), antaŭe.
Before (conj.), antaŭ ol.
Bracelet, ĉirkaŭmano.
Braces, ŝelko.
Bracket, tableto.
Brackish, saleta.
Bray, fanfaroni.
Braggart, fanfaronulo.
Brain, cerbo.
Brake (fern), filiko.
Brake (for wheels), haltigilo.
Bran, brano.
Branch (of tree), branĉo.
Branch (of roads, etc.), disvojo.
Brand (fire), brulaĵo.
Brandish, svingi.
Brandy, brando.
Brasier, fajrujo.
Brass, flava kupro.
Brave, brava.
Brave, bravulo.
Brave, kontraŭstari al.
Bravery, braveco.
Bravo! brave!
Brawl, malpaceco.
Brawny, muskola.
Bray (ass), bleki.
Bray (to pound), pisti.
Brazen, bronza.
Breach, breĉo.
Bread, pano.
Bread (unleavened), maco.
Breadth, larĝeco.
Break, rompi.
Break off, disrompi.
Break, to pieces, frakasi.
Breakfast, matenmanĝi.
Bream, bramo.
Breast, brusto.
Breast, mamo.
Breath, elspiraĵo.
Breathe, spiri.
Beforehand, antaŭe.
Beg (entreat), peti.
Beg (alms), almozon peti.
Beggar, almozulo.
Beggary, almozpeto.
Begin, ek, komenci.
Beginning (origin), deveno.
Begone! for de tie ĉi!
Beguile (deceive), trompi.
Beguile, amuzi.
Behalf, parto.
Behave, konduti.
Behaviour, konduto.
Behead, senkapigi.
Behind (prep.), post.
Behind (adv.), poste.
Behold, rigardi.
Beholder, rigardanto.
Behoof, profito.
Being, estaĵo.
Belabour, bategi.
Belch, rukti.
Belfry, sonorilejo.
Belgian, Belgo.
Belgium, Belgujo.
Belie, kalumnii.
Belief, kredo.
Believe, kredi.
Bell, sonorilo.
Bell (door, etc.), sonorileto.
Bell (ornament), tintilo.
Bell ringer, sonorigisto.
Belladonna, beladono.
Belle, belulino.
Bellow, blekegi.
Bellows, blovilo.
Belly, ventro.
Breathe (heavily), stertori.
Breathing, spirado.
Breech (of gun), ŝargujo.
Breeches, pantalono.
Breed (race), raso.
Breeze, venteto.
Brevity, mallongeco.
Brew, bierfari.
Brewer, bierfaristo.
Brewery, bierfarejo.
Bribe, subaĉeti.
Brick, briko.
Brick (fire), fajrŝtono.
Bride, novedzino.
Bridge, ponto.
Bridle, brido.
Brief, mallonga.
Brier, rozo sovaĝa.
Brigade, brigado.
Brigand, rabisto.
Brigandage, rabado.
Bright (clear), hela.
Bright, to get, heliĝi.
Brighten, briligi.
Brighten (polish), poluri.
Brightness, brilo.
Brilliant, brila.
Brilliant (jewel), brilianto.
Brimful, plenpota.
Brine, peklakvo.
Bring, alkonduki.
Bring back, rekonduki.
Bring down (of prices), rabati.
Bring forth (a child), naski.
Bring up (a child), elnutri.
Brink, rando.
Briny, sala.

Belong, aparteni.
Below (adv.), sube, malsupre.
Below (prep.), sub.
Belt, zono.
Bench (seat), benko.
Bench (work), stablo.
Bench (of judges), juĝistaro.
Bend, fleksi.
Beneath, sub.
Benediction, beno.
Benefactor, bonfaristo.
Beneficial, profita.
Benefit, profito.
Benevolence, bonfaro.
Bent, kurba.
Benumb, rigidigi.
Bequeath, testamenti.
Bequest, heredaĵo.
Bereave (of), senigi (je).
Berry, bero.
Berth (ship), kuŝejo.
Beseech, petegi.
Beset, ĉirkaŭi.
Beside, apud.
Besides, krom.
Besiege, sieĝi.
Besot, bestiĝi.
Besprinkle, ŝprucigi sur.
Best (adj.), la plej bona.
Best (adv.), la plej bone.
Bestial, besta.
Bestir, one's self, sin movetadi, vigliĝi.
Bestow, donaci.
Bet, veti.
Bet, veto.
Betimes, frue.
Betray, perfidi.
Betroth, fianĉigi.

Brisk (lively), vigla.
Brisk (quick), rapida.
Briskness, rapideco.
Bristle, harego.
Brittle, facilrompa.
Broach, trapiki.
Broad, larĝa.
Brochure, broŝuro.
Broil, rosti.
Broker, makleristo.
Broker, to act as, makleri.
Brokerage, maklero.
Bromine, bromo.
Bronchitis, bronkito.
Bronchial, bronka.
Brooch, broĉo.
Brood (fowl), kovi.
Brook, rivereto.
Broth, buljono.
Broom (sweeping), balailo.
Broom (shrub), ŝtipo.
Brother, frato.
Brotherhood, frateco.
Brotherly, frata.
Brougham, kaleŝo.
Brown, bruna.
Brownish, dubebruna.
Browse, sin paŝti.
Bruise (crush), pisti.
Bruise, kontuzi.
Bruit, bruego.
Brush, broso.
Brutal, bruta.
Brute, bruto.
Buccaneer, marrabisto.
Bucket, sitelo.
Buckle, buko.

Betrothing, fianĉiĝo.
Better (adj.), pli bona.
Better (adv.), pli bone.
Between, inter.
Bevel, tranĉi oblikve.
Beverage, trinkaĵo.
Bewail, ploregi.
Bewilder, konfuzi.
Bewitch, ensorĉi.
Bewitchment, ensorĉo.
Beyond, preter.
Beyond (across), trans.
Biassed, partia.
Bible, Biblio.
Biblical, Biblia.
Bicker, disputi.
Bicycle, biciklo.
Bid (good day, etc.), diri.
Bid (at auction), pliproponi.
Bid (order), ordoni.
Bidding, invito.
Bide, atendi.
Bifurcation, disduiĝo.
Big, granda.
Bigamy, bigamio.
Bigot, fanatikulo.
Bigotry, fanatikeco.
Bilberry, mirtelo.
Bile, galo.
Bilious, gala.
Bill (a/c), kalkulo.
Bill (of exchange), kambio.
Bill (beak), beko.
Bill (posted up), afiŝo.
Bill-poster, afiŝisto.
Billhook, branĉhakileto.
Billet (note), letereto.

Buckler, ŝildo.
Buckwheat, poligono.
Bud, burĝono.
Budget (finance), budĝeto.
Buffalo, bubalo.
Buffer, ŝtopilo.
Buffet, frapi.
Buffet (restaurant), bufedo.
Buffoon, ŝercemulo.
Bug, cimo.
Build, konstrui.
Building, a, konstruaĵo.
Bulb, bulbo.
Bulgarian, Bulgaro.
Bulk, dikeco.
Bulky, multdika.
Bull, bovoviro.
Bullet, kuglo.
Bulletin, noto, karteto.
Bullfinch, pirolo.
Bullion (ingot), fandaĵo.
Bullock, juna bovoviro.
Bulwark, remparo.
Bump, ĝibeto.
Bumper, plenglaso.
Bun, bulko.
Bunch (cluster), aro.
Bundle, fasko.
Bung, ŝtopilo.
Bungle, fuŝi.
Buoy, naĝbarelo.
Buoyant, naĝema.
Burden, ŝarĝo.
Burden (refrain), rekantaĵo.
Burden, ŝargi.
Burdensome, multepeza.
Bureau (office), oficejo.
Burgess, burgo.
Burglar, domorabisto.

Billet (wood), ŝtipo.
Billiard-ball, globo.
Billiards, bilardo.
Billow, ondego.
Bin, grenkesto.
Bind, ligi.
Bind (books), bindi.
Bind (together), kunligi.
Bind (wounds), bandaĝi.
Bind-weed, liano.
Biography, biografio.
Biology, biologio.
Biped, dupiedulo.
Birch (tree), betulo.
Bird, birdo.
Birth, naskiĝo.
Birthday, naskotago.
Biscuit, biskvito.
Bisect, bisekcii.
Bishop, episkopo.
Bismuth, bismuto.
Bit (piece), peco.
Bit (horse), enbuŝaĵo.
Bite, mordi.
Bitter, akra—ema.
Bitters, vermuto.
Bitumen, terpeĉo.
Bivouac, bivako.
Blab, babili.
Black, nigra.
Blackboard, nigra tabulo.
Black-currant, nigra ribo.
Black pudding, sangokolbaso.
Blackbird, merlo.
Blacken, nigrigi.
Blackguard, sentaŭgulo.
Blacking, ciro.
Blackish, dubenigra.
Blacksmith, forĝisto.

Burial, enteriĝo.
Buried, to be, enteriĝi.
Burn (trans.), bruligi.
Burn (intrans.), bruli.
Burner (gas), flamingo.
Burnish, poluri.
Burrow, kavigi.
Bury (something), enfosi.
Bury (inter.), enterigi.
Bush, arbetaĵo.
Bushel, buŝelo.
Buskin, duonboto.
Business (profession), profesio.
Business (in general), afero.
Business-man, aferisto.
Bust, busto.
Bustle, movo,—ado.
Busy, okupa.
But, sed.
But (prep.), krom.
Butcher, buĉisto.
Butler, kelisto.
Butt (end of gun), kapo de la pafilo.
Butter, butero.
Butterfly, papilio.
Button (verb), butonumi.
Button-hook, butonumilo.
Button, butono.
Button-hole, butontruo.
Buy, aĉeti.
By means of, per.

Bladder, veziko.
Blade (grass), trunketo.
Blade (knife), trancânto.
Blamable, mallaŭdinda.
Blame, mallaŭdi.

C

Cab, fiakro.
Cabal, kabalo.
Cabbage, brasiko.
Cabin, kajuto, ĉambreto.
Cabinet (room), ĉambreto.
Cabinet (ministry), kabineto.
Cabinet-maker, meblisto.
Cabinet-making, meblofarado.
Cable, ŝnurego.
Cackle, pepegi.
Cacophony, malbonsoneco.
Cadence, kadenco.
Cadet, kadeto.
Café (coffee house), kafejo.
Cage, kaĝo.
Cajoler, delogisto.
Cake, kuko.
Calcine, pulvorigi.
Calculate, kalkuli.
Calculation, kalkulo.
Caldron, kaldrono.
Calendar, kalendaro.
Calf, bovido.
Calf (of leg), tibiviando.
Calibre, kalibro.
Calico, kalikoto.
Calk, kalfatri.
Call, voki.
Call on (visit), viziti.
Call (a meeting), kunvoki.
Call, voko.
Call (visit), vizito.
Caller (visitor), vizitanto.
Calling, profesio.
Callous, kala.
Callosity, kalo.
Calm, kvietigi.
Calm, kvieta.
Calm, trankvila.
Calmness, kvieteco.
Calumniate, kalumnii.
Calumny, kalumnio.
Camel, kamelo.
Camelia, kamelio.
Camisole, kamizolo.
Camomile, kamomilo.
Camp, tendaro.
Campaign, militiro.
Camphor, kamforo.
Can (vb.), povas.
Canal, kanalo.
Canary, kanario.
Cancel (erase), surstreki.
Cancel (nullify), nuligi.
Candelabrum, kandelabro.
Candid, simplanima.
Candid, naiva.
Candidate (political), kandidato.
Candidate, aspiranto.
Candidature, kandidateco.
Candle, kandelo.
Candlestick, kandelingo.
Candour, verdiremo, sincereco.
[Error in book: sinsereco]
Candy, kando.
Come (after), postveni.
Come (back), reveni.
Comedian, komedianto.
Comedy, komedio.
Comely, gracia, beleta.
Comet, kometo.
Comfort, komforti.
Comfort, komforto.
Comic, komika, ridinda.
Coming, veno.
Comma, komo.
Command (milit.), komandi.
Command, ordoni.
Commandant, komandanto.
Commander, komandoro.
Commandment, ordono.
Commemorate, memorigi.
Commence, komenci.
Commend, laŭdi.
Commendation, laŭdo.
Comment, komentarii.
Commentary, komentario.
Commerce, komerco.
Commercial man, komercisto.
Commission, komisii.
Commission, komisio.
Commission (brokerage), maklero.
Commission agent, makleristo.
Commissioner, komisario.
Commit, fari.
Commit (to prison), aresti.
Committee, komitato.
Commodity, komercaĵo.
Common, komuna.
Common (vulgar), vulgara.
Commoner, malnobelo, burĝo.
Commonly, ordinare.
Commonwealth, respubliko.
Commotion, konfuzo.
Commune, mempensi.
Commune, komunumo.
Communicant, komuniiĝanto.
Communicate, komuniki.
Communicative, komunikema.
Communism, komunismo.
Communist, komunisto.
Community, komunumaro.
Community of interests, solidareco.
Compact, kontrakto.
Compact, densa.
Companion, kunulo.
Companion (travelling), kunvojaĝanto.
Company, kompanio.
Company (society), societo.
Company (theatrical), trupo.
Company (military), roto.
Company (troop), anaro.
Comparative, kompara.
Compare, kompari.
Compartment, fako.
Compartment (train), fakego, kupeo.
Compass, kompaso.
Compassion, kompato.
Compassionate, to be, kompati.
Compatriot, samlandano.
Compel, devigi.
Compend, resumo.
Compend, resumo.
Compensate, kompensi.
Compete, konkuri.
Competent, kompetenta.
Competition, konkurso.
Competitor, konkuranto.
Compile, redakti.
Complacency, komplezo, servemo.
Complainant, plendanto.
Complaint, plendo.
Complaisance, komplezo.
Complement, plennombro.
Complement (gram.), komple-
Cane, kano.
Cane (walking stick), bastono.
Cane, vergi.
Canine, huna.
Canker, mordeti.
Cannibal, hommanĝulo.
Cannon, pafilego.
Cannon (at billiards, etc.), karamboli.
Cannonade, pafilegado, bombardado.
Canon, kanono.
Canopy, baldakeno.
Cant, hipokrito.
Canteen, drinkejo.
Canter, galopeti.
Canticle, himno.
Canto, versaro.
Canton, kantono.
Canvas, kanvaso.
Canvass, subpostuli.
Cap, ĉapo.
Cap (military), kepo.
Capability, kapableco.
Capable, kapabla.
Capacious, vasta.
Capacity, enhavebleco.
Cape, promontoro.
Capital (city), ĉefurbo.
Capital (money), kapitalo.
Capital letter, granda litero.
Capital (of a column), kapitelo.
Capitalist, kapitalisto.
Capitulate, kapitulaci.
Capitulation, kapitulaco.
Capon, kapono.
Caprice, kaprico.

Capsize, renversiĝi.
Captain (ship), ŝipestro.
Captain (milit.), kapitano.
Captive, malliberulo.
Captive, mallibera.
Captivate (charm), ĉarmegi.
Captivity, mallibereco.
Capture, preno.
Capuche, kapuĉo.
Car, ĉaro.
Car (of balloon), korbego.
Carabine, karabeno.
Carafe, karafo.
Carat, karato.
Caravan, karavano.
Carbon, karbono.
Carbuncle, karbunkolo.
Card, karto.
Card (playing), ludkarto.
Card (visiting), karteto.
Cardboard, kartono.
Cardinal, Kardinalo.
Cardinal (adj.), ĉefa.
Care, zorgo.
Care of, take, zorgi pri.
Careful, zorga.
Careless, senzorga.
Caress, karesi.
Caress, kareso.
Cargo, ŝarĝo.
Carman, veturigisto.
Carmine, karmino.
Carnage, buĉado.
Carnation (flower), dianto.
mento.
Complete, plenigi.
Completely, plene.
Complex, malsimpla.
Complexion, vizaĝkoloro.
Compliant, ceda—ema.
Complicate, malsimpligi.
Complication, malsimpleco.
Complicity, kunkulpeco.
Compliment, komplimenti.
Comply, cedi.
Compose, verki.
Compose (soothe), trankviligi.
Compose one's self, kvietiĝi.
Composer, verkisto.
Composition (music), kompozicio.
Composition (mixture), kunmeto.
Compositor (printer), kompostisto.
Compound, kunmeti.
Comprehend, kompreni.
Comprehensible, komprenebla.
Comprehension, kompreneco.
Compress, kunpremi.
Compressible, kunpremebla.
Comprise, enhavi.
Compromise, kompromiti.
Compromise, kompromiso.
Compulsion, devigo.
Compunction,
Carnation (color), flavroza.
Carnival, karnavalo.
Carnivorous, viandomanĝanta.
Caricature, karikaturi.
Carousal, karuselo.
Carp, karpo.
Carpenter, ĉarpentisto.
Carpentering, to do, ĉarpenti.
Carpet, tapiŝo.
Carriage, veturilo.
Carriage (railway), vagono.
Carriage (cost), transsenda pago.
Carriage (of goods), transporto.
Carrion, mortintaĵo.
Carrot, karoto.
Carry, porti.
Carry away, forporti.
Carry back, reporti.
Carry off (by force), rabi, forrabi.
Carry (by vehicle), veturigi.
Cart, veturigi.
Cart, ŝarĝoveturilo.
Carter, veturigisto.
Cartilage, kartilago.
Cartridge, kartoĉo.
Cartridge-box, kartoĉujo.
Cartwright, veturilfaristo.
Carve (sculpture), skulpti.
Carve (cut), tranĉi, detranĉi.
memriproĉo.
Computation, kalkulo.
Compute, kalkuli.
Comrade, kamarado.
Concave, kaveta.
Conceal, kaŝi.
Consecutive, intersekva.
Concede, cedi.
Conceit, malmodesteco.
Conceited, malmodesta.
Conceive, gravediĝi.
Concentrate, koncentrigi.
Concentric, koncentra.
Conception (idea), elpenso.
Concern, koncerni.
Concern (anxiety), zorgemo, malkvieto.
Concerning, pri.
Concert, koncerto.
Concession, cedo, cedemo.
Conciliate, pacigi.
Conciliating, pacema.
Concise, mallonga.
Conclude (infer), konkludi.
Conclude (finish), fini.
Conclusion (inference), konkludo.
Concord, konsento.
Concordant, unuvoĉa.
Concordat, kontrakto.
Concourse, konkurso.
Concrete, konkreta.
Concubine,
Cascade, kaskado.
Case (gram.), kazo.
Case (cover), ingo.
Case (in court), proceso.
Casement, kazemato.
Cash, mono.
Cash (ready), kontanto.
Cashier, kasisto.
Cask, barelo.
Casket, skatoleto.
Cassock, pastra vesto.
Cast (throw), ĵeti.
Cast (iron, etc.), fandi.
Cast (skin, etc.), ŝanĝi felon.
Cast out, elĵeti.
Cast lots, loti.
Castaway, forĵetulo.
Castellan, kastelestro.
Caster, radeto.
Casting, fandaĵo.
Castigate (with a rod), vergi.
Cast-iron, ferfandaĵo.
Castle, kastelo.
Castrate, kastri.
Castration, kastro.
Casual, okaza.
Casually, okaze.
Casuality, okazeco.
Cat, kato.
Catacombs, subteraj galerioj.
Catafalque, katafalko.
Catalepsy, katalepsio.
Catalogue, katalogo.
Cataract (eyes), katarakto.
Catarrh, kataro.
kromvirino.
Concur, konsenti.
Concussion, skuego.
Condemn, kondamni.
Condemnation, kondamno.
Condense, densigi.
Condensed, mallonga, mallongigita.
Condescend, bonvoli.
Condition, kondiĉo.
Conditionally, kondiĉe.
Condole, simpatii, kondolenci.
Condolence, kondolenco.
Conduct, one's self, konduti.
Conduct, konduki.
Conduct, behaviour, konduto.
Conductor, kondukisto.
Conduit, tubo.
Cone, konuso.
Confectioner, konfitisto.
Confederate, konfederi.
Confederation, konfederacio.
Confer (holy orders), ordoni.
Conference, konferenco.
Confess, konfesi.
Confession, konfeso.
Confide, konfidi.
Confidence, konfidencio.
Confident, konfidema.
Confine, enfermi.
Confirm, certigi.
Confirm (religious), konfirmi.

Catch, kapti.
Catechise, kateĥizi.
Catechism, kateĥismo.
Catechist, kateĥisto.
Category, kategorio.
Cater, provizi.
Caterpillar, raŭpo.
Cathedral, katedro.
Catholic, Katoliko.
Catholicism, Katolikismo. [Error in book: Katolicismo]
Cattle, bestaro.
Cattle-pen, bestejo.
Caudal, vosta.
Cauldron, kaldrono.
Cauliflower, florbrasiko.
Cause, kaŭzo.
Cause, kaŭzi.
Cause, igi.
Cauterize, kaŭterizi.
Caution, averti.
Caution, singardemo.
Cautious, singardema.
Cavalcade, rajdantaro.
Cavalier, rajdanto.
Cavalry, kavalerio.
Cave, kaverno.
Caviare, kaviaro.
Cavil, ĉikani.
Cavity, kavo, kavaĵo.
Cease, ĉesi.
Cedar, cedro.
Cede, cedi.
Ceiling, plafono.
Celebrate (feast), festi.

Confirmation, certigo.
Confiscate, konfisiki.
Conflagration, brulado.
Conflict, konflikto.
Confluence, kunfluiĝo.
Conform, konformi.
Conformable, konforma.
Conformity, konformeco.
Confound, konfuzegi.
Confrère, kunfrato.
Confront, kontraŭstarigi.
Confuse, konfuzi.
Confusion, konfuzo—ado.
Confute, rifuti.
Congeal, firmigi.
Congestion, sangalfluo.
Congratulate, gratuli.
Congratulation, gratulo.
Congregate, kolekti.
Congregation, aŭdantaro.
Congress, kongreso.
Conical, konusa.
Conjecture, konjekti.
Conjoin, kuni.
Conjointly, kune.
Conjugate, konjugacii.
Conjunction, konjunkcio.
Conjunction (joining), kunigo.
Conjure, petegi.
Conjure, ĵongli.
Conjurer, ĵonglisto.
Connect, kunigi.

Celebrate (solemnize), solenigi.
Celebrated, fama.
Celerity, rapideco.
Celery, celerio.
Celestial, ĉiela
Celibacy, fraŭleco.
Cell (of honeycomb), ĉelo.
Cellar, kelo.
Cellular, ĉela.
Cement, cemento.
Cemetery, tombejo.
Censer, bonodorfumilo.
Censor, cenzuristo.
Censorious, cenzura.
Censure, cenzuri.
Censure (blame), riproĉo.
Census (take a), sumigi.
Cent, cendo.
Centenarian, centjarulo.
Centenary, centjara festo.
Centigramme, centigramo.
Centime, centimo.
Centimeter, centimetro.
Central, meza, centra.
Centralize, alcentrigi.
Centre, centro.
Centre-bit, turnborilo.
Centrifugal, decentrokura.
Centripetal, alcentrokura.
Century, centjaro.
Ceremonious, ceremonia.
Ceremony, ceremonio.
Certain (some), kelkaj.

Connection, kunigo.
Connections, parencaro.
Connoisseur, virtuozo.
Conquer, venki.
Conqueror, venkanto.
Conquest, venko.
Consanguineous, samsanga.
Conscience, konscienco.
Conscientious, konscienca.
Consecrate, dediĉi.
Consecutive, intersekva.
Consent, konsenti.
Consequence, sekvo.
Consequently, sekve.
Consequential, malmodesta.
Conserve (preserve), konservi.
Conservative, Konservativulo.
Consider, pripensi, konsideri.
Considerable, grandega.
Consideration, konsidero.
Consign, sendi.
Consignment, sendo.
Consist (of), konsisti (el).
Consistent, unuforma.
Consistory, konsistorio.
Console, konsoli.
Consolation, konsolo.
Consolidate, fortigi.
Consonant (letter), konsonanto.
Consonant, un-

Certain (sure), certa.
Certainly, certe, nepre.
Certainty, certeco.
Certify, certigi.
Certify, atesti.
Certitude, certeco.
Cessation (of hostilities), interpaco.
Cessation, ĉesado.
Cession, cedo.
Cetaceous, balena.
Chaff (ridicule), moki.
Chaff, pajlrestaĵo.
Chaffinch, fringo.
Chagrin, ĉagreno.
Chain, ĉeno.
Chain of mountains, montaro.
Chair, seĝo.
Chairman, prezidanto.
Chaise, veturileto.
Chalice, kaliko.
Chalk, kreto.
Chalky, kreteca.
Challenge, to, ekciti, al.
Chamber, ĉambro.
Chambermaid, ĉambristino.
Chamberlain, ĉambelano.
Chameleon, kameleono.
Chamois, ĉamo.
Chamois-leather, ŝamo.
Champagne, ĉampano.
Champion, probatalanto.
Chance, hazardo.
Chance (to happen), okazi.
Chancel, ĥorejo.
Chancellor, kanceliero.

uforma.
Consort, kunulo.
Conspicuous, videgebla.
Conspiracy, konspiro.
Conspire, konspiri.
Constant, konstanta.
Constellation, stelaro.
Consternation, konsterno.
Constipation, mallakso.
Constitution, konstitucio.
Constitutional, konstitucia.
Constraint, devigo.
Construct, konstrui.
Construction (building), konstruaĵo.
Consul, konsulo.
Consulate, konsulejo.
Consult, konsiliĝi kun.
Consultation, konsiliĝo.
Consume, konsumi.
Consumer, konsumanto.
Consummate, plenigi.
Consummation, plenigo.
Consumption (phthisis), ftizo.
Consumption, konsumiĝo.
Contact, kontakto.
Contagious, komunikebla.
Contain, enhavi.
Contaminate, malpurigi.
Contemn, malestimi.

Chandelier, lustro.
Change, ŝanĝi.
Changeable, ŝanĝebla.
Channel, kanalo.
Chant, kantado.
Chaos, ĥaoso.
Chaotic, ĥaosa.
Chapel, kapelo.
Chaplain, ekleziulo.
Chapter, ĉapitro.
Char, bruleti.
Character, karaktero.
Character (theatre), rolo.
Characterize, karakterizi.
Charge (attack), atakegi.
Charge (price), kosto.
Chariot, ĉaro.
Charitable, bonfarada.
Charity, bonfarado.
Charity (alms), almozo.
Charlatan, ĉarlatano.
Charm, ĉarmi.
Charm, ĉarmo.
Charm, talismano.
Charming, ĉarma.
Charnel house, karnejo.
Chart (geog.), karto geografia.
Chase, ĉasi.
Chase, ĉaso.
Chaste, ĉasta.
Chasten, korekti.
Chastise, puni.
Chastisement, puno.
Chastity, ĉasteco.
Chasuble, mesvesto.
Chat, interparoleti.
Chattels, bieno.

Contemplate, rigardadi.
Contemporary, samtempa.
Contempt, malestimo.
Contemptible, malestima.
Contend, batali.
Content, kontentigi.
Contentedness, kontenteco.
Contention, kontraŭstaro.
Contentious, malpacula.
Contentment, kontenteco.
Contents, enhavo.
Contest, disputi.
Contest, disputo.
Continence, sindetenemo.
Continent (geog.), kontinento.
Contingent (milit.), kontingento.
Contiguity, apudeco.
Contiguous, apuda.
Continue (to last), daŭri.
Continue (go on), daŭrigi.
Contortion (of face), grimaco.
Contour, konturo.
Contraband, kontrabando.
Contract, kontrakto.
Contract, make a, kontrakti.
Contract, kuntirigi.
Contractor, entreprenisto.
Contradict, kontraŭdiri.
Contrariwise, kontraŭe.
Contrary, kontraŭa.

Chatter, babili.
Cheap, malkara.
Cheat, trompi.
Cheat (trick), trompo.
Cheat (deceiver), trompanto.
Check (restrain), haltigi.
Check, kontraŭmarki.
Cheek, vango.
Cheekbone, vangosto.
Cheer, aplaŭdegi.
Cheer, konsoli.
Cheerful, gaja.
Cheerfulness, gajeco.
Cheer up, rekuraĝigi.
Cheese, fromaĝo.
Chemise, ĉemizo.
Chemist, apotekisto.
Chemist-shop, apoteko.
Chemistry, ĥemio.
Cheque, ĉeko.
Cherry, ĉerizo.
Cherub, kerubo.
Chess-pieces, ŝakoj.
Chess-board, ŝaka tabulo.
Chest of drawers, komodo.
Chest (box), kesto.
Chest, brusto.
Chestnut (edible), kaŝtano.
Chevalier, kavaliro.
Chew, maĉi.
Chicane, ĉikani.
Chicken, kokido.
Chicken-house, kokejo.
Chicory, cikorio.
Chide, riproĉi.
Chief, ĉefo.
Chief, ĉefa.
Chiffonier, ĉifonujo.

Contrary, on the, male, kontraŭe.
Contrast, kontrasti.
Contrast, kontrasto.
Contravention, malobeo.
Contribution, depago.
Contrite, penta.
Contrition, pento—eco.
Contrivance, elpensaĵo.
Contrive, elpensi.
Control, kontroli.
Controversy, disputado.
Contumacious, obstinema.
Contumacy, obstineco.
Contumely, malestimo.
Contuse, kontuzi.
Convalescence, resaniĝo.
Convalescent (man), resaniĝanto.
Convene, kunvoki.
Convenience, oportuneco.
Convenient, oportuna.
Convent, monaĥinejo.
Conventional, kutima.
Converge, konvergi.
Conversation, konversacio.
Converse, interparoladi.
Converse, mala.
Conversely, male.
Conversion (of one's self), konvertiĝo.
Conversion (of some one else), konverto.

Chignon, harligaĵo.
Chilblain, frostabsceso.
Child, infano.
Childhood, infaneco.
Childish, infana.
Childishness, infanaĵo.
Chill, malvarmigi.
Chill, malvarmo.
Chime, sonorilado.
Chimera, ĥimero.
Chimney, kamentubo.
Chimney-sweep, kamentubisto.
Chin, mentono.
China, Ĥinujo, Ĥinlando.
China, porcelano.
Chinese (man), Ĥino.
Chink, tinti.
Chink (crack), fendaĵo.
Chirp, pepi.
Chisel, ĉizi.
Chisel, ĉizilo.
Chivalrous, kavalira.
Chivalry, kavalireco.
Chocolate, ĉokolado.
Choice, elekto.
Choir, ĥoro.
Choke, sufoki.
Choke up, obstrukci.
Choler, kolero.
Cholera, ĥolero.
Choleric, kolera.
Choose, elekti.
Chop, haki.
Chop down, dehaki.
Chopper, hakilo.
Choral, ĥora.
Chorister, ĥoristo.
Chorus, ĥoraro.
Chrism, sankta oleo.

Convert (relig.), konverti.
Convex, malkaveta.
Convey, alporti.
Convey (by vehicle), veturigi.
Conveyance, veturilo.
Convict (man), kondamnulo.
Convict, kondamnato.
Conviction, kondamno.
Convince, konvinki.
Convocation, kunvoko.
Convolution, konvolvado—aĵo.
Convolvulus, konvolvulo.
Convoy, veturilaro.
Convulse, konvulsii.
Convulsion, konvulsio.
Cook, kuiri.
Cook (man), kuiristo.
Cookery, kuirado.
Cool, malvarmetigi.
Cool, malvarmeta.
Coolness, malvarmeto.
Coop, kaĝego.
Coop, kaĝigi.
Cooper, barelisto.
Co-operation, kunhelpo—ado.
Copeck, kopeko.
Copier, kopiisto.
Copious, plena, plenega.
Copper (boiler), kaldronego.
Copper (metal), kupro.
Copse, arbetaro.
Copy, kopii.
Copy, ekzem-

Christ, Kristo.
Christen, bapti.
Christendom, Kristanaro.
Christian, Kristano.
Christian-name, baptonomo.
Christianity, Kristanismo.
Christmas, Kristnasko.
Christmas-box, Kristnaskdono.
Chronicle, kroniko.
Chronology, kronologio.
Chrysanthemum, krizantemo.
Church, preĝejo.
Church-yard, preĝejkorto.
Churl, malĝentilulo. [Error in book: malgentilulo]
Churn, buterilo.
Churn, buterfari.
Cider, pomvino.
Cigar, cigaro.
Cigar-holder, cigaringo.
Cigarette, cigaredo.
Cinder, cindro.
Cinnabar, cinabro.
Cinnamon, cinamo.
Cipher, cifero.
Cipher, nulo.
Circle, rondo.
Circlet, rondeto.
Circuit, ĉirkaŭo.
Circular, cirkulero.
Circulate, ĉirkaŭiri.
Circumference, ĉirkaŭo.
Circumlocution, ĉirkaŭfrazo.
Circumscribe, ĉirkaŭskribi.

plero.
Copybook, kajero.
Copy (a corrected), neto.
Copyist, skribisto.
Coquet, koketi.
Coquetry, koketeco.
Coquette, koketulino.
Coral, koralo.
Cord, ŝnuro.
Cordage, ŝnuraĵo.
Cordial, kora.
Core, internaĵo.
Co-religionist, samreligiano.
Cork, korko.
Cork, ŝtopi.
Corkscrew, korktirilo.
Corn (on foot, etc.), kalo.
Corn, greno.
Corned, salita.
Corner, angulo.
Cornice, kornico.
Corolla, kroneto.
Coronation, kronado.
Corporal, korporalo.
Corporal, korpa.
Corporation, korporacio.
Corpse, malvivulo.
Corpulent, vastkorpa.
Correct, korekta.
Correction, korekto.
Correctness, korekteco.
Correspond, korespondi.
Correspondence, korespondado.
Corridor, koridoro.
Corrode, mordeti.
Corrupt, putrigi.
Corrupt (bribe), subaĉeti.
Corrupt (vicious),

Circumspect, singardema.
Circumstance, cirkonstanco.
Circus, cirko.
Cistern, akvujo.
Citadel, fortikaĵo.
Citation, citaĵo.
Cite, citi.
Citizen, urbano.
Citron, citrono.
City, urbo.
Civic, urba.
Civil, civila.
Civil (polite), ĝentila.
Civilian, nemilita.
Civility, ĝentileco.
Civilization, civilizacio.
Civilize, civilizi.
Claim, pretendo.
Claimant, pretendanto.
Clamber, suprenrampi.
Clammy, glua.
Clamour, bruego.
Clan, gento.
Clandestine, sekreta.
Clank, resoni.
Clap, manfrapi.
Clarify, klarigi.
Clarion, milita trumpeto.
Clarionet, klarneto.
Clasp (buckle), buko.
Clasp, preno.
Clasp, preni.
Class, klaso.
Class, ordigi.
Classify, ordigi.
Clatter, bruegado.
Claw, ungego.
Clay, argilo.
Clean, purigi.
Clean, pura.
Clean (boots, etc.), senkotigi.
Cleanliness, pureco.
Cleanse, purigi.

malvirta.
Corruption, putro.
Corsage, korsaĵo.
Corsair, korsaro.
Corse, malvivulo.
Corset, korseto.
Cortege, sekvantaro.
Cossack, Kozako.
Cosmopolite, kosmopolita.
Cosmography, kosmografio.
Cost, kosto.
Costiveness, mallakso.
Costly, multekosta.
Costume, kostumo.
Cosy, komforta.
Cot, liteto.
Cottage, dometo.
Cotton (raw), kotono.
Cotton (manufactured), katuno.
Cotton plant, kotonujo.
Couch, kuŝejo.
Cough, tusi.
Counsel, konsili.
Counsel, advokato.
Counsel, konsilo.
Counsel, to take, konsiliĝi kun.
Counsellor, konsilanto.
Count, kalkuli.
Count upon, konfidi al.
Count (title), grafo.
Countenance, vizaĝo.
Counter (token), ludmarko.
Counteract, malhelpi.
Counter-bass, kontrabaso.
Counterfeit, imiti.
Counterfeit, falsi.
Counterfeit, fal-

Clear, klara.
Clear (mental), malkonfuza.
Clearness, klareco.
Cleave (split), fendi.
Cleaver, fendilo.
Cleft, fendo.
Clemency, malsevereco.
Clement, malsevera.
Clergy, pastraro.
Clergyman, pastro.
Clerk (commercial), komizo.
Clerk (ecclesiastic), ekleziulo.
Clever, lerta.
Cleverness, lerteco.
Client, kliento.
Cliff, krutaĵo.
Climate, klimato.
Climb, suprenrampi.
Clinical, klinika.
Clink, tinti.
Clip (shear), tondi.
Clip off, detranĉi.
Clipper, tondisto.
Clique, fermita societo, kliko.
Cloak, mantelo.
Cloak-room, pakaĵejo.
Clock, horloĝo.
Clock-maker, horloĝisto.
Clod, bulo—aĵo.
Close (finish), fini.
Close, fermi.
Closet (w.c.), necesejo.
Cloth, a, drapo.
Cloth (material), tuko.
Clothe, vesti.
Clothes, vestaĵo.
Cloud, nubo.
Cloudy (not

saĵo.
Countermand (an order), kontraŭmendi.
Counterpane, litkovrilo.
Counterpart, kontraŭparto.
Counting-house, kontoro.
Country, lando.
Country (rural), kamparo.
Countryman, kamparano.
Countryman, fellow, samlandano.
Country-house, kampodomo.
Country-seat, somerloĝo.
County, graflando.
Couple, paro.
Couple, kunigi.
Couplet, strofo.
Courage, kuraĝo.
Courageous, to be, kuraĝi.
Courier, kuriero.
Course (race), kuro.
Course (of lessons), kurso.
Course (of course), kompreneble.
Court (royal), kortego.
Court (justice), juĝejo.
Court (yard), korto.
Court, amindumi.
Courteous, ĝentila.
Courtesy, ĝentileco.
Courtier, kortegulo.
Cousin (masc.), kuzo.
Covenant, kondiĉi.
Covenant, in-

clear), malklara.
Clove, kariofilo.
Clover, trifolio.
Clown, ŝercemulo.
Cloy, satigi.
Club (thick stick), bastonego.
Club (cards), trefo.
Club (society), klubo.
Clue, postsigno.
Clump (tuft), tufo.
Clumsy, mallerta.
Cluster (of berries), beraro.
Clutch, kapti, ekkaptigi.
Clyster, klistero.
Clyster-pipe, tubeto.
Coach, veturilo.
Coach-maker, veturilfaristo.
Coachman, veturigisto.
Coal, karbo.
Coalesce, kuniĝi.
Coalition, kuniĝo.
Coarse (manner), vulgara.
Coast, marbordo.
Coat, vesto.
Coat of arms, blazono.
Coat (walls, etc.), ŝmiri.
Coax, logi.
Cobalt, kobalto.
Cobweb, araneaĵo.
Cock (trigger), ĉano.
Cock (tap), krano.
Cock (rooster), koko.
Cockerel, kokido.
Cock's comb, kresto.
Cocoa, kakao.
Cocoa-nut, kokoso.
Cod, gado.
Code, leĝaro.

terkonsento.
Cover, kovri.
Cover (the head), surmeti.
Cover (roof), tegi.
Cover, kovrilo.
Covet, avidi.
Covetousness, avideco.
Covey, kovitaro.
Cow, bovino.
Coward, malkuraĝulo.
Cowardice, malkuraĝeco.
Cowherd, bovgardisto.
Cow shed, bovinejo.
Cowl, kapuĉo.
Cowslip, verprimolo.
Coxcomb, dando.
Coy, rezerva.
Coyness, rezerveco.
Cozen, trompi.
Crab, kankro.
Crack (split), fendi.
Crack (noise), kraki.
Crackle, kraketi.
Cradle, lulilo.
Craft, ruzo.
Craft (vessel), ŝipeto.
Crafty, to be, ruzi.
Crafty, ruza.
Cram (of food), supersatigi.
Cram, plenegigi.
Cramp (metal), krampo.
Crane (bird), gruo.
Crane, ŝarĝlevilo.
Crape, krepo.
Crater, kratero.
Cravat, kravato.
Crave, petegi.
Crawl, rampi.
Crayon, krajono.
Crazy, freneza.
Cream, kremo.

Codicil, kodicilo.
Coddle, dorloti.
Coerce, devigi.
Coercion, devigo.
Coffee, kafo.
Coffee-house, kafejo.
Coffee pot, kafkruĉo.
Coffee tin or box, kafujo.
Coffer, kesto.
Coffin, ĉerko.
Cogent, videbla.
Cognomen, alnomo.
Coherence, kunligo.
Coil, rulaĵo. volvaĵo.
Coin, monero.
Coincide, koincidi.
Coincident, samtempa.
Coke, koakso.
Colander, kribrilo.
Cold, malvarmo.
Cold in the head, nazkataro.
Cold, catch a, malvarmumi.
Coldness, malvarmeco.
Colic, koliko.
Collaborate, kunlabori.
Collaboration, kunlaborado.
Collar, kolumo.
Collation, manĝeto.
Colleague, kolego.
Collect, kolekti.
Collection, kolekto.
Collector (of taxes, etc.), kolektisto.
Collector (of stamps, etc.), kolektanto.
Collective, opa.

Create, krei.
Creation, kreitaĵo.
Creator, kreinto.
Creature, estaĵo.
Credence, kredo.
Credible, kredebla.
Credit, kredito.
Creditor, kreditoro.
Credulity, kredemo.
Creed, kredo.
Creep, rampi.
Creole, Kreolo.
Crest, tufo.
Crevice, fendo—aĵo.
Crew, maristaro.
Cricket (insect), grilo.
Crime, krimo.
Criminal, krimulo.
Criminally, kriminale.
Crimson, ruĝega.
Cripple, kripligi.
Cripple, kriplulo.
Crippled, kripla.
Crisis, krizo.
Crisp, friza.
Critic, kritikisto.
Criticism, kritiko.
Croak, bleki.
Crockery, fajenco.
Crocodile, krokodilo.
Crooked, hoka, malrekta.
Crop (harvest), rikolto.
Crosier, episkopa bastono.
Cross, kruco.
Cross, krucigi.
Cross (manner), malafabla.
Cross-over, transiri.
Cross-out, streki.
Crossing, krucigo.
Crotchet, kvarona noto.
Croup, krupo.

College, kolegio.
Collier, karbfosisto.
Colliery, karbejo.
Collision, interfrapo.
Colon, dupunkto.
Colonel, kolonelo.
Colonial, koloniano.
Colonist, koloniisto.
Colonize, koloniigi.
Colonnade, kolonaro.
Colony, kolonio.
Colossal, kolosa.
Color, koloro.
Color, kolori.
Color (complexion), vizaĝokoloro.
Colorless, senkolora.
Colt, ĉevalido.
Column, kolono.
Comb, kombi.
Comb, kombilo.
Combat, batalo.
Combat, batali.
Combatant, batalanto.
Combine, kombini.
Combustible, brulebla.
Combustion, brulado.
Come, veni.

Crow, korniko.
Crow, bleki.
Crow-bar, levilo.
Crowd, amaso.
Crown, krono.
Crown, kroni.
Crown (of head), verto.
Crucifix, krucifikso.
Crucifixion, krucumo.
Crucify, krucumi.
Crude, kruda.
Cruel, kruela.
Cruelty, kruelo—eco.
Cruet, oleujo.
Cruise, krozi.
Cruiser, krozŝipo.
Crumb (bread), panmolaĵo.
Crumble, elfali.
Crumple, ĉifi.
Crupper, postaĵo.
Crush, premegi.
Crust, krusto.
Crustaceous, kankrogenta.
Crutch, lambastono.
Cry (call out), krii.
Cry (weep), plori.
Cry out, ekkrii.
Cry (of animals, etc.), bleki.
Crypt, subteraĵo.
Crystal, kristalo.
Crystallise, kristaligi.
Cub (of lion), leonido.
Cube, kubo.
Cuckoo, kukolo.
Cucumber, kukumo.
Cudgel, bastonego.
Cuff, manumo.
Cuirass, kiraso.
Cull, kolekti.
Cullender, kribrilo.
Culpable, kulpa.

Culprit, kulpulo.
Cultivate, kulturi.
Culture, kulturo.
Cunning, ruzo.
Cunning, ruza.
Cup, taso.
Cupboard, ŝranko.
Cupidity, avideco.
Cupola, kupolo.
Curable, kuracebla.
Curacy, paroĥo.
Curate, vikaro.
Curator, kuratoro, gardisto.
Curb, haltigi.
Cure (act of curing), kuraco.
Cure (remedy), kuracilo.
Cure (a malady), kuraci.
Curious (inquisitive), sciama.
Curious (strange), stranga.
Curiosity, kuriozaĵo.
Curl, buklo.
Currant, ribo.
Current, fluo.
Currier, ledpretigisto.
Curse, malbeni.
Curt, mallonga.
Curtail, mallongigi.
Curtain, kurteno.
Curve, kurbigi.
Curve, kurbeco.
Cushion, kuseno.
Custard, flanaĵo.
Custom, kutimo.
Customary, kutima.
Customer, kliento.
Cut (with knife), tranĉi.
Cut (with scissors), tondi.
Cut off, detranĉi.
Cutaneous, haŭta.
Cute, ruza.

Cutlass, tranĉilego.
Cutlet, kotleto.
Cutter (blade), tranĉanto.
Cutting (underground), subtervojo.
Cycle, ciklo.
Cyclone, ciklono.
Cylinder, cilindro.
Cymbal, cimbalo.
Cypress, cipreso.
Czar, Caro.

D

Dab, bateto.
Daffodil, narciso.
Dagger, ponardo.
Dahlia, dalio.
Daily, ĉiutage, ĉiutaga.
Dainty, frandaĵo.
Dainty, frandema.
Dairy, laktovendejo.
Daisy, lekanto.
Dale, valeto.
Dally, malfrui.
Dam, bestopatrino.
Dam, akvoŝtopilo, digo.
Damage, difekti.
Damage, difektaĵo.
Damask, damasko.
Dame, sinjorino, patrino.
Damn, kondamni.
Damp, malseka.
Damsel, fraŭlino.
Dance, danci.
Dancing (the art of), dancarto.
Dandle, luleti.
Dandy, dando.
Dane, Dano.
Dandelion, leontodo.
Danger, danĝero.
Dangle, pendeti.
Dare, kuraĝi.
Daring, kuraĝa, maltima.

Dark (colour), malpala.
Dark, malluma.
Dark (to become), mallumiĝi.
Darken, mallumigi.
Darkness, mallumeco.
Darling, karegulo.
Darn, fliki.
Darning, flikado.
Dart, sago, pikilo.
Date (time), dato.
Date (fruit), daktilo.
Date, dati.
Dative, dativo.
Daub, fuŝi.
Daubing, fuŝoado.
Daughter, filino.
Daughter-in-law, bofilino.
Daunt, timigi.
Dauntless, sentima.
Dawn, tagiĝo.
Day, tago.
Day (a, per), laŭtage.
Day (before yesterday), antaŭhieraŭ.
Daybreak, tagiĝo.
Daybook, taglibro.
Daydream, revo.
Day laborer, taglaboristo.
Daze, duonesvenigi.
Dazzle, blindigi.
Deacon, diakono.
Dead (lifeless), senviva.
Deadly, pereiga.
Deadhouse, mortintejo.
Deaf, surda.
Deafen, surdigi.
Deafmute, surdamutulo.
Deafness, surde-

senkolorigi.
Discomfit, malvenkigi.
Discompose, malkvietigi.
Disconcert, konfuzi.
Disconnect, disigi.
Disconsolate, ĉagrenega.
Discontented, malkontenta.
Discontinuance, interrompo.
Discord, malpaco.
Discord (music), malakordo.
Discordant, malpaca, malakordo.
Discount, diskonto.
Discourage, senkuraĝigi.
Discouragement, senkuraĝeco.
Discourse, parolado.
Discourteous, malĝentila.
Discover, eltrovi.
Discovery, eltrovo.
Discredit, senkreditigi.
Discreet, diskreta.
Discretion, singardemo, diskreto.
Discriminate, distingi.
Discursive, tro skribema.
Discuss, diskuti.
Discussion, diskutado.
Disdain, malŝati.
Disease, malsano—ego.
Disembark, elŝipiĝi.
Disengage, liberigi.
Disentangle, liberigi.

co.
Deal (sell), komerci.
Deal out, disdoni.
Dealer, komercisto.
Dean, fakultestro.
Dear, kara.
Dear (person), karulo.
Dear (price), multekosta.
Dearth, seneco.
Death, morto.
Deathless, senmorta.
Debar, eksigi.
Debase, malnobligi.
Debate, disputo.
Debauch, diboĉigi.
Debauch, diboĉo.
Debility, malforteco.
Debit, debito.
Debris, rubo—aĵo.
Debt, to get into, ŝuldiĝi.
Debt, ŝuldo.
Debtor, ŝuldanto.
Debut, komenco.
Decadence, kadukeco.
Decalogue, dekalogo.
Decant, transverŝi.
Decanter, karafo.
Decapitate, senkapigi.
Decay, kadukeco.
Decaying, kaduka.
Decease (v.), morti.
Deceit, artifiko—eco.
Deceive, trompi.
Deceived, to be, trompiĝi.
December, Decembro.
Decent, deca.

Disfavour, malfavoro.
Disgrace, malhonori.
Disguise, alivesti.
Disgust, naŭzi.
Dish, plado.
Dishcloth, telertuko.
Dishearten, malkuraĝigi.
Dishonest, malhonesta.
Dishonesty, malhonesteco.
Dishonour, malhonori.
Dishonourable, malhonora.
Disillusion, elreviĝo.
Disinfect, dezinfekti.
Disinterested, malprofitema.
Disjoin, disligi.
Disjoint, elartikigi.
Disjunction, disigo.
Dislike, malŝati, malameti.
Dislike, antipatio.
Dislocate, elartikigi.
Dislocate (to take to pieces), dispecigi.
Dislocation, elartikigo.
Dislodge, transloki.
Disloyal, malfidela.
Disloyalty, malfidelo.
Dismal, funebra.
Dismay, konsterni.
Dismember, senmembrigi.
Dismiss, forsendi, eksigi.
Dismount, elseligi.

Deception, trompo.
Decide, decidi.
Decided, decida.
Decimal, decimalo.
Decipher, deĉifri.
Decisive, decidiga.
Deck (adorn), ornami.
Deck (ship), ferdeko.
Declaim, deklami.
Declaration, deklaracio.
Declaration (of love), amesprimo.
Declare, sciigi, anonci.
Declension, deklinacio.
Decline, ekfiniĝo.
Decline (health), ekmalfortiĝi.
Decline (refuse), rifuzi.
Decline (grammar), deklinacii.
Decline (in price), malplikariĝo.
Declivity, deklivo.
Decompose, dismeti.
Decorate, ornami.
Decorator, ornamisto.
Decorum, dececo.
Decorous, bonmora.
Decoy, trompi, delogi.
Decoy, kaptilo.
Decrease, malkreski.
Decree, dekreto.
Dedicate, dediĉi.
Dedication, dediĉo.
Deduce, depreni.
Deduct, depreni.
Deduction, depreno.
Deed, faro.
Deem, pensi.

Disobey, malobei.
Disobliging, neservema.
Disorder, malordo, senordeco.
Disorderly, malordema.
Disorganise, malorganizi.
Disown, forlasi, nei.
Disparity, neegaleco.
Dispatch, depeŝo.
Dispel, peli, forpeli.
Dispensary, kuracilejo.
Dispense (to give out), disdoni.
Disperse, dispeli.
Display, vidaĵo, montraĵo.
Display (show, pomp), lukso.
Displace, transloki.
Displease, malplaĉi.
Displeasure, malplaĉo.
Disport, ludi.
Dispose, disponi.
Disposable, disponebla.
Disposition, inklino.
Dispraise, mallaŭdi.
Disproof, refuto.
Disprove, refuti.
Dispute, disputo.
Dispute (quarrel), malpaci.
Disputatious, disputa. [Error in book: *Disputations*]
Disqualify, malkapabligi.
Disquiet, maltrankviligi.
Disrespectful, nerespekta.
Disappointment,

Deep (sound), basa.
Deep, profunda.
Deer, cervo.
Deface, forigi, surstreki.
Defame, kalumnii.
Defeat, venki.
Defeat (n.), malvenko—ego.
Defect, difekto—aĵo.
Defend, defendi.
Defer, prokrasti.
Deference, respektego.
Deficiency, deficito.
Defile (n.), intermonto.
Defile (soil), malpurigi.
Define, difini.
Definite, difinita.
Definitive, definitiva.
Deform, malbonformigi.
Deformed, malbelforma.
Defraud, trompi.
Defray, elpagi.
Defunct, mortinto.
Defy, kontraŭstari.
Degenerate, degeneri.
Degrade, degradi.
Degree, grado.
Deign, bonvoli.
Deism, diismo.
Deist, diisto.
Deity, diaĵo.
Deject, senkuraĝi.
Dejection, malĝojeco.
Delay (trans.), prokrasti.
Delay (intrans.), malfrui, tromalfrui.
Delay, prokrasto.
Delegate, delegi.
Delegate, delegi-

kontraŭaĵo.
Dissatisfied, malkontenta.
Dissect, dissekcii.
Dissection, dissekcio.
Dissemble, hipokriti, kaŝi.
Disseminate, dissemi.
Dissent, malkonsenti.
Dissenter, alireligiulo.
Dissertation, disertacio.
Dissimilar, malsama.
Dissimulate, kaŝi.
Dissimulation, kaŝemo.
Dissipate, malŝpari.
Dissipation, malŝparo.
Dissolute, diboĉa.
Dissolution, solvo.
Dissolve, solvi.
Disrespect, malrespekti.
Disrespect, malrespekto.
Dissuade, malkonsili.
Distaff, ŝpinilo.
Distance, interspaco.
Distant, malproksima.
Distaste, tedo, naŭzo.
Distend, plilarĝigi, ŝveli. [Error in book: ŝvelo]
Distil, distili.
Distinct (clear), klara.
Distinct, neta, klara.
Distinctive, distingiga.
Distinguish, distingi.
Distort, tordigi.

to.
Delegation, delegacio.
Deliberate, prikonsiliĝi.
Deliberation, prikonsiliĝo.
Delicacy, frandaĵo.
Delicate, delikata.
Delightful, rava, ĉarmega.
Delinquent, kulpulo.
Delirium, deliro.
Deliver (save), savi.
Deliver (liberate), liberigi.
Deliver (goods), liveri.
Delivery (childbirth), nasko.
Dell, valeto.
Delude, trompi.
Deluge, superakvego.
Delusion, trompo.
Demagogue, demagogo.
Demand, postulo.
Demean, humili.
Demeanour, konduto.
Demesne, bieno—aĵo.
Demise, morto.
Democrat, demokrato.
Democracy, demokrataro.
Demolish, detruegi.
Demon, demono.
Demoniac, demoniako.
Demonstrate, pruvi.
Demonstrative, montra.
Demoralized, to become, malkuraĝiĝi.
Demur, ŝanceliĝi.
Demure, modesta.

Distortion (grimace), grimaco.
Distract, distri.
Distraction, distreco.
Distress, ĉagreniĝi.
Distress, mizerigo.
Distribute (scatter), disŝuti.
Distribute (to share), disdoni.
District, kvartalo.
Distrust, malfidi.
Distrust, malfido.
Distrustful, malfidema.
Disturb, interrompi.
Disturbance, tumulto.
Disunite, disigi.
Disunion, disiĝo.
Ditch, defluilo.
Ditto, sama, idemo.
Ditty, kanteto.
Dive, subakviĝi.
Diver (bird), kolimbo.
Diverge, malkonvergi.
Divers (various), diversa.
Diverse, diversa.
Diversity, diverseco.
Divert, amuzi.
Divest, senvestigi.
Divide, dividi.
Dividend (finance), rento.
Dividend (arith.), dividato.
Divider, dividanto.
Divine, dia.
Divinity, dieco.
Divine service, Diservo.
Division, divido.
Division (arith.), dividado.
Divisor, dividon-

Den (animals, etc.), nestego.
Denial, neo.
Deniable, neigebla.
Denote, montri.
Denounce, denunci.
Dense, densa.
Density, denseco.
Dental, denta.
Dentist, dentisto.
Denude, senkovrigi.
Denunciation, denunco—ado.
Deny, nei.
Depart, foriri.
Depart (life), morti.
Department, fako, departemento.
Departure, foriro.
Depend, dependi.
Dependence, dependeco.
Depict, priskribi.
Deplore, bedaŭregi.
Deponent, atestanto.
Depopulate, senhomigi.
Depopulated, senhoma.
Deportment, konduto.
Depose (give evidence), atesti
Depose, eksigi, detroni.
Deposit, enmeti.
Depot, tenejo.
Deprave, malvirtigi.
Depravity, malvirto.
Depreciate, maltaksigi.
Depredation, rabado.
Depress, malleveti.
Deprivation, senigo.

to.
Divorce (judicial), eksedziĝo.
Divorce (judicial), eksedziĝi.
Divorced, to be, eksedziĝi.
Divulge, konigi.
Dizziness, kapturno.
Do, fari.
Do away with, to, forigi.
Docile, obea.
Docility, obeemo.
Dock, ŝipejo.
Docket, karteto, bileto.
Doctor, Doktoro.
Doctor (med.), kuracisto.
Doctrine, dogmaro.
Document, dokumento.
Doff, demeti.
Dog, hundo.
Dogged, obstina.
Doghouse, hundodometo.
Dog kennel, hundejo.
Dogma, dogmo.
Dole, disdoni.
Doleful, funebra.
Doll, pupo.
Dollar, dolaro.
Dolphin, delfeno.
Dolt, malsaĝulo.
Domain, bieno.
Dome, kupolo.
Domestic, hejma.
Domestic, servisto—ino.
Domicile, loĝejo.
Dominant, potenca.
Domination, potenco.
Dominion, regeco.
Dominion, regno.
Domino, domeno.
Donation, donaco, oferdono.

Depth, profundo—aĵo.
Depute, deputi.
Deputy, deputato.
Derail, elreliĝi.
Derange, malordigi.
Deride, moki, mokegi.
Derive, deveni.
Derivation, devenigado.
Descend, malsupreniri.
Descendant, ido, posteulo.
Describe, priskribi.
Desecration, malpiegaĵo.
Desert, forlasi.
Desert (place), dezerto.
Deserter, forkurinto.
Deserve, meriti.
Design (draw), desegni.
Design (intend), intenci.
Design (intention), intenco.
Designate, montr-, nomi.
Designing, ruza.
Desire, deziri.
Desist, ĉesi, ĉesigi.
Desk, skribtablo.
Desolate, ruinigi.
Despair, malesperi.
Despatch, ekspedi.
Desperate, furioza.
Despicable, malnobla.
Despise, malestimi.
Despond, malesperi.
Despot, tirano.
Despotism, tiraneco.

Donkey, azeno.
Donor, donanto.
Doom, kondamno, sorto.
Door, pordo.
Door curtain, pordo kurteno.
Doorkeeper, pordisto.
Dormant, ekdorma.
Dormer-window, fenestreto.
Dormitory, dormejo.
Dorsal, dorsa.
Dose, dozo.
Dot, punkto.
Dote, amegi.
Double, duobligi.
Doubt, dubi.
Doubter, dubanto.
Doubtful, duba.
Doubtlessly, sendube.
Douche, duŝo.
Dough, knedaĵo.
Dove, kolombo.
Dovecot, kolombejo.
Down, lanugo.
Downs, sablaj montetoj.
Downfall, falego.
Dowry, doto.
Downwards, malsupre.
Doze, dormeti.
Dozen, dekduo.
Draft (bill of exchange), kambio.
Drag, treni, tiri.
Dragon, drako.
Dragon fly, libelo.
Dragoon, dragono.
Drake, anaso.
Drama, dramo.
Dramatical, drama.
Dramatist, dramaŭtoro.
Drape, drapiri.
Draper,

Dessert, deserto.
Destine, for, difini (por).
Destiny, sorto.
Destitute, malriĉega.
Destroy, detrui.
Destruction, detruo.
Detach, apartigi.
Detachment (milit.), taĉmento.
Detail, detalo.
Details (minutes), detaleto.
Detain, malhelpi, deteni.
Detect, eltrovi.
Deter, malhelpi.
Deteriorate, difekti.
Determine, decidi.
Determination, decideco.
Determined, decida.
Detest, malami.
Dethrone, detroni.
Detonation, eksplodbruo.
Detract, kalumnii.
Detriment, malprofito, perdo.
Detrimental, malhelpa.
Devastate, dezertigi, ruinigi.
Develope, vastigi.
Development, vastigo.
Deviate, malrektiĝi.
Deviation, malrektiĝo.
Device, devizo.
Devil, diablo.
Devine, diveni.
Devious, malrekta.
Devise (invent), elpensi.
Devoid, senenhava.
Devote one's self, drapvendisto.
Drastic, drastika.
Draught-board, dama tabulo.
Draughts (pieces), damoj.
Draughtsman, desegnisto.
Draw (water from well), ĉerpi.
Draw (pull), tiri.
Draw after (load, etc.), posttiri.
Draw (near), proksimiĝi.
Draw (lots), loti.
Draw (together), kuntiri.
Drawer, tirkesto.
Drawers (garment), kalsono.
Drawing (lots), lotado.
Dray, ŝarĝveturilo.
Dread, timi, timegi.
Dread, teruro, timo.
Dreadful, terurega.
Dream, sonĝi.
Dreary, malgaja.
Dredge, skrapi.
Dredger, skrapilego.
Dregs, feĉo.
Drench, akvumi.
Dress (clothe), vesti.
Dress (wound), bandaĝi.
Dressing case, necesujo.
Dress coat, frako.
Dressing gown, negliĝa vesto.
Dressmaker, kudristino.
Dressing room, tualetejo, vestejo.
Drill, bori.
Drill (tool), borilo.
Drill (military), sin doni.
Devoted, sindona.
Devotion, sindono.
Devotee, religiulo.
Devoid, religia.
Devour, manĝegi.
Dew, roso.
Dexterity, lerteco.
Diadem, diademo.
Diagonal, diagonalo.
Diagram, diagramo.
Dial, ciferplato.
Dialect, dialekto.
Dialogue, dialogo.
Diameter, diametro.
Diamond, diamanto.
Diarrhœa, lakso.
Dice, ludkuboj.
Dictate, dikti.
Dictation, diktato.
Dictator, diktatoro.
Dictionary, vortaro.
Die, morti.
Die, presilo.
Diet, dieto.
Differ, diferenci.
Difference (dispute), malpaco.
Difficulty, malfacileco.
Diffusion, vastigo.
Dig, fosi.
Digest, digesti.
Digit, fingro, cifero.
Dignify, indigi.
Dignitary, rangulo.
Dignity, indeco.
Dignity (rank), rango.
Dilapidate, ruinigi.
Dilate, plilarĝigi.
Dilatory, prokrastema.
ekzerco.
Drink, trinki.
Drink (to excess), drinki.
Drink, trinkaĵo.
Drinkable, trinkebla.
Drip, guteti.
Drive away (expel), forpeli.
Drive (in carriage), veturi.
Drive back (repel), repeli, repuŝi.
Drivel (to slaver), kraĉeti.
Driver (car, etc.), veturisto.
Droll, ridinda, ŝerca.
Drollery, ŝerco—ado.
Dromedary, unuĝiba kamelo.
Drone, burdo.
Droop (pine), malfortiĝi.
Drop, guto.
Dropsy, akvoŝvelo.
Dross, metala ŝaŭmo.
Drought, senpluveco.
Drove (cattle), bestaro, brutaro.
Drown, droni.
Drown (trans.), dronigi.
Drowsy, dorma.
Drub (beat), bati.
Drudge, laboregi.
Drug, drogo.
Druggist, drogisto.
Drum, tamburo.
Drum, of ear, oreltamburo.
Drunkard, drinkulo.
Drunkenness, ebrieco.
Dry, seka.
Dry up, sekiĝi.
Diligence, diligento.
Diligent, diligenta.
Dim, dubeluma.
Diminish (length), mallongigi.
Diminish (price), rabati.
Diminutive, malgranda—eta.
Din, bruegado.
Dine (midday), meztagmanĝi.
Dine (evening), vespermanĝi.
Dining-room, manĝoĉambro.
Dining-room (public), restoracio.
Dinner-service, manĝilaro.
Dip, trempi.
Dip (in water), subakvigi.
Diphthong, diftongo.
Diploma, diplomo.
Diplomacy, diplomatio.
Diphtheria, difterio.
Dire, terura.
Direct (govern), direkti.
Direct (command), ordoni.
Direct (straight), rekta.
Directly (time), tuj.
Directly, rekte.
Director, direktoro.
Directory, adresaro.
Dirge, funebra kanto.
Dirt (soil), malpurigi.
Dirt, malpuraĵo.
Dirt (mud), koto.
Dirtiness,
Dry, one's self, sin sekigi.
Dry land, firmaĵo.
Dryness, sekeco.
Dual, duobla, dualo.
Dualism, dualismo.
Dubious, duba.
Ducat, dukato.
Duchess, dukino.
Duchy, duklando.
Duck, anasino.
Ducking, trempado.
Duct, tubo.
Ductile, etendebla.
Dude, dando.
Duel, duelo.
Duet, dueto.
Duke, duko.
Dukedom (duchy), duklando.
Dull (unpolished), malbrila.
Dull (sombre), malhela, nebula.
Dull (stupid), malklera.
Dull (blunt), malakra.
Dumb, muta.
Dumbness, muteco.
Dumb show, pantomimo.
Dunce, malklerulo.
Dung, sterko.
Dungheap, sterkaĵo.
Dungeon, malliberejo.
Dupe, trompi.
Duplicate, duobligi.
Duplicity, trompemo.
Durable, fortika.
Duration, daŭro.
During, dum.
Dusky, malhela.
Dust, polvo.

malpureco.
Dirty, malpura.
Disable, kripli.
Disadvantage, malutilo.
Disagree, malkonsenti.
Disagreement, malkonsento.
Disappear, malaperi.
Disappoint, malkontentigi.

Dust, grain of, polvero.
Duster, viŝilo.
Dustman, kotisto.
Dutchman, Holandano.
Duty, devo.
Duty (import), imposto.
Dutiful, respektema.
Dwarf, malgrandegulo.
Dwell, loĝi, restadi.
Dwelling, loĝejo.
Dwindle, malgrandiĝi.
Dye, kolorigi.
Dye, kolorigilo.
Dyer, kolorigisto.
Dying, to be, ekmorti.
Dying (person), mortanto.
Dyke, digo.
Dynamics, dinamiko.
Dynamism, dinamismo.
Dynamite, dinamito.
Dynasty, dinastio.
Dysentery, disenterio.
Dyspepsia, dispepsio.

E
Each (adj.), ĉia.
Each (pronoun), ĉiu.
Eager, avida.
Eagle, aglo.
Ear, orelo.
Ear (of corn), spiko.
Earl, grafo.
Earldom, graflando.
Early (adv.), frue.
Early (adj.), frua.
Earn, perlabori.
Earnest, diligenta.
Earnestly, forte, fervore.

Earnestness, seriozeco.
Earring, orelringo.
Earth, tero.
Earthenware, fajenco
Earthly, monda, tera.
Earthquake, tertremo.
Ease, komforto.
Ease, at, senĝene.
East, oriento.
Easter, Pasko.
Easterly, orienta.
Easy, facila.
Eat, manĝi.
Eatable, manĝebla.
Eaves, defluilo.
Ebb (and flow), forfluo (kaj alfluo).
Ebony, ebono.
Ebriety, ebrieco.
Ebullition, bolado.
Eccentric, stranga.
Ecclesiastic, ekleziulo.
Ecclesiastical, eklezia.
Echo, eĥo.
Eclipse, mallumiĝo.
Ecliptic, ekliptiko.
Eclogue, eklogo.
Economical, ŝparema.
Economics, ekonomio.
Economise, ŝpari.
Economist, ekonomiisto.
Economy, ŝparemo.
Ecstacy, ravo.
Eczema, ekzemo.
Eddy, turniĝadi.
Eddy, akvoturn.ĝo.
Eden, Edeno.

Epitomise, mallongigi.
Epoch, epoko.
Equable, egala.
Equal, egala.
Equality, egaleco.
Equalise, egaligi.
Equally, egale.
Equation, ekvacio.
Equator, ekvatoro.
Equilibrium, ekvilibro.
Equinox, tagnoktegaleco.
Equipment (milit.), armilaro.
Equitable, justa.
Equity, justeco.
Equivalent, ekvivalenta.
Equivocal, dusenca.
Era, tempokalkulo.
Eradicate, elradikigi.
Erase, surstreki.
Eraser, skrapileto.
Erasure, surstrekaĵo.
Ere, antaŭ (ol).
Erect, starigi.
Erect, vertikala.
Erection, konstruo.
Ermine (animal), ermeno.
Ermine (fur), ermenfelo.
Erotic, erotika.
Err, erari.
Errand, komisio.
Erratic, erara.
Erratum, eraro.
Erroneous, erara.
Error, eraro.
Eructation, rukto.
Erudite (person), instruitulo, klerulo.
Eruption, ekzantemo.

Edge, rando.
Edge (of tools), tranĉrando.
Edible, manĝebla.
Edict, ordono.
Edifice, konstruaĵo.
Edify, edifi.
Edit, eldoni, redakti.
Edition, eldono.
Editor, eldonisto.
Educate, eduki.
Educated, klera.
Education (given), edukado.
Education (received), edukiteco.
Educator, edukisto.
Eel, angilo.
Efface, surstreki.
Effect (result), efiko.
Effect (impression), efekto.
Effect, efektivigi.
Effective, efektiva.
Effectively, efektive.
Effectual, efektiva.
Effervesce, ŝaŭmadi.
Efficacious, efika.
Efficacy, efikeco.
Effigy, figuro.
Efflorescence, florado.
Effluvium, malbonodoro.
Efflux, defluado.
Effort, peno.
Effrontery, senhonteco.
Effulgent, radiluma.
Egg, ovo.
Egg-shaped, ovoforma.
Egoism, egoismo.
Egoist, egoisto.
Egress, eliro.

Eruption, volcanic, elsputo, vulkana.
Erysipelas, erisipelo.
Escape, forkuri.
Escarpment, krutegaĵo.
Eschew, eviti.
Escort, gardistaro.
Escort, gardi.
Escutcheon, blazono.
Especial, speciala.
Especially, precipe.
Espouse, edziĝi.
Espouse (adopt), alpreni.
Espy, vidi, ekvidi.
Essay (trial), provo.
Essay, provi.
Essence, esenco.
Essence (oil), oleo.
Essential, esenca.
Establish, fondi.
Estate, bieno.
Esteem, estimi.
Estimable, estiminda.
Estimate (appraise), taksi.
Estimate, estimi.
Estimate, appraisement, taksado.
Estimation, estimado.
Estrange, forigi.
Estuary, estuario.
Eternal, eterna.
Eternity, eterneco.
Ether, etero.
Ethereal, etera.
Ethical, etika.
Ethnography, etnografio.
Ethology, etologio.
Etiology, etiologio.
Etiquette, etiketo.

Egyptian, Egipto.
Eh! he!
Eider-down, lanugo.
Eider-duck, molanaso.
Eight, ok.
Either, aŭ.
Ejaculation, ekkrio.
Eject, elĵeti.
Elaborate, prilabori.
Elastic, elasta.
Elastic, elastaĵo.
Elasticity, elasteco.
Elbow, kubuto.
Elder (tree), sambuko.
Elder, pliaĝa.
Eldest (first born), unuanaskito.
Elect (choose), elekti.
Elect (by ballot), baloti.
Election, elekto.
Elector, elektanto.
Electric, elektra.
Electricity, elektro.
Electrify, elektrigi.
Elegance, eleganteco.
Elegant, eleganta.
Elegy, elegio.
Element, elemento.
Elementary, elementa.
Elephant, elefanto.
Elevate, altigi.
Elevation (height), altaĵo.
Elf, koboldo, feino.
Elicit, eltiri.
Elide, elizii.
Eligible, elektebla.
Eligibility, elektebleco.

Etymology, vortodeveno.
Eucharist, Eŭkaristo.
Eulogize, laŭdegi.
Eulogy, laŭdego.
Euphonic, bonsona.
Euphonious, belsona.
Europe, Eŭropo.
European, Eŭropano.
Evacuate, malplenigi.
Evade, eviti.
Evangelical, evangelia.
Evaporate, vaporiĝi.
Evaporation, vaporiĝo.
Evasion, forkuro.
Evasion, artifiko.
Eve, antaŭtago.
Eve, evening, vespero.
Even (number), parnombro.
Even, eĉ.
Even (level), ebena.
Even, to make, ebenigi.
Evening, vespero.
Evening party, vesperkunveno.
Event, okazo.
Eventful, okazplena.
Ever, ĉiam.
Ever (whoever, etc.), ajn (kiu ajn).
Everlasting, eterna.
Evermore, for, je eterne.
Every, ĉiu.
Every kind of, ĉia.
Every manner, ĉiel.
Everyone, ĉiu.
Everyone's, ĉies.
Every reason, for, ĉial.

Eliminate, elmeti.
Elision, elizio.
Elite, eminentularo.
Ell, ulno.
Ellipse, elipso.
Elm, ulmo.
Elocution, parolscienco.
Eloquence, elokventeco.
Eloquent, elokventa.
Elope, forkuri.
Else, alie.
Elsewhere, aliloke.
Elude, lerte eviti.
Emaciated, malgrasega.
Emanate, deveni.
Emancipate, liberigi.
Embalm, balzamumi.
Embankment, surbordo bordmarŝejo.
Embark, enŝipiĝi.
Embarrass, embarasi.
Embarrassment, embaraso.
Embellish, beligi, ornami.
Embers, brulaĵo.
Emblem, emblemo.
Embolden, kuraĝigi.
Embossment, reliefo.
Embrace, ĉirkaŭpreni.
Embroider, brodi.
Embryo, embrio.
Embryology, embriologio.
Emerald, smeraldo.
Emergency, ekokazo.
Emetic, vomilo.
Emigrant, elmigranto.

Everything, ĉio.
Everyway, ĉiel.
Everywhere, ĉie.
Evidence, evidenteco.
Evident, evidenta.
Evidently, evidente.
Evil, malbono, peko.
Evil, malbona, peka.
Evil doing, malbonfarado.
Evoke, elvoki.
Evolution, evolucio.
Ewe, ŝafino.
Ewer, kruĉego.
Exact, postuli.
Exact (precise), preciza.
Exact, ĝusta.
Exact, accurate, akurata.
Exactness, akurateco.
Exaggerate, trograndigi.
Exaggeration, trograndigo.
Exalt, laŭdegi.
Examination, ekzameno.
Examine, ekzameni.
Example, ekzemplo.
Exasperate, koleregigi.
Excavate, kavigi.
Excavate, kavigi, fosi.
Excavator, terfosisto.
Exceed, superi.
Excel, superi.
Excellence, boneco.
Excellency, Ekscelenco, Moŝto.
Excellent, bonega.
Except, krom.
Except, escepti.

Emigrate, elmigri.
Emigration, elmigrado, emigracio.
Eminence, altaĵo.
Eminence (title), Moŝto.
Eminent, eminenta.
Emissary, emisario, reprezentanto.
Emit, ellasi.
Emmet, formiko.
Emolument, salajro.
Emotion, kortuŝeco.
Emperor, imperiestro.
Emphatic, patosa, akcentega.
Emphasis, patoso, akcentego.
Emphasise, akcentegi.
Empire, imperio.
Employ (use), uzi.
Employ (hire), dungi.
Employment, ofico.
Empower, rajtigi.
Empress, imperiestrino.
Empty, malplenigi.
Empty, malplena.
Empty (unoccupied), neokupata.
Emulate, superemi.
Emulation, superemo.
Enable, ebligi.
Enact, reguli.
Enactment, regulo.
Enamel, emajlo.
Enamel, emajli.
Enamoured, enamiĝinta. [Error in book: emamiĝinta]
Encase, enkasigi.
Enchant, ravi.

Exception, escepto.
Excess, malmodereco.
Excessive, troa.
Excessively, troe.
Exchange, interŝanĝi.
Exchange, The, borso.
Excise officer, oficisto.
Excite, eksciti.
Excitement, ekscitego.
Exclaim, ekkrii.
Exclamation, point of, signo ekkria.
Exclude, eksigi.
Exclusion, eksigeco.
Exclusive, ekskluziva.
Excommunicate, ekskomuniki.
Excoriation, defrotaĵo.
Excrement, ekskremento.
Excrescence, elkreskaĵo.
Excruciate, turmentegi.
Exculpate, senkulpigi.
Excursion, ekskurso.
Excusable, pardonebla.
Excuse, pardoni, senkulpigi.
Execrable, abomena.
Execrate, malbenegi.
Execute (to do), fari.
Execute, ekzekuti.
Executioner, ekzekutisto.
Executive, regantaro.
Exemplar, ekzemplero.

Enchantment, ensorĉo.
Enclose, enfermi.
Enclosed (herewith), tie ĉi enfermita.
Encompass, ĉirkaŭi.
Encore, bis.
Encounter, renkonti.
Encourage, kuraĝigi.
Encyclopedia, enciklopedio.
Encroach, trudi.
End, fini.
End, fino.
Endearment, kareso.
Endeavour, peni.
Endeavour, peno.
Endless, eterna.
Endow, doti.
Endure (continue), daŭri.
Endure (tolerate), toleri.
Endure (suffer), suferi.
Enema, klisterilo.
Enemy, malamiko.
Energetic, energia.
Energy, energio.
Enervate, malfortigi.
Enfranchise, afranki, liberigi.
Engage, servigi, dungi.
Engage (to occupy), okupi.
Engagement (promise), promeso.
Engagement (milit.), ekbatalo.
Engine, maŝino.
Engineer, inĝeniero.
England, Anglujo, Anglolando.
English, Angla.

Exemplary, ekzempla.
Exemplify, ekzempligi.
Exempt, liberigi.
Exempt, libera.
Exercise, ekzerci.
Exercise, ekzerco.
Exercisbook, kajero.
Exhale, odori.
Exhaust, konsumi.
Exhaustion, konsumiteco.
Exhibit, elmontri.
Exhibition, ekspozicio.
Exhort, admoni.
Exhume, elterigi.
Exigence, postulo—eco.
Exigent, postula.
Exile, ekzili.
Exist, ekzisti.
Existence, ekzistaĵo.
Exit, eliro.
Exonerate, pravigi.
Exorbitant, supermezura.
Exotic, alilanda.
Expanse, etendeco.
Expand, etendi.
Expect, atendi.
Expectation, atendo.
Expectorate, kraĉi.
Expedite, ekspedi.
Expedition (milit.), militiro.
Expeditious, rapidega.
Expeditiously, rapide.
Expel, elpeli.
Expend, elspezi.
Expenditure, elspezado.
Expense, elspezo.
Expensive, multekosta.

Englishman, Anglo.
Engrave, gravuri.
Engraver, gravuristo.
Engraving, gravuraĵo.
Engross (fully occupy), priokupi.
Enhale, enspiri.
Enigma, enigmo.
Enjoin, ordoni.
Enjoy, ĝui.
Enlarge, pligrandigi.
Enlighten, klerigi.
Enlist, varbi.
Enlistment, varbo.
Enliven, gajigi.
Enmity, malamikeco.
Ennoble, nobeligi.
Enormous, grandega.
Enough, sufiĉe.
Enquire, informiĝi.
Enquiry, informiĝo.
Enrage, furiozigi.
Enrapture, ravi.
Enrich, riĉigi.
Enrichment, riĉigo.
Enrol, varbi.
Ensign-bearer, standardisto.
Enslave, sklavigi.
Ensue, sekvi.
Entangle, impliki.
Enter, eniri, enveni.
Enterprise, entrepreno.
Entertain, regali.
Entertain (amuse), amuzi.
Entertain (consider), konsideri.
Enthusiasm, entuziasmo.
Enthusiast, entuziasmulo.
Enthusiastic, entuziasma.

Experience, sperto.
Experience, senti.
Experienced, sperta.
Experiment, eksperimenti.
Experiment, eksperimento.
Expert, lerta.
Expert, an, kompetentulo.
Expiate, elpagi.
Expiation, elpago.
Expiration (of time), templimo.
Expire (to die), morti.
Expire (breathe out), elspiri.
Explain, klarigi.
Explanation, klarigo.
Explication, klarigo.
Explicit, klara.
Explode, eksplodi.
Exploit, heroaĵo.
Exploit, ekspluati.
Explore, esplori.
Explorer, esploristo.
Explosion, eksplodo.
Export, eksteren sendi.
Expose, montri.
Exposition, ekspozicio.
Expostulate, rezonegi.
Expound, klarigi.
Express, esprimi.
Express-train, rapida vagonaro.
Expression, esprimo.
Expressly, speciale.
Expulsion, elpelo.
Expunge, elstreki.
Exquisite, rava.
Extant, ekzistanta.
Extempore, sen-

Entice, allogi.
Entire, tuta.
Entirely, tute.
Entitle (to name), titoli.
Entomb, entombigi.
Entomology, entomologio.
Entr'acte, interakto.
Entrails, internaĵo.
Entrance, eniro.
Entrance, ĉarmi.
Entreat, petegi.
Entreaty, petego.
Entry, eniro.
Entwine, kunplekti.
Enumerate, denombri.
Enunciate, eldiri.
Envelop, envolvi.
Envelope, koverto.
Envenom, veneni.
Enviable, enviinda.
Envious, enviema.
Environs, ĉirkaŭaĵo.
Envoy, sendito.
Envy, envii.
Epaulet, epoleto.
Ephemeral, mallonga, efemera.
Epic, epopea.
Epic, epopeo.
Epicure, epikuristo.
Epidemic, epidemio.
Epidermis, epidermo.
Epigram, epigramo.

F

Fable, fablo.
Fabric (stuff), teksaĵo.
Fabric, fabriko.
Fabricate, fabriki.

prepara.
Extend, etendi.
Extension, etendo.
Extensive, vasta.
Exterior, eksteraĵo.
Exterminate, ekstermi.
External, ekstera.
Extinct, estingita.
Extinguish, estingi.
Extirpate, elradikigi.
Extol, laŭdegi.
Extort, eltiregi.
Extra, ekstra.
Extract, ekstrakti, eltiri.
Extract, ekstrakto, eltiro—aĵo.
Extraction (lineage), deveno.
Extraordinary, eksterorda.
Extravagance, malŝparo.
Extravagant, malŝparema.
Extreme, ekstrema.
Extremely, treege.
Extremity, ekstremaĵo.
Extricate, liberigi.
Exuberant, plenega.
Exude, guteti, malsorbiĝi, elsorbiĝi.
Exult, ĝojegi.
Exultation, ĝojego.
Eye, okulo.
Eyebrow, brovo.
Eyeglasses, lorno.
Eyelash, okulharo.
Eyelid, palpebro

Flail, draŝilo.
Flake, neĝero, floko.
Flambeau, torĉo.
Flame, flami.

Fabrication, fabrikado.
Fabulist, fablisto.
Fabulous, fabla.
Façade, antaŭa flanko.
Face, vizaĝo.
Facet, faceto.
Facetious, ŝerca.
Facilitate, faciligi.
Facility, facileco.
Facsimile, faksimilo.
Fact, fakto.
Fact, in (adv.), ja.
Faction, sekto.
Factious, malpaca.
Factor (agent), faktoro.
Factory, fabrikejo.
Faculty, fakultato.
Faculty, kapablo.
Fade, velki.
Fading, velkanto.
Fag, laboregi.
Fagot, branĉaro.
Fail, manki.
Fail, malprosperi.
Fail (bankruptcy), bankroti.
Failure, malprospero.
Failing (fault), kulpo.
Faint, sveni.
Faint (swoon), sveno.
Faint hearted, timema.
Fair (market), foiro.
Fair (complexion), blonda.
Fair, justa.
Fair copy, neto.
Fairly, juste.
Fairy, feino.
Faith, fido.
Faithful, fidela.
Falcon, falko.
Fall, fali.
Fall, falo.

Flame, flamo.
Flank, flanko.
Flannel, flanelo.
Flap, klapo.
Flare, brilego.
Flash (lightning), fulmo.
Flash (of wit), spritaĵo.
Flask, boteleto.
Flat, plata.
Flat (music), duontono sube.
Flatten, platigi.
Flatter, flati.
Flatterer, flatulo.
Flattering, flatema.
Flavour, gusto.
Flaw, difekto.
Flax, lino.
Flay, senhaŭtigi.
Flea, pulo.
Flee, flugi.
Fleece, ŝaflano.
Fleecy, laneca.
Fleet (quick), rapida.
Fleet, ŝiparo.
Flesh (meat), viando.
Flesh, karno.
Flexibility, fleksebleco.
Flexible, fleksebla.
Flexion, flekso.
Flicker, lumŝanceli.
Flight, forkuro.
Flight (birds), flugado.
Fling, ĵeti.
Flint (mineral), siliko.
Flippant, babila.
Flirt, amindumeti, koketi.
Flirt, koketulino.
Flirtation, koketeco.
Flit, flirti.
Float (intrans.), naĝi.
Float (trans.),

Fall (in price), malplikariĝo.
Fall off, away, defali.
Fall out (disagree), malpaci.
Fall (in ruins), ruiniĝi.
Fallacy, sofismo.
Fallow, senkulturega.
False, falsa.
Falsehood, mensogo.
Falsify, falsi.
Falsification, falsado.
Falsifier, falsinto.
Fame, famo.
Familiar, kutima.
Familiarize, kutimigi.
Familiarity, kutimeto.
Family, familio.
Famine, malsatego.
Famishing, to be, malsategi.
Famished, malsatega.
Famous, fama.
Fan, ventumi.
Fan, ventumilo.
Fanatic, fanatikulo.
Fanatical, fanatika.
Fanaticism, fanatikeco.
Fanciful, imaga.
Fancy, imagi.
Fanfaronade, fanfaronado.
Fang, kojna dento.
Fantastical, strangega.
Fantasy, fantazio.
Far, malproksima.
Far off (adv.), malproksime.
Farce, ŝerco.
Fare, bill of,

flosi.
Flock (congregation), zorgitaro.
Flock, aro.
Flog, skurĝi.
Flood, superakvego.
Floor, planko.
Floor (storey), etaĝo.
Florid, ruĝega.
Florin, floreno.
Florist, floristo.
Flotilla, ŝipareto.
Flour, faruno.
Flourish (brandish), svingi.
Flow, flui.
Flow (of blood), sangverŝo.
Flow away, deflui.
Flower, flori.
Flower-bed, florbedo.
Flower-garden, florejo.
Fluctuate, ŝanceliĝi.
Flue, kamentubo.
Fluent, elokventa, fluanta.
Fluid, fluaĵo.
Fluid, flua.
Flute, fluto.
Flutter, flugeti, flirti.
Flux, alfluo.
Fly, flugi.
Fly, muŝo.
Fly away, forflugi.
Foal, ĉevalido—ino.
Foam, ŝaŭmi.
Foam, ŝaŭmo—aĵo.
Foam (sea), marŝaŭmo.
Focus, fokuso.
Fodder, furaĝo.
Fœtid, malbonodora.
Foe, kontraŭulo, malamiko.

manĝokarto.
Farewell, adiaŭ.
Farm, farmi.
Farm, farmo.
Farmhouse, farmodomo.
Farmer, farma mastro.
Farrier, forĝisto.
Fascinate, ensorĉi.
Fascination, ensorĉo.
Fashion (to form), formi.
Fashion (manner), maniero.
Fashion (dress), fasono.
Fashion, in such a, tiel.
Fast, fasti.
Fast, fasto.
Fast, to make, alligi.
Fast, rapida.
Fast-day, fasta tago.
Fasten, alligi.
Fastidious, malŝatema.
Fasting, fastinte.
Fat, grasa.
Fatal, fatala.
Fatalism, fatalismo.
Fatality, fatalo.
Fatally, fatale.
Fate, sorto.
Father, patro.
Fatherland, patrolando.
Father-in-law, bopatro.
Fatherhood, patreco.
Fatherly, patra.
Fathom, sondi.
Fathom-line, sondilo.
Fatigue, lacigi.
Fatigue, laceco.
Fatigued, laca.
Fatiguing, laciga.
Fatten, grasigi.

Fog, nebulo.
Foil (weapon), rapiro, skermilo.
Fold, faldi.
Fold (sheep), ŝafejo.
Folding-screen, ventoŝirmilo.
Foliage, foliaro.
Follow, sekvi.
Following, the, sekvanta.
Follows, that which, jena.
Folly, malspriteco.
Fond, ama.
Foment, vivigi.
Fondle, dorloti.
Fondness, ameco.
Font, baptakvujo.
Food, nutraĵo.
Fool, simplanimulo.
Foolish, malsaĝa.
Foolishness, malsaĝeco.
Foot, piedo.
Foot (measure), futo.
Foot, on, piedire.
Foot-bridge, piedponto.
Footman, lakeo.
Footpath, trotuaro.
Footprint, piedsigno.
Foot-soldier, infanteriano.
Footway, piedvojo.
Fop, dando.
For, ĉar.
For (on account of), pro.
For, por.
Forage, furaĝo.
Forbear, toleri.
Forbearance, tolero.
Forbearing, tolerema.
Forbid, malpermesi.

Faucet, krano.
Fault (error), eraro.
Fault, kulpo.
Faulty, mankhava.
Favour, favori.
Favour, favoro.
Favourable, favora.
Fawn, cervido.
Fawn-coloured, brunruĝa.
Fay, feo (m.), feino (f.).
Fealty, fideleco.
Fear, timi.
Fear, timo.
Feasible, farebla.
Feast, regali.
Feast (meal), regalo.
Feast (holiday), festeno.
Feast, festeni.
Feat, heroaĵo.
Feather, plumo.
Feather-duster, plumbalailo.
Feature (trait), trajto.
Febrile, febra.
February, Februaro.
Fecundate, fruktigi.
Federal, federa.
Federation (act), federo.
Federation (state), federacio.
Federative, federa.
Fee, pagi.
Feeble, malforta.
Feebleness, malforteco.
Feed, nutri.
Feel (touch), palpi.
Feel, senti.
Feeling, sento.
Feeling, palpo.
Feel one's way, palpeti.

Force, devigi.
Forcible, devigebla.
Ford, transirejo.
Fore, antaŭa.
Forearm, antaŭbrako.
Foreboding, antaŭsento.
Forehead, frunto.
Foreign, alilanda.
Foreigner, alilandulo.
Foreman, submajstro.
Foremost, unua.
Forenoon, antaŭtagmezo.
Forepart (ship), antaŭparto.
Forerunner, antaŭulo.
Foresee, antaŭvidi.
Foresight, antaŭzorgo.
Forest, arbaro.
Foretell, antaŭdiri.
Forethought, antaŭzorgo.
Forewarn, averti.
Forge, forĝi.
Forge, forĝejo.
Forget, forgesi.
Forgetful, forgesa.
Forgetfulness, forgeseco.
Forget-me-not, miozoto.
Forgive, pardoni.
Forgiveness, pardono.
Fork, forko.
Form (to fashion), alformi.
Form (shape), formo.
Formal, ceremonia.
Formation, formo.
Former (the), tiu.
Formerly, iam,

antaŭe.
Formidable, timeginda.
Formulate, formuli.
Formulary, protokolo.
Formula, formulo.
Forsake, forlasi.
Fort, fortikaĵeto.
Fortify (milit.), fortikigi.
Fortify, fortigi.
Fortitude, kuraĝeco.
Fortnight, du semajnoj.
Fortress, fortikaĵo.
Fortune, riĉeco.
Forward! antaŭen!
Forward (in advance), antaŭe.
Forward, ekspedi, sendi.
Fossil, elfosataĵo.
Foster, nutri.
Foster child, suĉinfano.
Foul, malpura.
Foulard, silktuko.
Found, fondi.
Foundation, fondo, fondaĵo.
Founder (ship), ŝipperei.
Foundry, fandejo.
Fountain, fontano.
Four, kvar.
Fowl (domestic), kortbirdo.
Fox, vulpo.
Fraction, partumo.
Fracture, rompo.
Fragile, facilrompa.
Fragment, fragmento.
Fragrance, bonodoreco.
Frail, kaduka.

Feign, ŝajnigi.
Feint, ŝajnigo.
Felicity, feliĉeco.
Fell, faligi.
Fellow, a good, karulo.
Fellow-citizen, samurbano.
Felly (felloe), radrondo.
Felon, krimulo.
Felt, felto.
Female, virino, ino.
Feminine, virinseksa, ina.
Feminism, feminismo, inismo.
Fen, marĉejo.
Fence, skermi.
Fencing, skermo.
Fence, palisaro.
Fend, defendi.
Fender, fajrgardo.
Fennel, fenkolo.
Ferment, fermenti.
Ferment (disturbance), tumulto.
Fern, filiko.
Ferocious, kruelega.
Ferocity, kruelego, kruelegeco.
Ferret, ĉasputoro.
Ferry, prami.
Ferry-boat, pramo.
Fertile, fruktodona.
Fertilize, fruktigi.
Fervency, fervoreco.
Fervent, fervora.
Fervour, fervoro.
Festal, festa.
Fester, ulceriĝi.
Festival, festo.
Festoon, festono.
Fetch, alporti.
Fetich, fetiĉo.
Fetichism, fetiĉismo.
Fetid, malbonodora.

Fetter, kateno.
Feud, malpaceco.
Feudal, feŭdala.
Feudality, feŭdaleco.
Fever, febro.
Feverish, febra.
Few, kelkaj, malmultaj.
Fiancé, fianĉo.
Fiancée, fianĉino.
Fiasco, fiasko.
Fibre, fibro.
Fickle, ŝanĝebla.
Fictitious, fiktiva.
Fiddle, violono.
Fiddler, violonisto.
Fidelity, fideleco.
Fidget, movadiĝi.
Fie! fi!
Field, kampo.
Fierce, kruelega.
Fiery, fervorega.
Fife, fifro.
Fig, figo.
Fight, batali.
Figure (represent), figuri.
Figure (cipher), cifero.
Figure (image), figuro.
Filament, fibro.
Filch, ŝteli.
File, fajli.
File (tool), fajlilo.
File (newspapers), legaĵo.
Filial, filia.
Filiation, genealogio.
Filigree, filigrano.
Fill, plenigi.
Fillet, lumbaĵo.
Filly, ĉevalidino.
Film, membrano, ŝeleto.
Filter, filtrilo.
Filth, malpuraĵo.
Filthy, malpurega.
Fin, naĝilo.
Final, fina.
Finally, fine.
Finance, financo.

Frame, enkadrigi.
Frame, kadro.
Framework, trabaĵo.
Franc, franko.
France, Francujo, Franclando.
Frank, sincera.
Frank (letters), afranki.
Frankly, sincere.
Frankness, sincereco.
Frantic, furioza.
Fraternal, frata.
Fraternity, frateco.
Fraternize, fratiĝi.
Fraud, trompo.
Fraudulent, trompa.
Fray, batalo.
Freckle, lentugo.
Free, libera.
Free (gratis), senpage.
Freedom, libereco.
Freemason, framasono.
Freeze, glaciiĝi.
Freight (load), ŝarĝi.
Frenchman, Franco.
Frenzy, frenezeco.
Frequent, ofta.
Frequent, vizitadi.
Frequency, ofteco.
Fresco, fresko.
Fresh, freŝa.
Fret, malkvietiĝi.
Friar, monaĥo.
Friction, frotado.
Friend, amiko.
Friendly, amika.
Friendship, amikeco.
Frigate, fregato.
Fright, timo.
Frighten, timigi.
Frightful, terura.
Frigid, glaciiga.

Financial, financa.
Financier, financisto.
Find, trovi.
Fine, delikata.
Fine (penalty), mona puno.
Fine arts, belartoj.
Finery, ornamaĵo.
Finger, fingro.
Finish, fini.
Fir, abio.
Fire, fajro.
Fire, to set on, ekflamigi.
Fire-dog, kamenstableto.
Fire-engine, brulpumpilo.
Firing (guns, etc.), pafado.
Fireman (stoker), hejtisto.
Fireplace, kameno.
Fireside, hejmo.
Firework, fajraĵo, artfajraĵo.
Firm (fast), firma.
Firm (strong), fortika.
Firm (comm.), firmo.
Firmness, fortikeco.
Firmament, ĉielo.
First, unua.
Firstly, unue.
Firtree, pinarbo.
Fisc, fisko.
Fiscal, fiska.
Fish, fiŝo.
Fish, fiŝkapti.
Fisher, fiŝkaptisto.
Fishery, fiŝkaptado, fiŝkaptejo.
Fish-hook, fiŝhoko.
Fishing, fiŝkaptado.
Fishing-line, hokfadeno.

Fringe, franĝo.
Frisk, salteti.
Fritter, fritaĵo.
Frivolity, vaneteco. [Error in book: vanetco]
Frivolous, malserioza.
Friz (curl), frizi.
Frock-coat, frako.
Frog, rano.
Frolic, petoleco.
Frolicsome, petolema.
Front, antaŭa flanko.
Frontier, landlimo.
Frost, frosto.
Froth, ŝaŭmo.
Froward, malvirta.
Frown, sulkigi.
Fructify, fruktodoni.
Frugal, ŝparema.
Fruit, frukto.
Fruitery, fruktejo.
Fruitful, fruktoporta.
Fruit-garden, fruktejo.
Fruitless, vana.
Fruitlessly, vane.
Frustrate, malhelpi.
Fry, friti.
Fry (spawn), frajo.
Frying-pan, pato, fritilo.
Fuel, brulaĵo.
Fugitive, forkuranto.
Fugue (mus.), fugo.
Fulfil, plenumi.
Full, plena.
Full-aged, plenaĝa.
Fume, fumo.
Fun, ŝercado.
Function, funkcio.
Functionary, ofi-

Fish-market, fiŝvendejo.
Fishmonger, fiŝvendisto.
Fissure, fendeto.
Fist, pugno.
Fit (illness), atako.
Fit for, to be, taŭgi.
Fitly, alkonvena.
Five, kvin.
Fix, fiksi.
Fixed, fiksa.
Fixity, fikseco.
Flabby, mola.
Flag, standardo.
Flag (navy), flago.
Flagon, botelego.
Flagstone, ŝtonplato.
Flagrant, flagranta.

G
Gadfly, tabano.
Gaff, hokstango.
Gag, silentigi, buŝumi.
Gaiety, gajeco.
Gain, gajni.
Gain (of a watch), trorapidi.
Gainsay, kontraŭdiri.
Gait, irado.
Gaiter, gamaŝo.
Gale, ventego,

cisto.
Fundamental, fundamenta.
Fundholder, rentulo.
Funeral, enterigiro.
Funereal, funebra.
Funnel, funelo.
Funny, ridinda.
Fur, felo.
Furious, furioza.
Furnace, forno, fornego.
Furnish (provide), provizi.
Furnish (a house), mebli.
Furniture, meblaro.
Furniture (piece of), meblo.
Furrier, felisto.
Furrow (wrinkle), sulko.
Furrow, tersulko.
Further, plie.
Further, plimalproksima.
Fury, furiozo.
Fury (mythol.), furio.
Fuse, fandi.
Fusilade, pafado.
Fusion, fandiĝo.
Fustian, fusteno.
Futile, vana.
Future, estonta.
Futurity, estonteco.

Go away, foriri.
Go back, reiri.
Go before, antaŭiri.
Go beyond, trapasi, preterpasi.
Go in, eniri.
Go out, eliri.
Go out (of a light), estingiĝi, elbruli.
Go over, transiri.
Go through, trairi.

blovado.
Gall, galo.
Gall-nut, gajlo.
Gallant, amisto.
Gallant, ĝentila.
Gallant, brava.
Gallery, galerio.
Galley, remŝipego.
Gallicism, galicismo.
Gallop, galopi.
Gallows, pendigilo.
Galvanism, galvanismo.
Gambol, salteti.
Game (play), ludo.
Game, ĉasaĵo.
Game-bag, ĉasaĵujo.
Gamekeeper, ĉasgardisto.
Gamut, gamo.
Gander, anserviro.
Gang, bando.
Ganglion, ganglio.
Gangrene, gangreno.
Gaol, malliberejo.
Gaoler, gardisto.
Gap, breĉo.
Gap, manko.
Gape, oscedegi.
Garb, vesto.
Garden, ĝardeno.
Gardener, ĝardenisto.
Gardenia, gardenio.
Gardening, ĝardenlaborado.
Gargle, gargari.
Gargle, gargaraĵo.
Garland, girlando.
Garlic, ajlo.
Garment, vesto.
Garner, provizi.
Garnish, ornami.
Garniture, garnituro.

Go down (ship), ŝipperei.
Go on foot, piediri.
Go on a pilgrimage, pilgrimi.
Goad, instigilo.
Goal (aim), celo.
Goat, kapro.
Goatherd, kapristo.
Goblet, pokalo.
Goblin, koboldo.
God, Dio.
Godfather, baptopatro.
Godhead, Diaĵo.
Godless, malpia.
Godliness, sankteco.
Godly, sankta.
Gold, oro.
Golden, ora.
Goldfinch, kardelo.
Goldsmith, oraĵisto.
Goloche, galoŝo.
Gondola, gondolo.
Good, bona.
Good, to do, bonfari.
Good (welfare), bonstato.
Good-for-nothing, sentaŭgulo.
Good-bye, adiaŭ.
Goodness, boneco.
Goods (effects), posedaĵo.
Goods (merchandise), komercaĵo.
Goods train, by, malrapidire.
Goose, ansero.
Goose, anserino.
Gooseberry, groso.
Gorge, valego.
Gorge, supersatigi.
Gorgeous, belega.
Goshawk, akcip-

Garret, subtegmento.
Garrison, garnizono.
Garrote, ĉirkaŭligi.
Garter, ŝtrumpligilo.
Gas, gaso.
Gaseous, gasa.
Gash, trančadi.
Gasometer, gasometro.
Gasp, spiregi.
Gastric, stomaka.
Gate, pordego.
Gather, kolekti.
Gather together, kolekti.
Gathering, kolekto.
Gaudy, luksema.
Gauge, mezuri.
Gaunt, malgrasa.
Gauntlet, ferganto.
Gauze, gazo.
Gawky, mallerta.
Gay, to be, gaji.
Gay, gaja.
Gaze, rigardegi.
Gazelle, gazelo.
Gazette, gazeto.
Gear (machinery), ilaro.
Gehenna, Geheno.
Gelatine, gelateno.
Gem, brilianto, ĝemo.
Gendarme, ĝendarmo.
Gender, sekso.
Genealogy, genealogio.
General, ĝenerala.
General (milit.), generalo.
Generate, produkti, naski.
Generation, generacio.
Generosity, malavareco.
Generous, malavara.
Genial, bonvola.
Genitive, genitivo.
Genius, genio.
Genteel, ĝentila.
Gentle, dolĉa.
Gentleman, sinjoro.
Gently, dolĉe.
Genuflect, genufleksi.
Genuine, vera.
Genus, gento.
Geography, geografio.
Geology, geologio.
Geometry, geometrio.
Geranium, geranio.
Germ, ĝermo.
German, Germano.
German (adj.), Germana.
Germinate, ĝermi.
Gerund, gerundio.
Gesture, gesto.
Get (receive), ricevi.
Get (procure), havigi.
Get (with infinitive), igi, iĝi.
Get dirty, malpuriĝi.
Get ready, pretigi, pretiĝi.
Ghastly, palega.
Gherkin, kukumeto.
Ghost, fantomo.
Giant, grandegulo.
Gibbet, pendigilo.
Gibbous, ĝiba.
Gibe, moki.
Giddiness, kapturno.
Giddy, to make, kapturnigi.

Gosling, anserido.
Gospel, Evangelio.
Gossip, babilaĵo.
Gourd, kukurbo.
Gourmand, manĝegulo.
Gout, podagro.
Govern, regi.
Government, registaro.
Governess, guvernistino.
Governor, reganto.
Gown, robo.
Grace, gracio.
Graceful, gracia.
Gracious, gracia.
Gradation, gradeco.
Grade (rank), rango.
Gradual, grada.
Gradually, grade.
Graduate, gradigi.
Graduation, gradigo.
Graft, inokuli.
Grain of corn, grenero.
Grain of dust, polvero.
Grammar, gramatiko.
Gramme, gramo.
Granary, grenejo.
Grand, belega.
Grandfather, avo.
Grandson, nepo.
Granite, granito.
Grant, permesi.
Grape, vinbero.
Grapeshot, kugletaĵo.
Graphite, grafito.
Grapnel, ankreto.
Grapple, ekkapti.
Grasp, premi.
Grass, herbo.
Grass-plot, herbejo.
Grasshopper, akrido.
Grate, fajrujo.
Grate, raspi, froti.
Grateful, dankema.
Grater, raspilo.
Gratification, kontentigo.
Grating, krado.
Grating noise, akra sono.
Gratis, senpage.
Gratitude, dankeco.
Gratuitous, senpaga.
Gratuitously, senpage.
Gratuity (tip), trinkmono.
Grave, tombo.
Grave, grava.
Gravel, ŝtonetaĵo.
Graver, gravurilo.
Gravity, graveco.
Gravy, suko.
Gray, griza.
Graze (rub slightly), tuŝeti.
Graze cattle, paŝti.
Grazing ground, paŝtejo.
Grease, graso.
Grease, ŝmiri.
Great, granda.
Greatcoat, palto.
Great-grandfather, praavo.
Greatness, grandeco.
Greedy (eager), avida.
Greedy, manĝegema.
Green, verda.
Green (village), komunejo.
Greenhouse, varmejo.
Greenish, dubeverda.
Greek, Greko.
Greet, saluti.
Grenade, grenado.
Gift, donaco.
Gift, to make a, donaci.
Gifted, talenta.
Gild, orumi.
Gill (fish), branko.
Gilliflower, levkojo.
Gimlet, borileto.
Gin, ĝino.
Ginger, zingibro.
Gingerbread, mielkuko.
Gipsy, nomadulo.
Giraffe, ĝirafo.
Gird, zoni.
Girdle, zono.
Girl, knabino.
Give, doni.
Give back, redoni.
Give up, forlasi.
Give evidence, atesti.
Give notice, sciigi.
Glacier, glaciejo.
Glad, ĝoja.
Gladden, ĝojigi.
Glade, maldensejo.
Gladiator, gladiatoro.
Glance, ekrigardi.
Gland, glando.
Glare, brilego.
Glass (substance), vitro.
Glass (vessel), glaso.
Glass, pane of, vitraĵo.
Glass-case, vitromeblo.
Glass, looking, spegulo.
Glass-works, vitrofarejo.
Glassy, vitreca.
Glaucous (colour), marverda.
Glaze, vitrumi.
Glaze (pottery), glazuri.

Grenadier, grenadisto.
Grey, griza.
Greyhound, leporhundo.
Gridiron, kradrostilo.
Grief, malĝojo.
Grievance, plendkaŭzo.
Grieve, malĝoji.
Grieve (trans.), malĝojigi.
Grimace, grimaco.
Grime, malpureco.
Grin, grimaci.
Grind, pisti.
Grind the teeth, grinci.
Grind (corn), mueli.
Grip, premego.
Grit, sablego.
Groan, ĝemi.
Groats, grio.
Grocer, spicisto.
Groin, ingveno.
Groom, ĉevalisto.
Groove, kavo, radsigno.
Grope, palpeti.
Gross (in manner), maldelikata.
Grotesque, groteska.
Grotto, groto.
Ground, tero.
Ground-floor, teretaĝo.
Group, grupo.
Group, grupigi.
Grouse, tetro.
Grove, arbetaro.
Grow, kreski.
Grow (become), —iĝi.
Grow young, juniĝi.
Growl, bleki, blekadi.
Growth, kresko.
Grub (insect), ter-

Glaze (ice cakes, etc.), glaciumi.
Glaze (polish), poluri.
Glazier, vitrajîsto.
Gleam, lumeti.
Gleam, lumeto.
Glean, postrikolti.
Glee, ĝojo.
Glen, valeto.
Glide, gliti.
Glimmer, lumeto.
Glimpse, videto, ekvido.
Glisten, brili.
Glitter, brilegi.
Globe, globo.
Globe (earth), terglobo.
Globular, globa.
Globule, globeto.
Gloom, mallumo.
Gloom (sadness), malgajo.
Gloomy (sad), malgaja.
Gloomy, malluma.
Glorify, glori.
Glorious, glora.
Glory, gloro.
Gloss, poluri.
Glove, ganto.
Glow, brili.
Glow-worm, lampiro.
Glucose, glikozo.
Glue, gluo.
Glue, glui.
Glut, sato.
Glut, satigi.
Glutinous, gluanta.
Glutted, satega.
Glutton, manĝegulo.
Gluttonous, manĝegema.
Gluttony, manĝegemo.
Glycerine, glicerino.
Gnash, grinci.
Gnat, kulo.
Gnaw, mordeti.

vermeto.
Grudge, malameco.
Gruff, malĝentila.
Grumble, riproĉegi.
Grunt, bleki.
Guarantee, garantio.
Guarantee, garantii.
Guard, gardi.
Guard (milit.), gvardio.
Guardian, gardanto, zorganto.
Gudgeon, gobio.
Guess, diveni.
Guest, gasto.
Guide, gvidi.
Guide, gvidisto.
Guile, artifiko.
Guileless, senartifika.
Guillotine, gilotino.
Guilt, kulpo.
Guilty, to be, kulpiĝi.
Guinea, gineo.
Guitar, gitaro.
Gulf, golfo.
Gull, trompi.
Gullet, faringo, ezofago.
Gully, valeto.
Gulp, engluti.
Gum, gumo.
Gum, gumi.
Gun, pafilo.
Gun (cannon), pafilego.
Gun-carriage, subpafilego.
Gunpowder, pulvo.
Gunsmith, armilfaristo.
Gunnery, pafilado.
Gush, ŝpruci.
Gust, ekventego.
Gut, intestotubo.
Gutter, defluilo.
Gutter-spout, de-

Gnome, gnomo.
Go, iri.
Go along, vojiri.
Go astray, erari, vagadi.

H

Ha! ha!
Haberdasher, fadenisto.
Habit, kutimo.
Habit, vesto.
Habit of, to be in the, kutimi.
Habitation, loĝejo.
Habitual, kutima.
Habituate, kutimigi.
Hack, haki.
Hack (horse), ĉevaleto.
Hackney-coach, fiakro.
Hag, malbelulino.
Haggard, sovaĝa.
Haggle, marĉandi.
Hail, hajli.
Hail, hajlo.
Hailstone, hajlero.
Hair, haro.
Hair, head of, hararo.
Hairdresser, fizisto.
Hairy, haraĵa.
Halberd, halebardo.
Halcyon, alciono.
Hale, sana.
Half, duono.
Hall, vestiblo.
Hallow, sanktigi.
Hall-porter, pordisto.
Hallucination, halucinacio.
Halt, halti.
Halting-place, haltejo.
Halter, kolbrido.
Halves, by,

fluilo.
Gymnast, gimnastikisto.
Gymnasium, gimnastikejo.
Gypsum, gipso.
Gyrate, turniĝi.

Heretic, herezulo.
Heretical, hereza.
Herewith, tie ĉi aldonita.
Heritage, heredo.
Hermit, ermito.
Hernia, hernio.
Hero, heroo.
Heroic, heroa.
Heroine, heroino.
Heroism, heroeco.
Heron, ardeo.
Herring, haringo.
Hesitate, ŝanceliĝi.
Hesitation, ŝanceliĝo.
Hew, dehaki.
Hexagon, sesangulo.
Hexameter, heksametro.
Hiatus, manko.
Hiccough, singulto.
Hidden, kaŝita.
Hide, kaŝi.
Hide (skin), haŭto.
Hideous, malbelega.
Hiding-place, kaŝejo.
Hierarchy, hierarĥio.
Hieroglyphic, hieroglifo.
High, alta.
Highlander, montano.
Highness (title), moŝto.
High-tide, alfluo.
Highway, vojo.
Highwayman, rabisto.
Hill, monteto.

duone.
Ham, ŝinko.
Hamlet, vilaĝeto.
Hammer, martelo.
Hammer, martelumi.
Hammock, pendlito.
Hamper, korbo.
Hamper, malhelpi.
Hamstring, subgenuo.
Hand, mano.
Hand-barrow, puŝveturilo.
Handcuff, mankateno.
Handful, plenmano.
Handicraft, manfarado.
Handkerchief, naztuko.
Handle, manpreni.
Handle, tenilo.
Handmade, manfarita.
Handshake, manpremo.
Handsome, bela.
Handy, lerta, oportuna (of things).
Hang (intrans.), pendi.
Hang up, pendigi.
Hanker, deziregi.
Hansom, kabrioleto.
Hap, okazi.
Hapless, malfeliĉa.
Haply, eble.
Happen, okazi.
Happiness, feliĉo.
Happy, feliĉa.
Harangue, parolado.
Harass, enuigi, lacigi.
Harass (milit.), atakadi.
Harbinger, an-

Hillock, altaĵeto.
Hilt, tenilo.
Him, lin.
Himself, sin mem.
Hind, cervino.
Hinder, posta.
Hinder, malhelpi.
Hinderance, malhelpo.
Hindermost, lasta.
Hindoo, Hindo.
Hindrance, malhelpo.
Hindu, Hindo.
Hinge, ĉarniro.
Hint, proponeti.
Hip, kokso.
Hippodrome, hipodromo.
Hippopotamus, hipopotamo.
Hire, dungi.
Hire, cost of, salajro.
Hireling, salajrulo.
His, lia, sia.
Hiss, sibli.
Historian, historiskribanto.
History, historio.
History, natural, naturscienco.
Hit, frapi.
Hit against, ektuŝegi.
Hitch, malhelpaĵo.
Hive, abelujo.
Ho! ho!
Hoard, amaso.
Hoarfrost, prujno.
Hoarse, raŭka.
Hoarseness, raŭkiĝo. [Error in book: raukiĝo]
Hoax, mistifiki.
Hobble, lamiri.
Hobby, amuzaĵo.
Hoe, sarki.
Hoe, sarkilo.
Hog, porkviro.
Hoist, suprenlevi.
Hold, teni.
Hold one's

taŭulo.
Harbour, haveno.
Hard, malmola.
Hard (difficult), malfacila.
Hard (severe), severega.
Harden (to make hard), malmoligi, hardi.
Harden (to become hardy), hardiĝi.
Hardly, apenaŭ.
Hardness, malmoleco.
Hardwareman, kuirilvendisto.
Hardy, hardita.
Hark! aŭskultu.
Hare, leporo.
Hairbrained, sencerba.
Harem, haremo.
Haricot-bean, fazeolo.
Harlequin, arlekeno.
Harm, malutili.
Harm, malutilo.
Harmonica, harmoniko.
Harmonious, harmonia.
Harmonize, harmoniigi.
Harmony, harmonio.
Harness, jungi.
Harness, jungaĵo.
Harp, harpo.
Harpoon, harpuno.
Harpy, harpio.
Harrier, leporhundo.
Harrow (to rake), erpi.
Harrow, erpilo.
Harsh (rough), maldolĉa.
Harsh (severe), severega.
Harsh (of voice), raŭka.

tongue, silentiĝi.
Hole, truo.
Hole, to make a, truigi.
Holiday (feast), festo.
Holiday, libertempo.
Holiness, sankteco.
Holla, ho! he!
Hollow, kava.
Hollow, kavigi.
Holly, ilekso.
Holy, sankta.
Homage, riverenco.
Home, hejmo.
Home, at, hejme.
Homœopathy, homeopatio.
Homicide, hommortigo.
Homonym, samnoma.
Honest, honesta.
Honesty, honesteco.
Honey, mielo.
Honeycomb, mieltavolo.
Honeysuckle, lonicero.
Honour, honori.
Honour, honoro.
Honourableness, honorindeco.
Hood, kapuĉo.
Hoof, hufo.
Hook, hoko.
Hoop, ringego.
Hoot (of owl), pepegi, pepegadi.
Hope, espero.
Hope, esperi.
Hops, plant, lupolo.
Horizon, horizonto.
Horizontal, horizontala.
Horn, korno.
Horn (hunting), ĉaskorno.
Horoscope,

Hart, cervo.
Harvest (crop), rikolto.
Harvest-time, rikolto.
Hash, viandmiksaĵo.
Hasp, alkroĉi.
Hassock, kuseno.
Haste, rapideco.
Hasten, rapidi.
Hasten (trans.), rapidigi.
Hasty, rapida.
Hat, ĉapelo.
Hatch, elŝeligi.
Hatchet, hakilo.
Hate, malami.
Hateful, malaminda.
Hatred, malamo.
Haughty, aroganta.
Haunch, kokso.
Haunt, vizitadi.
Hautboy, hobojo.
Have, havi.
Haven, haveno.
Havoc, ruinigo.
Hawk, akcipitro.
Hawk (for sale), kolporti.
Hawthorn, kratago.
Hay, fojno.
Hay-loft, fojnejo.
Hazard, hazardi.
Hazard, hazardo.
Hazardous, hazarda.
Haze, nebuleto.
Hazel-nut, avelo.
He, li.
Head, kapo.
Headache, kapdoloro.
Head-dress (coiffure), kapvesto.
Headland, promontoro.
Headlong, senpripensa, e.
Headstrong, obstina.
Heal, kuraci.

horoskopo.
Horrible, teruriga.
Horrid, terura.
Horror, teruro.
Hors d'oeuvres, almanĝaĵoj.
Horse, ĉevalo.
Horsemanship, rajdarto.
Horse-radish, kreno.
Horseshoe, huferaĵo.
Horticulture, ĝardenkulturo.
Hose, ŝtrumpaĵo.
Hose, ledtubo.
Hosier, ŝtrumpvendisto.
Hospitable, gastama.
Hospital, malsanulejo, hospitalo.
Hospitality, gastamo.
Host, mastro.
Host, Hostio.
Hostage, garantiulo.
Hostile, kontraŭa, malamika.
Hot, varmega.
Hot air stove, hejtaparato.
Hothouse, varmejo.
Hotel, hotelo.
Hound, hundo.
Hour, horo.
House, domo.
House, to keep, mastrumi.
Housekeeping, mastraĵo.
Housewife, mastrino.
Hovel, kajuto, terdometo.
Hover, flirtegi.
How, kiel.
How (what manner), kiamaniere.
How many, kiom da.
How much, kiom

Health, sano.
Health, toast a, toasti.
Healthy, sana.
Heap, amaso.
Heap up, amasigi.
Hear, aŭdi.
Hearken, aŭskulti.
Hearse, ĉerkveturilo.
Heart, koro.
Heart (cards), kero.
Heart, by, parkere.
Heart, to learn by, parkeri.
Hearth, fajrujo, hejmo.
Heartrending, korŝiranta.
Heartsease, violo.
Hearty, korega.
Heat, hejti.
Heat, varmeco.
Heath, stepo, erikejo.
Heather (plant), eriko.
Heathen, idolano.
Heathenism, idolservo.
Heaven, ĉielo.
Heaviness, multepezeco.
Heavy, peza.
Hebdomadary, ĉiusemajna.
Hebraism, Hebreismo.
Hebrew, Hebreo.
Hectare, hektaro.
Hectogramme, hektogramo.
Hectolitre, hektolitro.
Hedge, plektobarilo.
Hedgehog, erinaco.
Heed, atenti.
Heedful, atenta.
Heedless, senatenta.
Heel, kalkano.

da.
However, tamen.
Howsoever, tamen.
Howl, hundblekegi.
Howitzer, bombardilo.
Hub (of wheel), radcentro.
Hubbub, bruado.
Huddle, kunproksimiĝi.
Hue (colour), nuanco.
Hug, ĉirkaŭprenegi.
Huge, grandega.
Hum, kanteti.
Hum, zumi.
Human, homa.
Humane, humana.
Humanity, humaneco.
Humanity (mankind), homaro.
Humble, humila.
Humble, humiligi.
Humble, to be, humiliĝi.
Humerus, humero.
Humid, malseka.
Humidity, malsekeco.
Humiliate, humiligi.
Humility, humileco.
Humming-bird, kolibro.
Humorous, humora.
Humour, humoro.
Hump, ĝibo.
Hunchback, ĝibulo.
Hunger, malsato.
Hungry, malsata.
Hungry, to be, malsati.
Hundred, 100, cent.
Hundredweight,

Heel (of shoe, etc.), kalkanumo.
Heifer, bovidino.
Height, alteco, altaĵo.
Heinous, kruelega.
Heir, heredanto.
Heliotrope, heliotropo.
Helix, ŝraŭbego.
Hell, infero.
Hellenism, Helenismo.
Hellish, infera.
Helm, direktilo.
Helmet, kasko.
Helmsman, direktilisto.
Help, helpi.
Helpful, helpema.
Helpmate, kunhelpanto.
Hem, borderi.
Hem, bordero.
Hemisphere, duonsfero.
Hemorrhage, sangado.
Hemorrhoids, hemorojdo.
Hemp, kanabo.
Hen (fowl), kokino.
Henbane, hiskiamo.
Hence, de nun.
Henceforth, de nun.
Hepatic, hepata.
Heptagon, sepangulo.
Her, ŝin.
Her (possessive), ŝia.
Hers, ŝia.
Herald, heroldo.
Heraldic, heraldika.
Heraldry (science), heraldiko.
Heraldry, blazono.
Herb, herbo.
Herbalist, herbovendisto.
Herbivorous, herbomanĝanta.
Herd, brutaro.
Herdsman, paŝtisto.
Here, tie ĉi, ĉi tie.
Here are, jen estas.
Here is, jen estas.
Hereafter, de nun.
Hereat, ĉi tie.
Hereditary, hereda.
Heresy, herezo.

I
I, mi.
Ibis, ibiso.
Ice, glacio.
Ice, an, glaciaĵo.
Iceberg, glacierego, glacimonto.
Icicle, pendglacio.
Icelander, Islandano.
Idea, ideo.
Ideal, idealo.
Identical, identa.
Identify, identigi.
Idiocy, idioteco.
Idiom (a peculiar expression), idiotismo.
Idiom (general sense), idiomo.
Idiot, idiotulo.
Idle, senokupa.
Idleness, senokupeco.
Idol, idolo.
Idolatry, idolservado.
Idolize, amegi, adori.
If, se.
Ignis fatuus, erarlumo.
Ignite, ekbruligi.
Ignoble, malnobla.
Ignominy, malnobleco.
Ignorance, nescio.

centfunto.
Hunt, ĉasi.
Hunting-lodge, ĉasdometo.
Hurdle, branĉbarileto.
Hurl, alĵeti.
Hurrah, hura.
Hurricane, uragano.
Hurry, rapidi.
Hurry (trans.), rapidigi.
Hurt (to wound), vundi.
Hurt, malutili.
Hurtful, malutila.
Husband, edzo.
Husbandman, terkulturisto.
Hush, silentigi.
Husk, ŝelo.
Hussar, husaro.
Hustle, puŝegi.
Hut, budo.
Hutch, kesto.
Hyacinth, hiacinto.
Hydra, hidro.
Hydrogen, hidrogeno.
Hydropathy, akvokuraco.
Hydrophobia, hidrofobio.
Hydrostatic, hidrostatika.
Hyena, hieno.
Hygrometer, higrometro.
Hygrometry, higrometrio.
Hymn, himno.
Hyperbole, hiperbolo.
Hyphen, streketo.
Hypnotic, hipnota.
Hypnotism, hipnotismo.
Hypnotize, hipnotigi.
Hypochondria, hipoĥondrio.
Hypocrisy,

bovendisto.
Hypocrite, hipokritulo.
Hypocritical, hipokrita.
Hypothesis, hipotezo.
Hypotenuse, hipotenuzo.
Hyssop, hisopo.
Hysterical, histeria.
Hysterics, histerio.

hipokriteco.
Ignorant of, to be, nescii.
Ignorant, malklera.
Ignore, neobservi.
Ill, malbono.
Ill, malbone.
Ill, to be, malsani.
Ill-bred, maledukita.
Illegal, malleĝa.
Illegible, nelegebla.
Illegitimate, nelaŭleĝa.
Illegitimate, malrajta.
Illiberal, avara.
Illicit, malpermesita.
Illiterate, malklera.
Illness, malsano.
Illogical, mallogika.
Illude, iluzii.
Illuminate, ilumini.
Illumination, iluminado.
Illusion, iluzio.
Illustrate, ilustri.
Illustrated, ilustrita.
Illustration, ilustraĵo.
Illustrious, fama.
Image, figuro.
Imaginary, fantazia.
Imagination, fantazio.
Imagine, imagi.
Imbecile, malspritulo.
Imbibe, sorbigi.
Imbue, penetri, inspiri.
Imitate, imiti.
Imitation, imito.
Immaculate, senmakula.
Immaterial, negrava.
Immature, ne-

Infinitive (gram.), infinitivo.
Infinity, multego.
Infirm, malforta.
Infirmary, malsanulejo.
Infirmity, malforteco.
Inflame, flamigi.
Inflammable, bruliĝema.
Inflammation, brulumo.
Inflate, ŝveligi. [Error in book: sveligi]
Inflect, fleksi.
Inflexible, nefleksebla, rigida.
Inflict, punon doni.
Influence, influi.
Influence, influo.
Influenza, gripo.
Inform, informi.
Inform, sciigi.
Informed, to be, sciiĝi.
Infrequent, malofta.
Infuze, infuzi.
Ingenious, sagaca.
Ingenuity, lerteco.
Ingenuous, naiva.
Ingot, fandaĵo.
Ingratitude, sendankeco.
Ingredient, elementaĵo.

Ingress, enigo.
Inhabit, loĝi.
Inhale, enspiri.
Inherit, heredi.
Inheritance, heredaĵo.
Inhuman, nehumana.
Iniquity, malboneco, maljusteco.
Initial (letter), ĉeflitero.
Initiate, iniciati.
Initiator, iniciatoro.
Inject, enŝprucigi.
Injection (medical), klistero.
Injurious, difektiga.
Injury, difektaĵo.
Injury (wound), vundo.
Injustice, maljusteco.
Ink, inko.
Inkstand, etc., inkujo.
Inmate, loĝanto.
Inn, gastejo.
Innocence, senkulpeco.
Innocent, senkulpa.
Innumerable, nekalkulebla.
In order to, por.
In order that, por ke.
Inoculate, inokuli.
Inodorous, senodora.
Inoffensive, neofendema.
Inopportune, neĝustatempa.
Inquest, enketo.
Inquietude, maltrankvileco.
Inquire, demandi.
Inquiry, demando.
Inquisition, inkvizicio.
Inquisitive, scia-

matura.
Immediate, tuja.
Immediately, tuj.
Immense, vasta.
Immense (size), grandega.
Immerge, trempi.
Immerse, subakvigi.
Immigrate, enmigri.
Immigrant, enmigranto.
Imminent, minaca.
Immobility, senmoveco.
Immoderate, malmodera.
Immodest, nemodesta.
Immolate, oferbuĉi.
Immoral, malbonmora.
Immorality, malbonmoreco.
Immortal, senmorta.
Immortality, senmorteco.
Immovable, senmova, nemovebla.
Immutable, neŝanĝebla.
Imp, diableto.
Impair, difekti.
Impart, komuniki, sciigi.
Impartial, senpartia.
Impartiality, senpartieco.
Impatience, malpacienco.
Impatient, malpacienca.
Impassive, kvieteｇa, stoika.
Impeach, kulpigi, denunci.
Impediment, baro.
Impel, antaŭen puŝi.
Impend, minaci.

ma.
Inquisitor, inkvizitoro.
Inroad, ekokupo.
Insalubrious, malsaniga.
Insane, freneza.
Insanity, frenezeco.
Insatiable, nesatigebla.
Inscribe, enskribi.
Inscription, surskribo.
Inscrutable, neserĉebla.
Insect, insekto.
Insecure, danĝera.
Insensible, sensenta.
Insert, enmeti.
Insert (print), enpresi.
Insertion, enpresaĵo.
Inseparable, sendisiĝa.
Inside, interne.
Inside out, returnite.
Insidious, insida.
Insight, elsciado.
Insignificant, sensignifa.
Insincere, nesincera.
Insinuate, proponeti.
Insipid, sengusta.
Insist, insisti.
Insnare, allogi, kapti.
Insobriety, malsobreco.
Insolent, insultema.
Insoluble, nesolvebla.
Insolvent, nepagokapabla.
Insomnia, sendormo.
Insomuch, tial ke.
Inspect, ekzameni.

Impenetrable, nepenetrebla.
Imperative, ordona.
Imperfect, neperfekta.
Imperfection, difektaĵo.
Imperial, imperia.
Imperishable, nepereema.
Impermeable, nepenetrebla.
Impersonal, nepersona.
Impertinent, malrespekta.
Imperturbable, stoika.
Impetuous, vivega.
Impetus, antaŭenpuŝo.
Impiety, malpieco.
Impious, malpia.
Implacable, venĝema.
Implant, enradiki.
Implement, ilo.
Implicate, impliki.
Implied, neesprimita.
Implore, petegi.
Impolite, malĝentila.
Impolitic, nesaĝema.
Import, enporti.
Importance, graveco.
Important, grava.
Importunate, trudema.
Importune, trudi, trudiĝi.
Impose (put on), trudi.
Impose on, trompi.
Impossible, neebla.
Impost, imposto.
Impostor,

Inspector, inspektoro.
Inspiration, inspiro.
Inspiration (breath), enspiro.
Inspire, enspiri.
Inspire, inspiri.
Instalment, partpago.
Install, loĝigi.
Instance, ekzemplodoni.
Instance, ekzemplo.
Instant, momento.
Instant, in an, momente.
Instantaneous, subita.
Instead of, anstataŭ.
Instead of, to put, anstataŭi.
Instep, piedartiko.
Instigate, instigi.
Instill, infuzi.
Instinct, instinkto.
Institute, fondi.
Institute, instituto.
Institution, institucio.
Instruct, instrui.
Instruction, instrukcio.
Instruction (teaching), instruado.
Instructive, instrua.
Instructor, instruisto.
Instrument (mus.), muzikilo.
Instrument (wind), blovinstrumento.
Instrument (string), kordinstrumento.
Instrument (tool), ilo.
Insubordination, ribeleto—ado.
Insufferable, ne-

trompanto.
Impotence, neebleco.
Impoverish, malriĉigi.
Impracticable, nefarebla.
Impregnable, fortika.
Impress, impresi.
Impress (print), presi.
Impression (printing), presaĵo.
Impression, impreso.
Impressionable, impresebla.
Impressive, impresa.
Imprison, malliberigi.
Improbable, neverŝajna.
Improper, nedeca.
Impropriety, nedececo.
Impromptu, senprepara.
Improve, plibonigi.
Improvement, plibonigo.
Improvident, malspxarema.
Improvise, improvizi.
Imprudent, nesingardema.
Impudent, senhonta.
Impulse, puŝo.
Impure, malpura.
Impurity, malpureco.
Impute, alkalkuli.
In, en.
In front, antaŭe.
In place of, to put, anstataŭi.
In that manner, tiamaniere.
Inability, neebleco.
Inaccessible,

suferebla.
Insufficient, nesufiĉa.
Insular, insula.
Insulate, soligi, izoli.
Insult, insulti.
Insurance, asekuro.
Insure, asekuri.
Insurgent, ribelanto.
Insurrection, ribelo.
Insusceptible, sensentema.
Intact, sendifekta.
Integer, tutcifero.
Integral (math.), integrala.
Integrity, rekteco.
Intellect, inteligenteco.
Intelligence, inteligenteco.
Intelligence (news), sciigo.
Intelligent, inteligenta.
Intemperance, malsobreco.
Intemperate, malsobra.
Intend, intenci.
Intense, ega.
Intensity, egeco.
Intent, celo.
Intention, intenco.
Intentional, intenca.
Inter, enterigi.
Intercalate, intermeti.
Intercede, propeti.
Intercept, interkapti.
Intercession, propeto.
Intercessor, propetulo.
Intercourse, interrilato.
Interdict, malpermesi.
Interest, procento.

neatingebla.
Inaccurate, neakurata.
Inaction, senokupo.
Inactive, senokupa.
Inadvertence, malatenteco.
Inane, malplena.
Inanimate, senviva.
Inappreciable, netaksebla.
Inappropriate, nedeca.
In as much as, tial ke.
Inattention, neatenteco.
Inaudible, neaŭdebla.
Inauspicious, nefavora.
Incalculable, nekalkulebla.
Incapable, nekapabla.
Incapacity, nekapableco.
Incarnate, korpigi.
Incarnation, korpiĝo.
Incendiary, brulkrimulo.
Incense, bonodorfumo.
Incense, furiozigi.
Incest, sangadulto.
Incentive, kaŭzo.
Inch, colo.
Incident, okazaĵo.
Incision, tranĉo.
Incite, instigi, inciti.
Inclination, inklino.
Incline, inklini.
Incline (slope), deklivo.
Include, enhavi.
Incoherent, sensenca.

Interest, interesi.
Interest one's self in, interesiĝi je.
Interesting, interesa.
Interfere, sin intermeti.
Interior, interno.
Interjection, interjekcio.
Interline, interlinii.
Interlocutor, interparolanto.
Interloper, trudulo.
Interlude, interakto.
Intermeddle, enmiksiĝi.
Intermediate, intera, intermeza.
Interment, interigo.
Interminable, senfina.
Intermission, intermito.
Intermit, intermiti.
Intermittent, intermita.
Internal, interna.
Internally, interne.
International, internacia.
Internationalist, Internaciisto.
Internationality, internacieco.
Interpose, intermeti.
Interprete, traduki.
Interpreter, tradukisto.
Interrogate, demandi.
Interrogation, denotes, ĉu.
Interrogation, note of, signo demanda.
Interrogatory, de-

Income, rento.
Incommode, ĝeni.
Incomparable, nekomparebla.
Incompatible, nekunigebla.
Incompetent, nekompetenta.
Incomplete, neplena.
Incomprehensible, nekomprenebla.
Inconceivable, neimagebla.
Inconsistent, nekonsekvenca.
Inconsolable, nekonsolebla.
Inconstant, ŝanĝema.
Incontestable, nedisputebla.
Inconvenient, maloportuna.
Incorporeal, spirita.
Incorrect, malkorekta.
Incorrigible, plimalobea, nerebonigebla.
Incorrupt, honesta.
Incorruptible, neputrebla.
Incorruption, senputreco.
Increase (grow), kreskiĝi.
Increase, plimultigi.
Incredible, nekredebla.
Incredulous, nekredema.
Incriminate, kulpigi.
Inculcate, enradiki.
Incurable, neresanigebla.
Indebtedness, ŝuldeco.
Indecent, maldeca.

manda.
Interregnum, interregno.
Interrupt, interrompi.
Intersect, intersekcii.
Interval (space), interspaco.
Interval (time), intertempo.
Intervene, sin intermeti.
Intervention, intermeto.
Interview, intervidiĝo.
Interweave, kunplekti.
Intestate, sentestamenta.
Intestine, internaĵo.
Intimacy, intimeco.
Intimate, intima, intimulo.
Intimate, sciigi.
Intimation, sciigo.
Intimidate, timigi.
Into, en (with accusative).
Intolerable, netolerebla.
Intolerant, netolerema.
Intoxicate, ebriigi.
Intoxicated, ebria.
Intoxication, ebrieco.
Intractable, nedresebla.
Intransitive, netransitiva.
Intrepid, kuraĝega.
Intricate, malsimpla.
Intrigue, intrigi.
Intrinsic, vera.
Introduce, prezenti, enkonduki.
Introduction, enkonduko.
Introduction

Indecision, nedecideco.
Indeed, do, efektive, ja.
Indefatigable, senlaca.
Indefinite, nedifinita.
Indemnify, kompensi.
Indemnity, kompenso.
Independence, sendependeco.
Independent, sendependa.
Indeterminate, nedifinita.
Index (names), nomaro.
Index, tabelo.
India-rubber, kaŭĉuko.
Indicate, montri.
Indicative (gram.), indikativo.
Indict, kulpigi.
Indifferent, indiferenta.
Indigenous, enlanda.
Indigent, malriĉa.
Indigestible, nedigestebla.
Indigestion, malbona digestado.
Indignant, to be, indigni.
Indirect (through an intermediary), pera.
Indirectly (through an intermediary), pere.
Indirect (devious), malrekta.
Indiscreet, maldiskreta.
Indispensable, necesega.
Indisposed (ill), malsaneta.
Indisposition, malsaneto.
Indisputable,

(preface), antaŭparolo.
Intruder, trudulo.
Intrusion, trudo.
Intrust, komisii.
Inundate, superakvi.
Inure, kutimigi.
Inutility, senutilo.
Invade, enpenetri.
Invalid, nula.
Invalid, malsanetulo.
Invalidate, nuligi.
Invaluable, netaksebla.
Invariable, neŝanĝebla.
Invasion, ekokupado.
Invent, elpensi.
Invention, elpenso.
Inventory, katalogo.
Invert, interŝanĝi.
Invest (money), procentdoni.
Investigate, esplori.
Inveterate, enradikita.
Invigorate, vivigi.
Invincible, nevenkebla.
Invisible, nevidebla.
Invitation, invito.
Invite, inviti.
Invoice, fakturo.
Invoke, alvoki.
Involuntary, senvola.
Iodine, jodo.
Irascible, ekkolerema.
Ire, kolero.
Iris (anat.), iriso.
Iris (bot.), irido.
Irishman, Irlandano.
Irksome, peniga, enuiga.
Iron, fero.
Iron (linen, etc.),

nedisputebla.
Indissoluble, nesolvebla.
Indistinct, malklara.
Individual, individuo.
Individual, individua.
Indivisible, nedividebla.
Indolent, senenergia.
Indomitable, nedresebla.
Indorse, dorseskribi.
Indubitable, neduba.
Induce, decidigi, alkonduki.
Indulge, indulgi.
Indulge (one's self), indulgiĝi.
Indulgence, indulgo.
Industrious, diligenta.
Industry (business), industrio.
Inebriate, ebrii.
Ineffectual, vana.
Ineligible, neelektebla.
Inert, senmova.
Inertia, inercio.
Inestimable, netaksebla.
Inevitable, neeviteble.
Inexact, malĝusta.
Inexhaustible, nekonsumebla.
Inexpedient, nenecesa, nekonvena.
Inexperience, malsperteco.
Inexplicable, neklarigebla.
Inexpressible, neesprimebla.
Inextricable, nemalplektebla.
Infallible, neer-

gladi.
Iron, an, gladilo.
Ironer (fem.), gladistino.
Ironmonger, patvendisto.
Irony, ironio.
Irradiate, radii.
Irregular, neregula.
Irreligious, malpia.
Irreparable, neriparebla.
Irrepressible, nehaltigebla.
Irreproachable, neriproĉinda.
Irresolute, ŝanceliĝa, nedecida.
Irreverence, malriverenco.
Irritable, incitebla.
Irritate, inciti.
Is, estas.
Island, insulo.
Islander, insulano.
Isle, insulo.
Isolate, izoli.
Israelite, Izraelido.
Issue, eldoni.
Issue (offspring), idaro.
Issue, elflui.
Isthmus, terkolo.
It, ĝi, ĝin.
Italian, Italo.
Italic (writing), kursiva.
Itch, juki.
Itching, juko.
Item, ero.
Iteration, ripetado.
Itinerant, vojaĝanta.
Ivory, elefantosto.
Ivy, hedero.

arebla.
Infallibility, neerarebleco.
Infallibly, neerareble.
Infamous, malglora, malfama.
Infamy, malgloro, malfamo.
Infancy, infaneco.
Infant, infaneto.
Infantile, infana.
Infantry, infantario.
Infatuation, delogiteco.
Infect, infekti.
Infelicity, malfeliĉeco.
Infer, impliki.
Inferior, an, suzulo.
Inferior, malsupera.
Inferiority, malsupereco.
Infernal, infera.
Infidelity, malfideleco.
Infinite, senlima.

J

Jabber, babili.
Jack, roasting, turnrostilo.
Jackass, azenviro.
Jackal, ŝakalo.
Jacket, jako, jaketo.
Jade (tire), lacgadi.
Jaded, laca.
Jagged, denta.
Jaguar, jaguaro.
Jail, malliberejo.
Jailer, gardisto.
Jam, fruktaĵo.
January, Januaro.
Japan (polish), laki.
Japan, Japanujo.
Japanese, Japano.
Jar, botelego.
Jasmine, jasmeno.
Jaundice, flavmalsano.

Javelin, ĵetponardo.
Jaw, makzelo.
Jawbone, makzelosto.
Jay garolo.
Jealousy, ĵaluzo.
Jeer, mokadi.
Jelly, ĝelateno.
Jeopardy, danĝero.
Jerk, ekskuo.
Jersey (garment), trikoto.
Jessamine, jasmeno.
Jest, ŝerci.
Jest, ŝerco.
Jesuit, Jezuito.
Jesus, Jesuo.
Jetsam, fuko.
Jetty, digo.
Jew, Hebreo.
Jewel, juvelo.
Jewel-box, juvelujo.
Jeweller, juvelisto.
Jewess, Hebreino.
Jilt, koketulino.
Jingle, tinti.
Job, tasketo.
Jockey, rajdisto.
Jocose, ŝercema.
Jocular, ŝercema.
Join, kunigi.
Join hands, manplekti.
Join together, kuniĝi.
Join with, kunigi.

K

Kaleidoscope, kalejdoskopo.
Kangaroo, didelfo.
Keel, kilo.
Keen (sharp), akra.
Keep, teni, gardi.
Keep silence, silentiĝi.
Keeper, gardanto.
Keepsake, memoraĵo.

Joiner, lignaĵisto.
Jointly, kune.
Joint (anatomy), artiko.
Joint (carpentering), kuniĝo.
Joist, trabo.
Joke, ŝerci.
Jolly, gajega.
Jolt, ekskui.
Jostle, puŝegi.
Jot, joto.
Journal (book keeping), taglibro.
Journal (a paper), ĵurnalo.
Journey (by car, etc.), veturi.
Journey (travel), vojaĝi.
Journey, vojaĝo.
Journeyman, taglaboristo.
Jovial, ĝojega.

Jowl, buŝego.
Joy, ĝojo.
Joyous, ĝoja.
Jubilant, ĝojega.
Jubilee, jubileo.
Judge, juĝi.
Judge (legal), juĝisto.
Judge, juĝanto.
Judgment (legal), juĝo.
Judicial, juĝa.
Judicious, prudenta.
Jug, kruĉo.
Juggle, ĵongli.
Juggler, ĵonglisto.
Jugglery, ĵonglado.
Juice, suko.
Juicy, suka.
July, Julio.
Jumble, miksi.
Jump, salti.
Junction, kuniĝo.
June, Junio.
Junior, neplenaĝa.
Juror, ĵurinto.
Jury, juĝantaro.
Juryman, ĵurinto.
Just (time), ĵus.
Just (fair), justa.
Justice, justeco.
Justice (correctness), praveco.
Justify, pravigi.
Justly, juste.
Juvenile, juna.
Juxtaposition, apudmeto.

Kinsman, parenco.
Kiss, kisi.
Kitchen, kuirejo.
Kitchen-garden, legoma ĝardeno.
Kitchen-gardener, legomĝardenisto.
Kitchen-jack, turnrostilo.
Kitchen utensils, kuirilaro.
Kite (bird), milvo.

Keg, bareleto.
Kennel, hundejo.
Kernel, kerno.
Kettle, bolilo.
Key, ŝlosilo.
Key (of piano, etc.), klavo.
Keyboard, klavaro.
Keystone, ĉefŝtono.
Kick, piedfrapo.
Kid, kaprido.
Kidnap, forŝteli.
Kidney, reno.
Kill, mortigi.
Kill (animals), buĉi.
Kilogramme, kilogramo.
Kilolitre, kilolitro.
Kilometre, kilometro.
Kin, parenceco.
Kind (species), speco.
Kind, bona.
Kindle, ekbruligi.
Kindness, boneco.
Kindred, parencaro.
King, reĝo.
Kingdom, reĝolando, reĝlando.
Kingfisher, alciono.
Kingly (adj.), reĝa.
Kingly (adv.), reĝe.
King's evil, skrofolo.
Kinsfolk, parencaro.

L
Label, surskribeto.
Laborious, laborema.
Laboratory, laborejo.
Labour, laboro.
Labour, labori.

Kite (toy), flugludilo.
Knack, lerteco.
Knacker, defelisto.
Knapsack, tornistro.
Knave, fripono.
Knave (cards), lakeo.
Knavery, friponeco.
Knead, knedi.
Kneading-trough, knedujo.
Knee, genuo.
Kneecap, genuosto.
Kneel, genufleksi.
Knell, mortsonorado, funebra sonorado.
Knife, tranĉilo.
Knife-blade, tranĉanto.
Knight, kavaliro.
Knit, triki, trikoti.
Knitting-needle, trikilo.
Knob, butono.
Knock, frapi.
Knock down, disĵeti, deĵeti.
Knot, ligtubero.
Knot (bow), banto.
Knot (in wood), lignotubero.
Knout, skurĝo.
Know, scii.
Know (to be acquainted with), koni.
Knuckle, artiko.
Kopeck, kopeko.
Koran, Korano.

Libretto, libreto.
License, permeso.
Licentiate, licencato.
Licentious, malbonmora.
Lichen, likeno.
Lick (lap), leki.

Labour, manual, manlaboro.
Labourer, laboristo.
Labyrinth, labirinto.
Lac (lacquer), lako.
Lace, laĉi.
Lace, pasamento.
Lace (of shoe, etc.), laĉo.
Lacerate, disŝiri.
Lack, bezono.
Lacker, lacquer, laki.
Lackey, lacquey, lakeo.
Laconic, lakona.
Laconism, lakonismo.
Lad, knabo, junulo.
Ladder, ŝtuparo.
Lade, ŝarĝi.
Lading, bill of, garantiita letero.
Lading, ŝarĝo—ado.
Lady, sinjorino, nobelino.
Lag, malakceli.
Laical, nereligia.
Lair, nestego.
Laity, nereligiuloj.
Lake, lago.
Lamb, ŝafido.
Lame, to be, lami.
Lament, bedaŭri.
Lamentable, bedaŭrinda.
Lamp, lampo.
Lampoon, satiro.
Lamprey, petromizo.
Lance, lanco.
Lancet, lanceto.
Land (goods), elŝipigi.
Land (a country), lando.
Land (of persons), elŝipiĝi.
Land (soil), tero.

Lie (rest on), kuŝi.
Lie down, kuŝiĝi.
Lie, mensogo.
Lien, garantiaĵo.
Lieu (in lieu of), anstataŭ.
Lieutenant, leŭtenanto.
Life, vivo.
Lifeguard, korpogardisto.
Lifelong, dumviva.
Lifetime, dumvivo.
Lift, levi.
Lift up, altlevi.
Lift, homlevilo.
Ligament, tendeno.
Ligature, bandaĝilo.
Light, lumi.
Light, lumo, lumeco.
Light (weight), malpeza.
Lighten, malpeziĝi.
Lightning, fulmo.
Lightning-conductor, fulmoŝirmilo.
Lighthouse, lumturo.
Like, ameti.
Like, simila.
Like (adv.), tiel.
Likelihood, verŝajno.
Likeness (similarity), simileco.
Likeness (portrait), portreto.
Likely (adj.), ebla, verŝajna.
Likely (adv.), eble, verŝajne.
Likewise, simile.
Lilac, siringo.
Lilac (colour), siringkolora.
Lily, lilio.
Limb, membro.
Lime, kalko.

Landgrave, landgrafo.
Landing (place), plataĵo.
Landlord, bienulo, landsinjoro.
Landmark, terlimŝtono.
Landscape, pejzaĝo.
Landslip, terdisfalo.
Lane, strateto.
Language, lingvo.
Language (speech), lingvaĵo.
Languid, malfortika.
Languish, malfortiĝi.
Lank, maldika.
Lantern, lanterno.
Lap, leki, lekumi.
Lapis lazuli, lapis lazuro.
Lapse (of time), manko, daŭro.
Larceny, ŝtelo.
Larch, lariko.
Lard, porkograso.
Larder, manĝaĵejo.
Large, granda.
Largely, grandege.
Lark, alaŭdo.
Larva, larvo.
Larynx, laringo.
Lascivious, voluptema.
Lash (to tie), alligi.
Lash (to whip), skurĝi.
Lass, junulino.
Lassitude, laciĝo.
Lasso, kaptoŝnuro.
Last (continue), daŭri.
Last, lasta.
Last but one, antaŭlasta.
Latch, pordrisor-

Lime tree, tilio.
Limestone, kalkŝtono.
Limit, limigi.
Limit, limo.
Limp, lami, lameti.
Limpid, klarega.
Linden, tilio.
Line, linio.
Line, subŝtofi.
Linen, tolo.
Linen (the washing), tolaĵo.
Linen, baby, vestaĵeto.
Linen-room, tolaĵejo.
Linger, prokrastiĝi.
Lining, subŝtofo.
Link (of chain), ĉenero.
Link, torĉo.
Lint, ĉarpio.
Lion, leono.
Lip, lipo.
Liquefy, fluidigi.
Liquid, fluida.
Liquid, fluidaĵo.
Liquidate, likvidi.
Liquidation, likvido.
Liquidator, likvidanto.
Liquor, likvoro.
Liquorice, glicirizo.
Lisp, lispi.
List, registro.
List of names, nomaro.
List (index), tabelo.
Listen, aŭskulti.
Listless, senvigla.
Litany, litanio.
Literal, laŭlitera.
Literally, laŭlitere.
Literary, literatura.
Literateur, literaturisto.
Literature, liter-

to, fermilo.
Late, malfrua.
Late, to be, malfrui.
Late (deceased), mortinto.
Lately, antaŭ ne longe.
Lateness, malfrueco.
Latent, kaŝita.
Lateral, flanka.
Lath, paliseto.
Lathe, tornilo.
Lather, sapumi.
Lather, sapumaĵo, ŝaŭmaĵo.
Latin, Latina.
Latter, lasta, tiu ĉi.
Lattice, palisplektaĵo.
Laud, laŭdi.
Laudable, laŭdebla.
Laudation, laŭdego.
Laugh, ridi.
Laughable, ridinda.
Laughter, ridado.
Laundress, lavistino.
Laundry, lavejo.
Laurel, laŭro.
Lava, lafo.
Lavish, malŝpara.
Law, a, regulo, leĝo.
Law, the, leĝoscienco.
Lawful, rajta.
Lawn, herbejo.
Lawsuit, proceso.
Lawyer, legisto.
Lax, laksa.
Laxative, laksilo.
Lay (song), kanto.
Lay (trans. v.), meti.
Lay (eggs), demeti (ovojn).
Lay bare, senigi.
Lay hold of, ekkapti.

aturo.
Lithe, aktiva.
Lithograph, litografi.
Lithographer, litografisto.
Lithography, litografarto.
Litigation, procesado.
Litigious, procesema.
Litre, litro.
Litter (animals), kuŝejo. [Error in book: kueŝjo]
Litter, pajlaĵo.
Little, a, iom.
Little (not much, not many), malmulte.
Little (small), malgranda.
Littleness, malgrandeco.
Littoral, marbordo.
Liturgy, liturgio.
Live, vivi.
Live (dwell), loĝi.
Live long! vivu!
Lively, vigla.
Liver, hepato.
Livery, livreo, uniformo.
Living, viva.
Lizard, lacerto.
Lo! jen.
Load, ŝarĝi.
Load (weapon), ŝargi.
Load, ŝarĝo.
Loadstone, magneto.
Loaf, bulkego.
Loan, prunto.
Loathe, malamegi.
Loathsome, naŭziza.
Lobby, vestiblo.
Lobster, omaro.
Local, loka.
Locality, loko.
Loch, lago.

Lay open, malkovri.
Lay waste, ruinigi.
Layer (stratum), tavolo.
Layman, nereligiulo.
Laziness, mallaboreco.
Lazy, mallaborema.
Lead, konduki.
Lead (metal), plumbo.
Lead astray, deturni.
Lead away, dekonduki.
Leaf (tree), folio.
Leaf, folio.
League (union), ligo.
Leaguer, ligano.
Leak, guteti.
Lean, klini.
Lean, malgrasa.
Lean, to grow, malgrasiĝi.
Leap, salti.
Leap forward, antaŭensalti.
Leap year, superjaro.
Learn, lerni.
Learn (news, etc.), sciiĝi.
Learn (thoroughly), ellerni.
Learned (man), klerulo, sciencuulo.
Lease, lukontrakto.
Leash, ligilo.
Least, malplej.
Least, at, almenaŭ.
Leather, ledo.
Leave, lasi.
Leave (bequeath), testamenti.
Leave (depart), deiri.
Leave off, ĉesi.
Leaven, fermenti-

Lock, ŝlosi.
Lock, seruro.
Lock (hair), buklo.
Lock (of canal, etc.), kluzo.
Lockjaw, tetano.
Locomotive, lokomotivo.
Locksmith, seruristo.
Lodge (small house), dometo.
Lodge (dwell), loĝi.
Lodger, luanto.
Lodgings, loĝejo.
Loft (corn), grenejo.
Loftiness (character), nobleco.
Lofty, altega.
Log, ŝtipo.
Logarithm, logaritmo.
Logic, logiko.
Logogriph, logogrifo.
Loins, lumboj.
Loiter, vagi.
Lone, lonely, sola.
Loneliness, soleco.
Long, longa.
Long for, sopiri pri.
Longitude, longo.
Long time, longatempe.
Long while, longatempe.
Look, mieno, vizaĝo.
Look at, rigardi.
Look for, serĉi.
Looking-glass, spegulo.
Look out (man), observisto.
Loom, teksilo.
Loop (of ribbons), banto.
Loose, ellasa.
Loosen, ellasi.
Lop, ĉirkaŭhaki.

lo.
Leavings (food), manĝrestaĵo.
Lecture, parolado.
Leech, hirudo.
Leer, flanken rigardi.
Lees, feĉo.
Left, on the, maldekstre.
Leg (limb), kruro.
Leg (of a fowl, etc.), femuro.
Leg of mutton, ŝaffemuro.
Legacy, heredaĵo.
Legal, leĝa.
Legation (place), senditejo.
Legation, senditaro.
Legend, legendo.
Legible, legebla.
Legion, legio.
Legislate, leĝdoni.
Legislative, leĝdganta.
Legislator, leĝfaranto.
Legitimate, rajta.
Legitimate, laŭleĝa.
Leisure, libertempo.
Lemon, citrono.
Lemonade, limonado.
Lemon tree, citronarbo.
Lend, prunti, pruntedoni.
Lender, pruntanto.
Length, longeco.
Length, in, laŭlonge.
Lengthen, plilongigi.
Leniency, malsevereco.
Lenient, malsevera.
Lent (40 days before Easter), gran-

Lord, the, la Sinjoro.
Lord's Supper, Sankta vespermanĝo.
Lordly, nobla.
Lose, perdi.
Lose, at play, malgajni.
Lose time (of a watch, etc.), malrapidi.
Lose one's self, perdiĝi.
Lose one's way, vojperdi.
Loss, perdo.
Lot (destiny), sorto.
Lot, lotaĵo.
Lots, to cast, loti.
Lottery, loterio.
Loud, laŭta.
Loudly, laŭte.
Loudness, laŭteco.
Lough, lago.
Lounger, vagulo.
Louse, pediko.
Love, ami.
Love, to make, amindumi.
Lover, amanto, amisto.
Low (cry of a cow), bleki.
Low (sound), basa.
Low (not loud), mallaŭta.
Low (not high), malalta.
Lower, mallevi.
Lower price, rabati.
Lowly, humila.
Lowliness, humileco.
Loyal, fidela.
Loyalty, fideleco.
Lozenge (geom.), lozanĝo.
Lozenge, pastelo.
Lucid, klara.
Luck, ŝanco,

da fasto.
Lentil, lento.
Leopard, leopardo.
Leper, leprulo.
Leprosy, lepro.
Leprous, lepra.
Less, malpli.
Lessee, luanto.
Lessen, plimalgrandigi.
Lesson, leciono.
Lessor, luiganto.
Let (house, etc.), luigi.
Let (before an infinitive), lasi.
Let down, mallevi.
Lethargy, letargio.
Letter, capital, granda litero.
Letter (alphabet), litero.
Letter (epistle), letero.
Letter (registered), rekomendita letero.
Letter of advice, ricevavizo.
Letter of exchange, kambio.
Letter-box, poŝta kesto, leterkesto.
Letter-carrier (postman), leteristo.
Letter-case, leterujo.
Lettuce, laktuko. [Error in book: latuko]
Level (instrument), nivelilo.
Level, nivela.
Level (flat), ebena.
Lever, levilo.
Levity, malseriozo.
Lewd, malĉasta.
Lexicon, leksikono.
Liable, responda.

Liability, respondeco.
Liar, mensogulo.
Libation, oferverŝo.
Libel, kalumnii.
Liberal (generous), malavara.
Liberate, liberigi.
Libertine, malĉastulo.
Liberty, libereco.
Librarian, bibliotekisto.
Library, biblioteko.

M

Macadam, makadamo.
Macaroni, makaronio.
Machine, maŝino.
Machine, sewing, stebilo.
Machinery, radaro, maŝinaro.
Machinist, maŝinisto.
Mad, freneza.
Madam, sinjorino.
Madden, frenezigi.
Madly, freneze.
Madness, frenezeco.
Madrigal, madrigalo.
Magazine, revuo, gazeto.
Magazine (storehouse), magazeno.
Maggot, akaro.
Magic, magio.
Magician, magiisto.
Magisterial, majstrata.
Magistrate, magistrato.
Magnanimous, grandanima.
Magnet, magneto.
Magnetise, magnetizi.

bonŝanco.
Lucky, ŝanca, bonŝanca.
Lucrative, profita.
Ludicrous, ridinda.
Luggage, pakaĵo.
Lukewarm, varmeta.
Lull, kvietigi.
Lullaby, lulkanto.
Luminary, lumigilo.
Luminous, lumiga.
Lump, bulo.
Lunacy, lunatikeco.
Lunar, luna.
Lunatic, lunatikulo.
Lunch, tagmezomanĝo.
Lung, pulmo.
Lurch, ŝanceliĝi.
Lure, trompi, logi.
Lurid, malhela.
Lurk, sin kaŝi (insideme).
Luscious, bongusta.
Lust, avideco.
Lustre (lamp), lustro.
Lustre, brilo.
Lusty, fortega.
Lute, liuto.
Lutheran, luterano.
Luxury, lukso.
Luxurious, luksa.
Lyceum, liceo.
Lye, lesivo.
Lymph, limfo.
Lynx, linko.
Lyre, liro.

Middle, meza.
Midnight, noktomezo.
Midsummer, duonjaro, somermezo.
Midwife, akuŝistino.
Mien, mieno.
Might, potenco.
Mighty, potenca.
Mignonette, resedo.
Migrate, migri.
Milch, laktodona.
Mild, dolĉa.
Mildew, ŝimo.
Mildness, dolĉeco.
Mile, mejlo.
Militant, milita.
Military, milita.
Military man, militisto.
Militia, militantaro.
Milk, melki.
Milk, lakto.
Mill, muelilo.
Mill-house, muelejo.
Miller, muelisto.
Millenium, miljaro.
Millet, milio.
Milligram, miligramo.
Millimeter,

Magnetism, magnetismo.
Magnificent, belega.
Magnify, pligrandigi.
Magnitude, grandeco.
Magpie, pigo.
Mahogany, mahagono.
Mahomet, Mahometo.
Mahometan, Mahometano.
Maid, fraŭlino.
Maiden, virgulino.
Maidenly, virga.
Maid-servant, servistino.
Mail, poŝto.
Mail (armour), maŝo.
Maim, vundegi.
Mainly, ĉefe.
Maintain, subteni.
Maintain (assert), pretendi.
Maintenance, subtenado.
Maize, maizo.
Majestic, majesta.
Majesty, majesto.
Major (milit.), majoro.
Major (mus.), dura.
Majority (age), plenaĝo.
Majority, plimulto.
Make, fari.
Make glad, ĝojigi.
Make good, rebonigi.
Make haste, rapidiĝi.
Make holy, sanktigi.
Make known, sciigi.
Make longer, plilongigi.
Make an obei-

milimetro.
Milliner, ĉapelistino.
Millinery, galanterio.
Million, miliono.
Milt, laktumo.
Mimic, imiti.
Mince, haketi.
Mind (heed), atenti.
Mind (a patient), flegi.
Mind, spirito.
Mind (see after), zorgi.
Mindful, zorga.
Mine, mia, mian.
Mine (pit), mino.
Mine, subfosi.
Miner, ministo.
Mineral, mineralo.
Mineralogy, mineralogio.
Mingle, miksi.
Miniature, miniaturo.
Minimum, minimumo.
Minister (religious), pastro.
Minister (polit.), ministro.
Ministry, ministraro.
Minor (age), neplenaĝa.
Minor (mus.), molo, mola.
Minority (age), neplenaĝo.
Minority, malplimulto.
Minstrel, bardo, kantisto.
Mint, mento.
Minute, menueto.
Minuet (time), minuto.
Minute (note), noto.
Minute, malgrandega.
Minutiæ, detaleto.

sance, riverenci.
Make public, publikigi.
Make stronger, plifortigi.
Make younger, plijunigi.
Malachite, malakito.
Malady, malsano.
Malcontent, malkontentulo.
Male, viro.
Malediction, malbeno.
Malefactor, krimulo.
Malevolence, malbonvolo.
Malicious, malica.
Malign, kalumnii.
Malignant, malicema.
Malleable, etendebla.
Mallet, martelego.
Mallow, malvo.
Malt, bierhordeo, hordeo trempita.
Maltreat, bati.
Mama, patrineto.
Mammal, mamsuĉbesto.
Man, homo.
Man (male), viro.
Manage, administri.
Management, administrado.
Manager, administranto.
Mandate, skribordono, komando.
Mandarin, Mandarino.
Mane, kolhararo.
Manganese, mangano.
Mange, bestjuko—skabio.
Manger, manĝujo.
Mangle (to maim), senmemb-

Miracle, miraklo.
Miraculous, mirakla.
Mire, ŝlimo, koto.
Mirror, spegulo.
Mirth, gajeco, kun—.
Miry, ŝlimhava.
Misapply, eraralmeti.
Misapprehend, malkompreni.
Misapprehension, malkompreno.
Misanthrope, homevitulo.
Misbehave, malbonkonduti.
Miscalculation, kalkuleraro.
Miscarry, malsukcesi.
Miscellaneous, miksita, diversa.
Mischance, malfeliĉo.
Mischief, malboneco, malpraveco.
Mischievous, malbonema.
Misconception, malkompreno—eco.
Misconduct, malbonkonduti.
Miscreant, malbonulo.
Misdeed, malbonfaro.
Misdemeanour, krimeto.
Miser, avarulo.
Miserable, malgaja.
Miserly, avara.
Misery, mizero.
Misfortune, malfeliĉo.
Misgiving, dubo.
Mishap, malfeliĉo.
Misinform,

rigi.
Manhood, vireco.
Mania, manio.
Maniac, frenezulo.
Manifest, elmontri.
Manifest, evidenta.
Manifest, klara.
Manifesto, manifesto.
Manifold, multenombra.
Manikin, kvazaŭhomo.
Mankind, homaro.
Manly, vira.
Manliness, vireco.
Manna, manao.
Manner, maniero.
Manner, in this, tiamaniere.
Manner, in that, tiel.
Mannered, bonmora.
Manners, moroj.
Manœuvre (milit.), manovro.
Manometer, manometro.
Mansion, domego.
Manslaughter, mortbato.
Mantle, mantelo.
Manual, mana.
Manual, lernolibro.
Manufactory, fabrikejo.
Manufacture, fabriki.
Manufacture, fabriko.
Manure, sterko.
Manuscript, manuskripto.
Many, multo.
Many, multaj.
Many of, multe da.
Many, how, kiom.
Many, so, tiom.

malsciigi.
Mislay, erarigi, neĝustmeti, trompi.
Mislead, erarigi.
Mislead (deceive), trompi.
Misplaced, neĝustloka.
Misprint, preseraro.
Misrepresent, falsreprezenti.
Miss, manki.
Miss, Fraŭlino.
Missile, ĵetarmilo.
Missing, manka.
Mission, misio.
Missionary, misiisto.
Mist, nebuleto.
Mistake, eraro.
Mistaken, to be, trompiĝi.
Mistletoe, visko.
Mistress (house), mastrino.
Mistress (lover), amantino.
Mistress (school), instruistino.
Mistrust, malfido.
Mistrust, suspekti.
Misty, nebuleta.
Misunderstand, malkompreni.
Misuse, maluzi, malbonuzi.
Mite, akaro.
Mite (coin), monereto.
Mitre, mitro.
Mitigate, moderigi.
Mix, miksi.
Mixture, miksaĵo.
Moan, ĝemi.
Moat, fosaĵo.
Mob, amaso.
Mobile, movebla.
Mobilise, mobilizi.
Mock, moki.
Mockery, moko—eco.

Map, karto, geografikarto.
Mar, difekti, malbonformigi.
Maraud, rabeti.
Marble, marmoro.
Marble (plaything), globeto.
March (month), Marto.
March, marŝi.
March, marŝado.
Marchioness, markizino.
Mare, ĉevalino.
Margin, marĝeno.
Marguerite (daisy), lekanto.
Marigold, kalenduło.
Marine, mara.
Marine, marsoldato.
Mariner, maristo.
Marionette, marioneto.
Maritime, mara.
Mark (sign), signo.
Mark, marko.
Market, vendejo.
Marl, kalkargilo.
Marmalade, fruktaĵo.
Marmot, marmoto.
Marquis, Markizo.
Marriage (state), edzeco.
Marriage (ceremony), edziĝo, edziniĝo.
Marriageable, edzigebla.
Married, to get, edz(in)iĝi.
Marry a man, edzigi.
Marry a woman, edzinigi.
Marry (unite), geedzigi.
Marry, geedziĝi.
Marsh, marĉo.

Mode, modo.
Model, modelo.
Model, modeli.
Moderate, modera.
Moderate, moderigi.
Moderation, modereco.
Modern, moderna.
Modest, modesta.
Modesty, modesteco.
Modify, ŝanĝi.
Modulate, moduli.
Modulation, modulado.
Moiety, duono.
Moist, malseketa.
Moisten, malseketigi.
Moisture, malseketaĵo.
Molasses, mielsiropo.
Molar, vanga dento.
Mole (animal), talpo.
Molest, turmenti, lacigi.
Mollify, moderigi
Mollusk, molusko.
Moment (time), momento.
Momentous, gravega.
Monarch, monarĥo.
Monarchy, monarĥejo.
Monastery, monaĥejo.
Monday, Lundo.
Monetary, mona.
Money, mono.
Money-order, poŝtmandato.
Mongrel, hibrida.
Monitor, avertulo, avertanto.
Monk, monaĥo.

Marshal, marŝalo.
Marsh mallow, alteo.
Mart, vendejo.
Martial, militama—ema.
Marten, mustelo.
Martingale, kapdetenilo.
Martyr, turmentito.
Martyr, suferanto.
Martyrdom, turmento.
Martyrdom, sufero.
Marvel, miri.
Marvel, mirindaĵo.
Marvellous, mirinda.
Masculine, vira.
Masculine, virseksa.
Mash, miksaĵo.
Masher, dando.
Mask, masko.
Mask, maski.
Mason, masonisto.
Masquerade, maskitaro.
Mass, meso.
Mass, amaso.
Massacre, elmortigi.
Massacre, buĉado.
Massive, masiva.
Mast, masto.
Master (of house), mastro.
Master (teacher), instruisto.
Master (of profession), majstro.
Mr., sinjoro.
Masterpiece, ĉefverko.
Mastic, mastiko.
Masticate, maĉi.
Mastication, maĉado.
Mastiff, korthundo.

Monkey, simio.
Monograph, monografo.
Monogram, monogramo.
Monologue, monologo.
Monomania, monomanio.
Monopolise, monopoligi.
Monopoly, monopolo.
Monosyllable, unusilabo.
Monotonous (of form), unuforma.
Monotonous (of tone), unutona.
Monster, monstro.
Monstrous, monstra.
Month, monato.
Monthly (adj.), ĉiumonata.
Monument, monumento.
Mood, modo.
Moody, silentema.
Moon, luno.
Moonlight, lunbrilo.
Moor, stepo.
Moor (a ship, etc.), alligi per ŝnurego.
Moot, disputebla.
Mope, malĝojiĝi.
Moral, morala.
Morality, moraleco.
Morals, etiko, moro.
Morass, marĉejo—aĵo.
Morbid, malsana.
Mordant, morda.
More (than), pli (ol).
More, plu.
More, the—the more, ju pli—des pli.
Moreover, plie.
Morgue, mortulejo.

Mat, mato.
Match, alumeto, egaligi.
Match-box, alumetujo.
Match, kompari, egaligi.
Matchless, nekomparebla.
Matchmaker, alumetisto.
Match (marriage), svatisto.
Mate, ŝipoficiro.
Mate, kunulo.
Material (cloth), ŝtofo.
Material, materialo.
Materialism, materialismo.
Materialist, materialisto.
Maternal, patrina.
Maternity, patrineco.
Mathematician, matematikisto.
Matrimony, geedzeco.
Matrix, utero.
Matron, patrino.
Matron, patronino, estrino. [Error in book: potronino]
Matter, ŝtofo.
Matter, materialo.
Matter (pus), puso.
Mattock, pikfosilo.
Mattress, matraco.
Mature, matura.
Mature, maturiĝi—iĝi.
Maturity, matureco.
Maul, bategi.
Maxillary, makzela.
Maxim, proverbo.
Maximum, maksimumo.

jo.
Moribund, mortanto.
Morning, mateno.
Morocco (leather), marokeno.
Morose, malgaja.
Moroseness, malgajeco.
Morrow, morgaŭtago.
Morsel, peceto.
Mortal (subject to death), mortema.
Mortal (deadly), mortiga.
Mortal, a, mortonta—o.
Mortality (effect), mortado.
Mortality (state), morteco.
Mortar, a, pistujo.
Mortar (milit.), bombardilo.
Mortar (building), mortero.
Mortgage, hipoteko.
Mortification, humiligo.
Mortification, gangreno.
Mortify, gangreni.
Mortify, humiligi.
Mosaic, mozaiko.
Mosquito, kulo.
Moss, musko.
Most, plej.
Mostly, pleje.
Moth, tineo.
Mother, patrino.
Motion, movo.
Motionless, senmova.
Motive, kaŭzo.
Motive, moviga.
Motor, movilo, motoro.
Motto, devizo.
Mould, modelilo.
Mould (soil), tero.
Mouldy, ŝima.
Mouldy, to get,

May (month), Majo.
May-bug, majskarabo.
Mayhap, eble.
Mayor, urbestro.
Maze, labirinto.
Mazurka, mazurko.
Me, (al) mi, min.
Meadow, herbejo.
Meagre (poor), malriĉa.
Meal (flour), faruno.
Meal, manĝo.
Mean (math.), mezakvanto.
Mean (paltry), malgrandanima.
Mean (stingy), troŝpara.
Mean, signifi.
Meaning, signifo.
Meaning (of a word), senco.
Means of, by, per.
Means, by no, neniel.
Measles, morbilo.
Measure, mezuri.
Measure (quantity), mezuro.
Measure, mezurilo.
Measure (time, mus.), takto.
Measurement, mezuraĵo—eco.
Meat, viando.
Mechanic, metiisto.
Mechanic (engineer), meĥanikisto.
Mechanism, meĥanismo.
Mechanics, meĥaniko.
Mechanical, meĥanika.
Medal, medalo.
Medallion, medaliono.
Meddle, enmik-

ŝimiĝi.
Moult, ŝanĝi plumojn.
Moult (birds), ŝanĝi plumojn.
Mound, remparo, digo.
Mount, supreniri.
Mount, monteto.
Mountain, monto.
Mountaineer, montano.
Mountainous, monta.
Mountain-range, montaro.
Mountebank, ĵonglisto.
Mourn, malĝoji, ploregi.
Mournful, funebra.
Mourning (dress), funebra vesto.
Mouse, muso.
Mouse, shrew, soriko.
Mouse-trap, muskaptilo.
Moustache, lipharoj.
Mouth, buŝo.
Mouth (of river), enfluo.
Movable, movebla.
Move, movi.
Move (furniture), transloĝiĝi.
Move in (dwelling), enloĝi.
Move out (dwelling), elloĝiĝi.
Move (feelings), kortuŝi.
Moved (to be), kortuŝiĝi.
Movement, movado.
Mow, falĉi.
Much, multe da.
Much, multa.
Much, so, tiom.

siĝi.
Mediæval, mezepoka.
Mediate, peri.
Mediate, pera.
Mediator, perulo.
Medical, medicina.
Medicament, kuracilo.
Medicinal, medicina.
Medicine, kuracilo.
Medicine (art), medicino.
Mediocre, malboneta.
Meditate, mediti.
Meditation, medito.
Mediterranean, Mezomaro.
Medium (spiritualism), mediumo.
Medium, meza.
Meek, humilega.
Meet, renkonti.
Meeting, renkonto.
Meeting (of club, etc.), kunveno.
Meeting-place, kunvenejo.
Melancholy, melankolio.
Melancholy, melankolia.
Mellow, matura.
Melodious, melodia.
Melody, melodio.
Melodrama, melodramo.
Melon, melono.
Melt, fluidiĝi.
Member (limb), membro.
Member (of club), klubano.
Membrane, membrano.
Memento, memoraĵo.
Memorable,

Much, how, kiom da.
Much, too, tro multe.
Mucus, muko.
Mud, ŝlimo, koto.
Muddle (of liquors), malklarigi.
Muddle (bungle), fuŝi, konfuzi.
Muddle (bungle), konfuzo.
Mudguard, kotŝirmilo.
Muff, mufo.
Muffle, envolvi.
Mug, pokaleto, poteto.
Mulberry, moruso.
Mulct (fine), mona puno, monpuno.
Mule, mulo.
Muleteer, mulisto.
Mulish, obstina.
Multiple, multoblo.
Multiplicand, multigato.
Multiplication, multigado.
Multiplied, multigita.
Multiplier, multiganto.
Multiply (trans.), multigi.
Multiply (intrans.), multiĝi.
Mumble, murmuri.
Mummy, mumo.
Munch, maĉi.
Mundane, monda.
Municipal, urba.
Munificence, malavareco.
Munificent, malavara.
Murder, mortigi.
Murder, mortigo.
Murderer, mortiganto.

memorinda.
Memorandum, noto.
Memorial, memoraĵo.
Memory, memoro.
Menace, minaci.
Menacing, minaca.
Menagery, bestejo.
Mend, fliki. [Error in book: fleki]
Mendacity, mensogeco.
Mendicant, almozulo.
Menial, servulo.
Menses, monataĵo.
Mental, spirita.
Mention, citi, nomi.
Menu, manĝokarto.
Mercantile, komerca.
Mercenary, dungato.
Mercenary, subaĉetebla.
Merchandise, komercaĵo.
Merchant, negocisto.
Merciful, kompata—ema.
Mercury, hidrargo.
Mercy, kompato—eco.
Mere, nura.
Merely, nure.
Meridian, meridiano.
Merino, merinolano. [Error in book: merinoslano]
Merit, merito.
Merit, meriti.
Mermaid, sireno.
Merriment, gajeco.

Murky, malhela, malluma.
Murmur, murmuri.
Muscat wine, muskatvino.
Muscle, muskolo.
Muscular, muskola.
Muse, muzo.
Muse, revi.
Museum, muzeo.
Mushroom, fungo.
Music, muziko.
Musical, muzika.
Musician, muzikisto.
Music (to play), muziki.
Muskrat, miogalo.
Musket, pafilo.
Muslin, muslino.
Mussel, mitulo.
Must (verb), devas.
Must, mosto.
Mustard, mustardo.
Mustard plant, sinapo.
Mustard-plaster, sinapa kataplasmo.
Muster, kunvenigi.
Musty, malfreŝa.
Mutation, ŝanĝado.
Mute, muta.
Mute, mutulo.
Mutilate, vundegi.
Mutinous, ribela.
Mutiny, ribelo.
Mutter, murmuri.
Mutton, ŝafaĵo.
Mutton, leg of, ŝaffemuro.
Mutual, reciproka.
Mutually, reciproke.
Muzzle (for a dog), buŝumo.
Muzzle, buŝumi.
My, mia, mian.

Merry, gaja.
Mesh, maŝo.
Mess, kunmanĝi.
Message, depeŝo.
Messenger, sendito.
Messiah, Savonto, Mesio.
Messmate, kunmanĝanto.
Metal, metalo.
Metallic, metala.
Metallurgy, metalurgio.
Metaphor, metaforo.
Mete, dividi, disdoni.
Meteor, meteoro.
Meteorology, meteorologio.
Meter, mezurilo.
Method, metodo.
Metre, metro.
Metric, metra.
Metropolis, ĉefurbo.
Mettle, fervoro, kuraĝo.
Mew, katbleki.
Miasma, miasmo.
Mica, glimo.
Microbe, mikrobo.
Microscope, mikroskopo.
Midday, tagmezo.
Middle, centro.
N
Nadir, nadiro.
Nail (of finger, etc.), ungo.
Nail, najli.
Naive, naiva.
Naked, nuda.
Name, nomi.
Name, Christian, baptonomo.
Namely, nome.
Namesake, samnomulo.
Nankeen, nankeno.
Nap (doze), dormeti.

Myoptic, miopa, miopema.
Myopy, miopeco.
Myosotis, miozoto.
Myriad, miriado.
Myriametre, miriametro.
Myrrh, mirho.
Myrtle, mirto.
Mysterious, mistera.
Mystery, mistero.
Mystify, mistifiki.
Mystification, mistifiko.
Myth, mito.
Mythology, mitologio.

Niece, nevino.
Niggard, avarulo.
Nigh, proksima.
Nigh (time), baldaŭa.
Night, nokto.
Nightly, nokta.
Night, by, nokte.
Nightingale, najtingalo.
Night-watch, nokta patrolo.
Nightmare, terursonĝo.
Nimble, vigla.
Nimbus, glorkro-

Nape, nuko.
Napkin, buŝtuko.
Narcissus, narciso.
Narcotic, narkotiko.
Narrate, rakonti.
Narrative, rakonto.
Narrow, mallarĝa.
Narrowly, mallarĝe.
Narrowness, mallarĝeco.
Nasal, naza.
Nasty, malagrabla.
Natation, naĝarto.
Nation, nacio.
National, nacia.
Nationality, nacieco.
Native, landano, enlandulo.
Native, enlanda.
Native-land, patrujo.
Nativity, naskiĝo.
Natural (music), naturo.
Natural, natura.
Naturalism, naturalismo.
Naturalist, naturalisto.
Naturally, nature.
Naturally (of course), kompreneble.
Naturalness, naturaleco.
Nature, naturo.
Naught, nulo.
Naughty, malbona.
Nausea, naŭzo.
Nauseate, naŭzi.
Nauseous, naŭza.
Nautical, ŝipa.
Naval, ŝipa.
Nave (church), navo.
Nave (wheel), aksingo.
Navigable, ŝipirebla.
Navigate, marveturi.
Navigation, marveturado.
Navy, ŝiparo.
Navvy, terfosisto.
Nay, ne.
Near, proksima.
Near by, apud.
Nearly, preskaŭ.
Nearness, proksimeco.
Neat, pura, deca.
Neatness, pureco, dececo.
Nebulous, nebula.
Necessary, necesa.
Necessity, neceseco.
Neck, kolo.
Neck (of vase), nazeto.
Neck (of land), terkolo.
Neckcloth, koltuko.
Necklace, ĉirkaŭkolo.
Necktie, kravato.
Necrology, nekrologio.
Necromancer, nekromancisto, sorĉisto.
Nectar, nektaro.
Need, bezoni.
Need, malriĉeco.
Needful, bezona, necesa.
Needle, kudrilo.
Needy, malriĉa.
Negation, neado.
Negative, nea.
Neglect, ne zorgi pri.
Neglected, nezorgita.
Neglectful, senzorga.
Negligent, malatenta.
Negligence, malatento.
Negotiate, negoci.
Negotiation, negocado.
Negro, nigrulo.
Neigh, ĉevalbleki.
Neighbour, najbaro.
Neighbourhood, ĉirkaŭajo.
Neighbouring, samlima.
Neither, nek.
Neo-Latin, novlatina.
Neologism, neologismo.
Nephew, nevo.
Nepotism, nepotismo.
Nerve, nervo.
Nervous, nerva.
Nervousness, nerveco.
Nest, nesto.
Nestle, kuŝiĝeti.
Nestling, birdido.
Net, reto.
Netting, retaĵo.
Nettle, urtiko.
Network, retaĵo.
Neuralgia, neŭralgio.
Neuter, neŭtra.
Neutral, neŭtrala.
Neutrality, neŭtraleco.
Never, neniam.
Nevertheless, tamen.
New, nova.
News, sciigo, novaĵo.
Newspaper, ĵurnalo.
New Year's Day, novjartago.
Next, sekvanta.
Next (near), plejproksima.
Nibble, mordeti.
Nice, agrabla.
Niche, niĉo.
Nick (notch), tranĉeti.
Nickel, nikelo.
Noviceship, noviceco.
Novitiate, provtempo.
Novitiate (place), novicejo.
Now, nun.
Nowadays, nuntempe.
Nowhere, nenie.
Noxious, malutila, venena.
Nozzle, nazeto.
Nude, nuda.
Nudity, nudeco.
Null, nuliga.
Nullify, nuligi.
Numb, rigidigi.
Numbness, rigideco.
Number (quantity), nombro.
Number, numero.
Numeral, numero.
Numerical, nombra.
Numerous, multa.
Numerously, multege.
Nun, monaĥino.
Nuncio, nuncio.
Nunnery, monaĥinejo.
Nuptial, edziĝa.
Nurse (a child), varti.
Nurse, nutristino.
Nurse, flegistino.
Nurse (hospital), malsanulistino.
Nurse (wet), suĉigistino.
Nurseling, suĉinfano.
Nursemaid, vartistino, infanistino.
Nursery (horticulture), plantejo, florkulturejo.
Nursery, infanĉambro.
Nurture, elnutri.
Nut, nukso.
Nut (of a screw),

Nine, naŭ.
Ninny, simplanimulo.
Nip, pinĉi.
Nippers, prenileto.
Nitre, salpetro.
Nobility, nobelaro.
Noble, nobla.
Nobleman, nobelo.
Nobleness, nobleco.
Nobody, neniu.
Nocturnal, nokta.
Nocuous, pereiga.
Nod (beckon), signodoni.
No, ne.
No one, neniu.
Noise, bruo.
Noisome, naŭza, malbonodora.
Noisy (of children), petola.
Nomad, migranto.
Nomadic, migranta.
Nom-de-plume, pseŭdonomo.
Nomenclature, nomaro.
Nominal, nominala.
Nominative, nominativo.
Nonchalance, apatio.
Nonconformist, nekonformisto.
Nondescript, nepriskriba.
None, neniom.
Nonentity, neestaĵo.
Nonsense, sensencaĵo, malsaĝeco.
Non-success, malprospero.
Nook, anguleto.
Noon, tagmezo.
Noose, ligotubero.
Nor, nek.

No, bla.
Normal, normala.
North, nordo.
Northerly, norda.
Northern, norda.
Nose, nazo.
Nosebag, manĝujo.
Nosegay, bukedo.
Nostril, naztruo.
Not, ne.
Notable, fama, grava.
Notary, notario.
Note, noti, rimarki.
Note (music), noto.
Note (letter), letereto.
Notbook, notlibreto.
Note of exclamation, signo ekkria.
Note of interrogation, signo demanda.
Nothing, nenio.
Notice, rimarki.
Notice (public), surskribo.
Notice, avizo.
Notification, sciigo.
Notify, sciigi.
Notion, ekkono.
Notoriety, konateco.
Notorious, malglora.
Notwithstanding, tamen.
Nought, nulo.
Nought, nenio.
Noun, substantivo.
Nourish, nutri.
Nourishing, nutra.
Nourishment, nutraĵo.
Novel (romance), romano.
Novelty, novaĵo.
November, Novembro.
Novice, novulo.

Nickname, moknomo.
Nicotine, nikotino.

O

Oaf, idiotulo.
Oak, kverko.
Oakum, stupo.
Oar, remilo.
Oasis, oazo.
Oath (legal), ĵuro.
Oath (curse), blasfemo.
Oatmeal, grio.
Obduracy, obstineco.
Obdurate, obstina.
Obedience, obeo.
Obedient, obea.
Obeisance, riverenco.
Obelisk, obelisko.
Obese, grasega.
Obesity, vastkorpeco.
Obey, obei.
Obituary, nekrologio.
Object (end, aim), celo.
Object, kontraŭparoli.
Object, objekto.
Objection, kontraŭparolo.
Objectionable, riproĉeblinda.
Objective (purpose), celo.
Oblation, ofero.
Obligation, devo.
Obligatory, deviga.
Oblige (compel), devigi.
Oblige (render service), fari komplezon.
Obliged, to be, devi.
Obliging, servema.
ŝraŭbingo.
Nutmeg, muskato.
Nutriment, nutraĵo.
Nutritious, nutra.
Nymph, nimfo.

Open-hearted, malkovranima.
Openly, nekaŝeme, tutkora.
Opera, opero.
Opera-glass, lorneto.
Opera-house, operejo.
Operate (surgery), operacii.
Operate, funkcii.
Operatic, opera.
Operation, operacio.
Operative, metiisto.
Operative, agebla.
Operetta, opereto.
Opinion, to be of an, opinii.
Opium, opio.
Opponent, kontraŭulo.
Opportune, ĝustatempa.
Opportunity, okazo.
Oppose, kontraŭmeti, kontraŭbatali.
Opposed to, to be, kontraŭstari.
Opposite (in opposition), kontraŭa.
Opposite facing, kontraŭe.
Opposition, kontraŭmeto—ado.
Oppress, subpremi.
Oppressor, tirano, subpremanto.
Opprobrium, malnobleco, malglo-
Oblique, oblikva.
Obliquity, oblikveco.
Obliterate, surstreki.
Oblivion, forgeso.
Oblivious, forgesa.
Oblong, longforma.
Obnoxious, ofendega.
Obscene, malbonmora, malĉasta.
Obscure, mallumigi.
Obscure, malhela.
Obscurity, senlumeco, mallumeco.
Obsequies, enterigiro.
Observance (rite), ceremonio—ado.
Observant, observema.
Observation, observo—ado.
Observatory, observatorio.
Observe (make a remark), rimarki.
Observe (see), vidi.
Obsolete, troantikva.
Obstacle, baro, kontraŭaĵo.
Obstinacy, obstineco.
Obstinate, to be, obstini.
Obstinate, obstina.
Obstruct, obstrukci.
Obstruction, baro, obstrukco.
Obtain, ricevi, atingi.
Obtrude, trudi.
Obtrusion, trudo—eco.
Obtrusive, trudema.
ro.
Optics, optiko.
Optical, optika.
Optician, optikisto.
Optimism, optimismo.
Optimist, optimisto.
Option, elekto—aĵo.
Opulence, riĉeco.
Opulent, riĉa.
Opusculum, libreto, broŝuro.
Or, aŭ.
Oracle, orakolo.
Oral, voĉa, parola.
Orange, oranĝo.
Orange (colour), oranĝkolora.
Orangery, oranĝerio.
Oration, parolado.
Orator, oratoro, parolisto.
Oratory (chapel), preĝejeto.
Oratory, elokventeco.
Orchard, fruktarbejo.
Orchestra, orkestro.
Ordain, ordeni.
Ordeal, provo, ekzameno.
Order, to put in, ordigi.
Order (goods), mendi.
Order (command), ordoni.
Orders (instructions), instrukcio.
Order (for goods), mendo.
Order (postal), mandato.
Order (a decoration), ordeno.
Order (arrangement), ordo.
Obtuse, malakra, malinteligenta.
Obverse, antaŭa flanko.
Obviate, malhelpi.
Obvious, videbla, evidenta.
Occasion, okazo.
Occasional, okaza.
Occult, kaŝata.
Occupant, okupanto, loĝanto.
Occupation, okupo.
Occupy, okupi.
Occupied with, to be, okupiĝi pri.
Occur, okazi.
Occurrence, okazo.
Ocean, oceano.
Oceania, Oceanio.
Ochre, okro.
Octave, oktavo.
October, Oktobro.
Ocular, okula.
Ocularly, okule.
Oculist, okulisto.
Odd (peculiar), stranga.
Odd (number), nepara.
Oddly, strange.
Ode, odo.
Odious, malaminda.
Odium, malamo.
Odour, odoro.
Odorous, odora.
Of, de.
Of (after noun of measure, etc.), da.
Off, be! foriru!
Offence, peketo, ofendo.
Offend, ofendi.
Offender, ofendanto.
Offensive, ofenda.
Offer (propose), proponi.
Offer (present),
Orderly, orda.
Orderly (military), servosoldato.
Ordinance, ordono.
Ordinary, kutima, ordinara.
Ordnance, artilerio.
Ore, minaĵo.
Organ (music), orgeno.
Organ, organo.
Organic, organa.
Organism, organismo.
Organize, organizi.
Organization, organizo.
Orient, oriento.
Oriental, orienta.
Orifice, truo, buŝo.
Origin, deveno.
Original, originala.
Originate, devenigi—iĝi.
Ornament, ornamo.
Ornament, ornami.
Ornaments (jewellery, etc.), juvelaro.
Ornamentation, ornamaĵo.
Ornithology, ornitologio.
Orphan, orfo—ino.
Orphanage, orfejo.
Orthodox, ortodoksa.
Orthography, ortografio.
Ortolan, hortulano.
Oscillate, vibri, balanciĝi.
Osier, saliko.
Ossify, ostiĝi.

prezenti.
Offer (sacrifice), oferi.
Offering, oferdono, oferaĵo.
Offertory, mona kolektado.
Office (divine), Diservo.
Office (function), ofico.
Office, printing, presejo.
Office, oficejo.
Office, post, poŝta oficejo.
Officer (military), oficiro.
Officer, non-commissioned, subofíciro.
Official, oficisto.
Official, oficiala.
Officiate, agi.
Officious, agama.
Offspring, ido, idaro.
Often, ofte.
Oh! ho!
Oil, oleo.
Oilcloth, vakstolo.
Ointment, ŝmiraĵo.
Old (not new), malnova.
Old (aged), maljuna.
Old, to grow, maljuniĝi.
Old, to make, maljunigi.
Old age, maljuneco.
Olden (time), antikva.
Oldness, malnoveco.
Oligarchy, oligarkio.
Olive, olivo.
Olive-shaped, olivforma.
Olive tree, olivarbo.

Ostensible, videbla.
Ostentation, fanfaronado, trudpompo.
Ostentatious, trudpompa.
Ostracism, ostracismo.
Ostrich, struto.
Other, alia.
Otherwise, alie, cetere.
Otter, lutro.
Ought (should), devus (devi).
Ounce, unco.
Our, ours, nia.
Oust, forpeli.
Out (prep.), ekster.
Out (prefix), el.
Outbid, plioferi, superoferi.
Outcast, ekzilo, elpelito.
Outcome, elveno.
Outer, ekstera.
Outermost, plejekstera.
Outfit, vestaro.
Outlaw, forpeli.
Outlaw, elpelito.
Outlay, elspezo.
Outlet, eliro.
Outline, skizo, konturo.
Outlive, postvivi.
Outpost, antaŭposteno.
Outrage, insultegi, perforti.
Outrage, perforto.
Outright, tute.
Outset, komenco.
Outskirts, ĉirkaŭaĵo.
Outside, ekstere.
Outstanding (unpaid), nepagita.
Oval, ovala.
Ovary, ovujo.
Ovation, laŭdado.
Oven, forno.
Over (above), su-

Omelet, ovaĵo.
Omen, antaŭsigno.
Ominous, graveg a.
Omission, formetado.
Omit, formeti, forigi.
Omnibus, omnibuso.
Omnipotent, ĉiopova.
Omnipresence, ĉieesto.
Omniscient, ĉioscia.
On, sur.
Once, foje, unu fojon.
Once upon a time, iam.
One, unu.
One day (sometime), iam.
One-eyed, unuokula.
Oneness, unueco.
Onion, bulbo.
Only, nur.
Onset, atako.
Ontology, ontologio.
Onward, antaŭe, n.
Onyx, onikso.
Ooze, traguteti.
Opal, opalo.
Opaque, maldiafana.
Open, malfermi.
Open, to throw, malfermegi.
Open (candid), nekaŝema.
Open (uncork, etc.), malŝtopi.
Open (of flowers), ekflori.

per.
Overall, surtuto.
Overbearing, aŭtokrata, fierega.
Overcast, malklara, nuba.
Overcharge, supertakso.
Overcoat, supervesto.
Overcome, venki.
Overflow, superflui.
Overhaul (examine), ekzameni.
Overhead, supre.
Overlook (inspect), viziti, ekzameni, esplori.
Overlook (excuse), senkulpigi, pardoni.
Overlook, malatenti, malintenci.
Overplus, preteraĵo, plimultaĵo.
Overpower, venki, submeti.
Overrun, enpenetri.
Overseer, observisto, oficisto.
Overstep, transpaŝi.
Overtake, atingi.
Overthrow, renversi.
Overture (music), uverturo.
Overture (proposal), propono.
Overturn, renversi.
Overweening, tromemfida.
Overwhelm, premegi.
Owe, ŝuldi.
Owl, strigo, gufo.
Own, propra.
Own (possess), posedi, havi.
Owner (of property, etc.), bienulo.
Ox, bovo.

Oxide, oksido.
Oxygen, oksigeno.
Oyster, ostro.

P

Pa, patreto, paĉjo.
Pace, paŝi.
Pace (step), paŝo.
Pacific, pacema.
Pacifically, pace, paceme.
Pacification, pacigo.
Pacify, trankviligi, pacigi.
Pachydermatous, dikhaŭta.
Pack, paki.
Pack up, enpaki.
Pack (hounds), hundaro.
Package, pakado, pakaĵo.
Packer, pakisto.
Packet, pako—aĵo.
Packet-boat, kurierŝipo.
Pack-saddle, ŝarĝselo.
Pad, vati.
Padding, vato—aĵo.
Paddle (to row), remeti.
Paddock, kampeto.
Padlock, penda seruro.
Pagan, idolano.
Page-boy, paĝio, lakeeto.
Page, paĝo.
Pageant, vidaĵo, parado.
Pagoda, pagodo.
Pail, sitelo.
Pain, dolori.
Painful, dolora.
Painless, sendolora.
Paint, pentri, kolori.
Paint, kolorilo, kolorigilo.

Planet, planedo.
Plank, tabulo.
Plant, planti.
Plant, kreskaĵo.
Plantation, plantejo.
Plaster, plastro, gipso.
Plastron, brustoŝirmilo.
Plate, stanumi.
Plate, telero.
Plate (stereotype), kliŝaĵaro, kliŝaĵo.
Plateau, plataĵo.
Platform, plataĵo, estrado.
Platinum, plateno.
Platitude, plateco.
Platter, pladego.
Plaudit, aplaŭdego.
Plausible, verŝajna, aprobebla.
Play (a game), ludi.
Play (piano, etc.), ludi.
Play about, ludeti, petoli.
Play (joke), ŝerci.
Play (theatrical), teatraĵo.
Player, ludanto.
Playful, petola.
Playhouse (theatre), teatro.
Plaything, ludilo.
Playtime, ludtempo.
Plead, procesi, proparoladi.
Pleasant, plaĉa.
Pleasant (manner), dolĉega.
Please, plaĉi.
Please, if you, se vi bonvolas, se plaĉos al vi.
Pleasure, to give,

Paint (rouge), ruĝilo.
Painter (artist), pentristo.
Painter (workman), kolorigisto.
Painting (art), pentrarto.
Painting, pentrado.
Painting (picture), pentraĵo.
Pair, kunigi.
Pair, paro.
Palace, palaco.
Palanquin, palankeno.
Palate, palato.
Palatable, bongusta.
Pale, to become, paliĝi.
Pale, pala.
Paleness, paleco.
Paleography, paleografio.
Paleontology, paleontologio.
Paletot, palto.
Paling, palisaro—aĵo.
Palisade, palisaro—aĵo.
Pall, supersati.
Pall, ĉerkokovrilo.
Palliasse, pajla matraco.
Pallid, palega.
Pallet, paletro.
Palm (of hand), manplato.
Palm, palmobranĉo.
Palm-tree, palmarbo.
Palpable, palpebla.
Palpitate, korbati, palpiti.
Palpitation, korbato—ado.
Palsy, paralizeto.
Paltry, triviala.
Pamper, dorloti.

Pamphlet, pamfleto.
Pan, tervazo.
Pane, vitraĵo.
Panegyric, laŭdado.
Panegyrist, laŭdegisto.
Panel, enkadraĵo.
Pang, doloro.
Panic, teruro.
Pannier, korbego.
Pansy, violo.
Pant, spiregi.
Pantaloons, pantalono.
Pantheism, panteismo.
Pantheist, panteisto.
Panther, pantero.
Pantomime, pantomimo.
Pantry, manĝajejo.
Pap, kaĉo.
Papa, patreto, paĉjo.
Papal, papa.
Paper, papero.
Paper-hanger, paperkovristo, tapetisto.
Paper-maker, paperisto.
Paper-manufactory, paperfarejo.
Paper-mill, paperfarejo.
Paper-shop, ĵurnalvendejo.
Papyrus, papiruso.
Parable, komparaĵo.
Parabola, parabolo.
Parade, paradi.
Parade (place), promenejo.
Parade, vidaĵo, luksaĵo.
Paradise, paradizo.
Paradox,

placi.
Pleasure, with, plezure.
Plebeian, malnobelo.
Pledge, garantiaĵo.
Plenitude, pleneco.
Plenteous, sufiĉega.
Plenty, sufiĉa, sufiĉega. [Error in book: sufiĉelga]
Pleonasm, pleonasmo.
Pliable, fleksebla.
Pliant, fleksebla.
Pliantness, flekseblaeco.
Pliers, prenilo—eto.
Plod on, diligentiĝi.
Plot, konspiri, intrigi.
Plot (league), intrigo, konspiro.
Plot (of land), terpeco.
Plough, plugi.
Plough, plugilo.
Ploughshare, plugfero.
Pluck (fowl), plumtiregi, senplumigi.
Pluck (courage), kuraĝo.
Plug, ŝtopilego.
Plum, pruno.
Plumage, plumaro, plumaĵo.
Plumbago, grafito.
Plumber, plumbisto.
Plume, plumfasko.
Plummet, sondilo.
Plump, dika.
Plumpness, dikeco.
Plunder, rabadi.
Plunge, sub-

akviĝi.
Plural, multenombro.
Plush, pluŝo.
Poach, ĉasoŝteli.
Poach (eggs, etc.), boleti.
Poacher, ĉasoŝtelisto.
Pocket, poŝo.
Pod, ŝelo.
Poem, poemo.
Poesy, poezio.
Poet, poeto.
Poetize, versi.
Poetry, poezio, poeziaĵo.
Poetry, a piece of, versaĵo.
Poignant, dolorega.
Point, punkto.
Point (cards), poento.
Point (tip of), pinto.
Point (to sharpen), pintigi.
Point out, montri, signali.
Points (railway), relforko.
Poise, balanci, ekvilibri.
Poison, veneno.
Poisonous, venena.
Poke the fire, inciti la fajron.
Poker, fajrincitilo.
Polar, polusa.
Pole (wooden), stango.
Pole (shaft of car), timono.
Pole (geography), poluso.
Polecat, putoro.
Polemic, disputo, polemiko.
Police, polico.
Policeman, policano.
Polish, poluri.
Polish (sub-

paradokso.
Paragon, perfektmodelo, perfektaĵo.
Paragraph, paragrafo.
Parallel, paralela.
Paralyze, paralizi.
Paralysis, paralizo—ado.
Paralytic, paralizito—ulo.
Paramount, superega.
Paramour, kromviro—ino.
Parapet, randmuro.
Paraphrase, parafrazo.
Parasite, parazito.
Parasitic, parazita.
Parasol, sunombrelo.
Parboil, duonboli.
Parcel, pako, pakaĵo.
Parcel out, dispecigi, dividi.
Parcels-office, pakaĵejo.
Parcel-post, poŝta paketo.
Parch, sekigi.
Parchment, pergameno.
Pardon, pardoni, senkulpigi.
Pardon, pardono.
Pardonable, pardonebla.
Pare, ŝeli.
Parenthesis, parentezo.
Parents, gepatroj.
Parentage, naskiĝo, deveno.
Parental, gepatra.
Paring, ŝelo—aĵo.
Parish, paroĥo.
Parishioner, paroĥano.
Parish-priest, paroĥestro.

stance), poluraĵo.
Polished (manners), ĝentila.
Polite, ĝentila.
Politic, saĝa.
Political, politika.
Politician, politikisto.
Politics, politiko.
Poll (vote), voĉdoni, baloti.
Poll (of head), verto.
Pollen, florsemo.
Pollute, malpurigi.
Poltroon, timulo—egulo.
Poltroonery, timeco—egeco.
Polygon, multangulo.
Polyp, polipo.
Polypus, polipo.
Polytechnic, politekniko, a.
Pomade, pomado.
Pomatum, pomado.
Pomegranate, pomgranato.
Pompous, pompa.
Pond, lageto.
Ponder, pripensi, reveti.
Ponderous, multepeza.
Poniard, ponardo.
Pontiff, ĉefpastro.
Pontoon, boatoponto.
Pony, ĉevaleto.
Poodle, pudelo.
Pool, marĉlageto.
Poop, posta parto.
Poor, malriĉa.
Pope, papo.
Poplar, poplo—arbo.
Poppy, papavo.
Poppy-coloured, punca.
Populace, popolo—amaso.
Popular, popu-

Parity, egaleco.
Park, parko.
Parley, paroladi.
Parliament, house of, parlamentejo.
Parliamentary, parlamenta.
Parlour, parolejo.
Parochial, paroĥa.
Parody, parodio.
Parole, parolo je la honoro.
Paroxysm, frenezo, frenezado.
Parricide, patromortiginto.
Parroquet, papageto.
Parrot, papago.
Parry, lerte eviti, skermi.
Parsimony, parcimonio.
Parsley, petroselo.
Parsnip, pastinako.
Parson, pastro.
Parsonage, pastra domo.
Part, parto, porcio.
Part, on my part, miaflanke.
Part, to depart, foriri.
Part, to separate, disiĝi, malkuniĝi.
Partake, partopreni.
Parterre, florbedo.
Parterre (theatre), partero.
Partial, partia.
Partiality, partieco.
Participant, partoprenanto.
Participate, partopreni.
Participle, participo.
Particle, pecero, lara.
Population, loĝantaro.
Populous, popola.
Porcelain, porcelano.
Porch, vestiblo.
Porcupine, histriko.
Pore, trueto.
Pork, porkaĵo.
Porous, trueta.
Porphyry, porfiro.
Porpoise, fokseno.
Port (harbour), haveno.
Portable, portebla.
Portend, antaŭsciigi.
Porter (doorkeeper), pordisto.
Porter, portisto.
Portfolio, paperujo.
Portion (allot), dividi.
Portion, porcio, parto, doto.
Portmanteau, valizo, vestkesto.
Portrait, portreto.
Portraiture (art), pentrarto.
Position (place), loko.
Position, situacio.
Positive, pozitiva.
Possess, posedi.
Possessive, poseda.
Possessor, posedanto.
Possible, to render, ebligi.
Possible, ebla.
Possibility, ebleco.
Possibly, eble.
Post (military), posteno.
Post (wooden pole), stango, fosto.
pecereto.
Particular, speciala.
Partisan, partiano.
Partition, dividi.
Partition, divido, partituro.
Partition-wall, maldika muro.
Partly, parte.
Partner, partoprenanto, kunulo.
Partridge, perdriko.
Party, partio.
Parvenu, elsaltulo.
Pass (intrans.), pasi.
Pass (trans.), pasigi.
Pass, to let, preterlasi.
Pass by, preteriri.
Pass on, preterpasi.
Pass over, across, transpasi.
Pass through, trapasi.
Pass (passport), pasporto.
Passable, nebona.
Passage (a way), aleo.
Passage, trairejo.
Passage (voyage), vojiro, vojaĝo.
Passenger, vojaĝanto.
Passer-by, pasanto.
Passion, manio, pasio.
Passion, kolera, kolerega, pasio.
Passionate, pasia, kolerema.
Passive, pasiva.
Passport, pasporto.
Password, signaldiro.
Post (position), ofico.
Post (letters, etc.), poŝto.
Postal, poŝta.
Postcard, poŝtkarto.
Postman, poŝtisto, leteristo.
Post-office, poŝta oficejo.
Poster (placard), afiŝo, kartego.
Poste-restante, poŝtrestante.
Posterior, posta, malantaŭ.
Posterity, idaro, posteularo.
Postillion, kondukisto.
Postscript, postskribaĵo.
Postulate, petado.
Posture, teniĝo.
Pot, poto.
Potash, potaso.
Potato, terpomo.
Potency, potenco.
Potent, potenca.
Potential, potencebla, poviga.
Potter, potisto.
Pottery (art), potfarado.
Pottery, a, potfarejo.
Pouch, saketo.
Poultice, kataplasmo.
Poultry, kortbirdaro.
Poultry-yard, kortbirdejo.
Pound (grind), pisti.
Pound (money), livro.
Pound (weight), funto.
Pour out (liquids), verŝi.
Pour out, ŝuti.
Pout, kolereti.
Poverty, malriĉeco.
Past, estinta.
Past, estinteco.
Paste, pasto.
Pasteboard, kartono.
Pastel, paŝtelo.
Pastille, pastelo.
Pastime, amuzaĵo.
Pastor, pastro.
Pastoral, kampa.
Pastry, pasteco.
Pastry-shop, kukejo.
Pasture, herbejo, paŝtejo.
Pasturage, paŝtaĵo, paŝtejo.
Pat, frapeti.
Patch, fliki.
Patchwork, flikaĵo.
Patella, genuosto.
Patent, patento.
Patentee, patentito.
Paternal, patra.
Paternity, patreco.
Path, vojo, vojeto.
Pathetic, kortuŝanta.
Pathology, patologio.
Pathos, patoso.
Patience, pacienco.
Patient, pacienca.
Patient, a, malsanulo—ino.
Patois, provinca lingvaĵo.
Patriarch, patriarko.
Patrimony, hereda propraĵo.
Patriot, patrioto.
Patriotism, patriotismo.
Patrol, patrolo.
Patrol (night), nokta patrolo.
Patron, proktektanto, patrono.
Patronage, proco.
Powder (hair, etc.), pudri.
Powder (gun), pulvo.
Powder, pulvro, pudro.
Power, povo, potenco.
Power (of attorney), konfidatesto.
Powerful, multepova.
Powerless, senpotenca.
Practical, praktika.
Practice (custom), kutimo.
Practice, praktiko, kutimo, uzado.
Practise, praktiki.
Prairie, herbejo.
Praise, laŭdi.
Prank, petolecoaĵo.
Prate, babili.
Prattle, babili.
Pray (religious), preĝi.
Pray (to request), peti.
Prayer, preĝo.
Prayer-book, preĝlibro.
Preach, prediki.
Preacher, predikisto.
Preaching, predikado.
Preamble, antaŭparolo.
Prebendary, kanoniko.
Precarious, duba, necerta.
Precaution, antaŭzorgo, singardo.
Precede, antaŭiri.
Precedence, antaŭeco.
Precedent, an-

tekto.
Patronize, favori, protekti.
Patron saint, patrona sanktulo.
Patrons (clients), klientaro.
Patter, guteti.
Pattern, patrono, modelo.
Paunch, ventro.
Pauper, malriĉulo, almozulo.
Pause, paŭzo.
Pave, pavimi.
Pavement, pavimo.
Paving-stone, pavimero.
Pavilion, tendo, paviliono.
Paw, piedego.
Pawn (chess), soldato.
Pawn, garantiaĵo.
Pawnbroker, pruntisto.
Pawnbroker's, pruntoficejo.
Pawn-office, pruntoficejo.
Pay, pagi.
Pay (military), soldo.
Pay (in full), elpagi.
Payable, pagebla.
Payment (wages, etc.), pago.
Pea, pizo.
Peace, paco.
Peace, to make, pacigi.
Peaceable, pacema.
Peaceably, pace.
Peaceful, pacema.
Peacefully, pace.
Peach, persiko.
Peacock, pavo.
Peak, pinto, pintaĵo.
Peak (of cap, etc.), ŝirmileto.
Peal (of bells),
taŭaĵo.
Precentor, kantoro.
Precept, ordono.
Preceptor, guvernisto.
Precinct, limo.
Precious, multekosta.
Precipice, krutegaĵo.
Precipitancy, trorapideco.
Precipitate, trorapida.
Precipitation, trorapideco.
Precise, preciza.
Precisely, ĝuste.
Precision, precizeco, akurateco.
Preclude, eksigi, malhelpi.
Precocious, frumatura.
Precocity, frumaturo—eco.
Precursor, antaŭulo.
Predatory, rabadega.
Predecessor, antaŭulo.
Predestination, sortdifino.
Predetermination, antaŭdecido.
Predict, antaŭdiri, profetadi.
Prediction, antaŭdiro.
Predisposition, inklino.
Predominate, superregi.
Preface, antaŭparolo.
Prefect, prefekto.
Prefer, preferi.
Preferable, preferinda.
Preferably, prefere.
Preference, prefero.
sonorilaro.
Pear, piro.
Pear-tree, pirarbo.
Pearl, perlo.
Pearl, mother of, perlamoto.
Peasant, vilaĝano, kamparano.
Peat, torfo.
Pebble, marŝtono, ŝtoneto.
Peccadillo, peketo.
Peculiar, stranga.
Pecuniary, mona.
Pedagogue, pedagogo.
Pedagogy, pedagogio.
Pedal, pedalo.
Pedant, pedanto.
Peddler, kolportisto.
Peddle, kolporti.
Pedestal, piedestalo.
Pedestrian, piediranto.
Pedigree, deveno, genealogio.
Pediment, fruntaĵo.
Peel (fruit, etc.), ŝelo.
Peel, senŝeligi.
Peep, rigardeti.
Peer, nobelo.
Peer, esplori, serĉi.
Peerage, nobelaro.
Peerless, senegala, nekomparebla.
Peevish, malafabla, ĉagrena.
Peevishness, malafableco.
Peg (a hook), krocilo, lignarajlo.
Peg, ŝtopileto
Pelerine, mantele-
Prefix, prefikso.
Pregnancy, gravedeco.
Pregnant, graveda.
Prehension, preno.
Prehistoric, pratempa.
Prejudice, antaŭjuĝo.
Prejudge, antaŭjuĝi.
Prejudicial, malutila.
Prelate, episkopo, ĉef—.
Preliminary, antaŭafero, antaŭpreparo.
Prelude, antaŭludaĵo.
Premature, antaŭtempa.
Premeditate, pripensi.
Premeditation, pripensado.
Premier, ĉefa, unua.
Premises, propreco—aĵo.
Premium, at a, premie.
Premium (reward), premio.
Premonitory, antaŭsciiga.
Pre-occupation, priokupado.
Prepare, prepari, pretigi.
Preparation, preparo—ado.
Prepay, antaŭpagi, afranki.
Preponderance, superrego.
Preposition, prepozicio.
Presage, antaŭsigno.
Presbyter, pastro.
Presbytery, pastrejo.
to.
Pelf, mono.
Pelican, pelikano.
Pelisse, pelto.
Pellet, kugleto, buleto.
Pellicle, membraneto.
Pell-mell, intermiksita, e.
Pellucid, diafana.
Pelt, felo.
Pen, plumo.
Pen (to enclose), barĉirkaŭi, enfermi
Pen (sheep fold), ŝafejo.
Pen-name, pseŭdonomo.
Penal, puna.
Penal servitude, punlaboro.
Penalty, puno, monpuno.
Penance, to do, pentofari.
Penance, puno.
Penchant, inklinc—emo.
Pencil (lead), krajono.
Pencil (slate), grifelo.
Pendant, pendaĵo.
Pendulum, pendolo.
Penetrate, penetri.
Penetrable, penetrebla.
Penetration, akrasento.
Penholder, plumingo.
Peninsula, duoninsulo.
Penitence, pento.
Penitent, a, konfesanto.
Penitent, penta.
Penitentiary, pentfarejo.
Penknife, tranĉileto.
Prescribe, ordoni.
Prescription (med.), recepto.
Presence, apudesto, ĉeesto.
Present, to be, ĉeesti, apudesti.
Present, to make a, donaci.
Present, prezenti.
Present (gift), donaco.
Present (time), nuntempa, estanteco.
Present, at, nune.
Presentative, donaco, prezento.
Presentiment, antaŭsento.
Presently, tuj.
Preserve (jam, etc.), konservi.
Preserve, antaŭgardi.
Preservation, antaŭzorgo.
Preservative, antaŭgardo—ado.
Preside, prezidi.
President, prezidanto.
Press (squeeze), premi.
Press (machine), premilo.
Press (newspapers), gazetaro.
Press forward, antaŭiri.
Press-gang, varbigistaro.
Pressure, premo—ado.
Pressing (urgent), neprokrastebla, urĝa.
Presumably, supozeble.
Presume, supozi.
Presumption, tromemfideco, tromemfido.
Presumptuous, tromemfida.

Pennant, flageto.
Penny, penco.
Penniless, senmona.
Pension, pensio.
Pensioner, pensiulo.
Pensive, pensa, pensema.
Pentagon, kvinangulo.
Pentecost, pentekosto.
Penultimate, antaŭlasta.
Penurious, avara.
Penury, malriĉeco.
Peony, peonio.
People, popolo, homoj.
Peopled, homhava.
Pepper, pipro.
Pepper-box, piprujo.
Pepper-caster, piprujo.
Peradventure, eble, hazarde.
Perambulate, promeni, trairi.
Perambulator, infanveturilo.
Perceive (to see), ekvidi.
Perceive, senti.
Percentage, procento.
Perceptible, palpebla, sentebla.
Perception (by sight), vido, videco.
Perception, sento.
Perch (for birds, etc.), stango.
Perch (fish), perko.
Percolate, traguti.
Perdition, ruinego, perdego.
Peremptory, absoluta.

Pretence, pretaksto.
Pretend (to claim), pretendi.
Pretend, preteksti.
Pretend (to feign), ŝajnigi.
Pretentious, afektema.
Preternatural, supernatura, preternatura.
Prbook, preteksto.
Pretty, beleta.
Prevail, superi.
Prevalent, ĝenerala, rega.
Prevaricate, malveriĝi.
Prevent, malhelpi, eksigi.
Previous, antaŭa.
Prey, kaptaĵo.
Price, prezo, kosto.
Price—current, prezaro.
Priceless (valuable), senpreza, netaksebla.
Price lists, prezaro.
Prick, piki.
Prick, pikilo.
Prickly, pika.
Pride, malhumileco, fiereco.
Priest, pastro.
Priesthood, pastreco.
Prim, afekta, preciza.
Primary, elementa, unua.
Primeval, primitiva.
Primitive, primitiva, originala.
Primrose, primolo.
Prince, reĝido, princo.
Principal, estro, ĉefo.
Principal, preci-

Perennial, persista.
Perfect, perfektigi.
Perfect, perfekta.
Perfection, perfekteco.
Perfidious, perfida.
Perfidy, perfido, perfideco.
Perforate, trabori, trapiki.
Perform (to do), efektivigi, fari.
Perform (fulfil), plenumi.
Performer, faranto.
Perfume, parfumi.
Perfume, parfumo, odoro.
Perfumer, parfumisto.
Perfumery (manufactory), parfumfarado.
Perhaps, eble.
Perigee, perigeo.
Peril, danĝero.
Perimeter, perimetro, ĉirkaŭmetro.
Period, periodo.
Periodic—al, perioda.
Periodicity, periodeco.
Periphrase, ĉirkaŭfrazo.
Periphery, ĉirkaŭo, periferio.
Perish, perei.
Perishable, pereema.
Peristyle, peristilo.
Peritoneum, peritoneo.
Periwig, peruko.
Periwinkle (plant), vinko.
Perjury, ĵurrompo.
Permanent, kon-

pa.
Principality, princlando.
Principle, principo.
Print, presi.
Print (picture), gravuraĵo.
Printer, presisto, preslaboristo.
Printed matter, presaĵo.
Printing-press, presilo.
Prior (title), ĉefabato.
Prior, antaŭa.
Priority, antaŭeco.
Prism, prismo.
Prison, malliberejo.
Prisoner, malliberulo.
Prisoner of war, militkaptito.
Private, privata.
Privateer, marrabisto.
Privation, senigo.
Privilege, privilegio.
Privily, sekrete.
Prize, premio.
Prize, ŝati.
Probable, kredinda—ebla.
Probability, kredebleco, kredindeco, iĝebleco.
Probation, provtempo.
Probationer, novico.
Probe, sondi, esplori.
Probity, honesteco.
Problem, problemo.
Proboscis, rostro.
Proceed, procedi.
Proceedings (law), proceso—ado.

stanta, daŭra.
Permeable, penetrebla.
Permission, permeso.
Permissive, permesa.
Permit, permesi.
Permutation, interŝanĝo.
Pernicious, pereiga.
Perpendicular, perpendikulara.
Perpetrate, elfari.
Perpetual, eterna.
Perpetuate, daŭrigi.
Perplex, konfuzi, ĉagrenegi.
Perplexity, konfuzeco, ŝanceliĝo.
Perron, perono.
Perruquier, perukisto.
Persecute, persekuti.
Persecution, persekutado.
Perseverance, persisto.
Persevere, persisti.
Persist, persisti.
Persistance, persisto—ado.
Persistent, persista.
Persistency, persisteco.
Person, persono.
Personage, persono.
Personal, persona.
Personality, personeco.
Personate, reprezenti.
Personate, personiĝi, imiti.
Personification, personiĝo.
Perspective, perspektivo.

Proceeding, procedo.
Procession, procesio.
Process, procedo, rimedo.
Proclaim, proklami.
Procrastinate, prokrasti.
Procure, havigi.
Procuration, konfidatisto.
Prodigal, malŝpara.
Prodigality, malŝparemo.
Prodigious, mireginda.
Prodigy, miregindaĵo.
Produce, produkti.
Produce, produktaĵo.
Product, produktaĵo.
Production, produkto.
Productive, fruktoporta.
Proem, antaŭdramo, antaŭdiro.
Profanation, malpiegaĵo.
Profane, malpia.
Profanity, malpieco.
Profess, anonci, profesi.
Profession (occupation), profesio.
Professor, profesoro.
Proffer, proponi, prezenti.
Proficient, kompetenta.
Profile, profilo.
Profit, profito, gajno.
Profitable, profita.
Profligate, diboĉulo.

Perspicuous, sagaca.
Perspicacity, sagaceco.
Perspiration, ŝvito.
Perspire, ŝviti.
Persuade, konvinki.
Persuasive, konvinka.
Pert, malrespekta.
Pertinacious, trudpeta.
Pertinacity, obstineco, persisteco.
Perturb, konfuzi, turmenteti.
Perturbation, turmentado.
Peruke, peruko.
Perusal, legado.
Peruse, legadi, ellegi.
Pervade, penetri.
Perverse, obstina, kontraŭa.
Pervert, malkonverti, malverigi.
Perversion, malkonverto, malverigo, malveriĝo.
Pervious, penetrebla.
Pest, pesto.
Pester, enui, turmenteti.
Pestiferous, pesta.
Pestilence, pesto.
Pestilential, pesta, pestiga.
Pestle, pistilo.
Pet, dorloti.
Petal, florfolieto.
Petard, petardo.
Petition, petegi.
Petition, petskribo.
Petrify, ŝtonigi.
Petroleum, petrolo.
Petticoat, subjupo.

Profound (deep), profunda.
Profound (learned), lernega, klerega.
Profundity, profundeco.
Profuse, sufiĉega, supermezura.
Progeny, ido, idaro.
Prognostic, antaŭsigno.
Programme, programo.
Progress, progreso.
Progression, progresado.
Prohibit, malpermesi.
Prohibition, malpermeso.
Project (protrude), elstari.
Project, projekto.
Projectile, ĵetaĵo, pafaĵo.
Proletarian, proletaria, o.
Prolific, multinfana, fruktoporta.
Prolix, trolonga.
Prologue, antaŭskribaĵo, antaŭverko.
Prolong, plilongigi.
Promenade, promeni.
Promenade (act), promenado.
Promenade (place), promenejo.
Prominent, eminenta, rimarkinda.
Promiscuous, miksa, konfuza.
Promise, promesi.
Promontory, promontoro.
Promote (advance), antaŭenigi.

Pettish, malĝenila.
Petty, malgranda.
Petulance, petoleco.
Petulant, petola.
Pew, preĝbenko.
Pewter, stano.
Phantom, aperc, fantomo.
Pharmacist, farmaciisto.
Pharmacy (place), farmaciejo, apoteko.
Pharmacy (science), farmacic.
Pharos, lumturo.
Pharynx, faringo.
Phase, fazo.
Pheasant, fazano.
Pheasantry, fazanejo.
Phenomenon, fenomeno.
Phial, boteleto.
Philanthropist, filantropo.
Philanthropy, filantropeco.
Philatelic, filatela.
Philatelist, filatelisto.
Philately, filatelo.
Philologist, filologiisto.
Philology, filologio.
Philosopher, filozofo.
Philosophise, filozofii.
Philosophy, filozofio.
Phlegm, flegmo, muko.
Phlegmatic, flegma.
Phoenix, fenikso.
Phonetic, fonetika.
Phonograph, fonografo.
Phosphorus, fos-

foro.
Photograph, fotografaĵo.
Photographer, fotografisto.
Photography, fotografarto.
Phrase, frazero.
Phraseology, frazeologio.
Phthisis, ftizo.
Phthisical, ftiza.
Physic, kuracilo.
Physical, fizika.
Physician, fizikisto, kuracisto.
Physics, naturscienco, fiziko.
Physiognomy, fizionomio.
Physiology, fiziologio.
Piano, fortepiano.
Piaster, piastro.
Pick (choose), elekti.
Pick (implement), pikfosilo.
Pickaxe, pikfosilo.
Picket (military), pikedo.
Pickle (to salt), pekli.
Pickle (liquid), peklakvo.
Pickpocket, fripono.
Picnic, kampfesteno.
Picquet (cards), pikedo.
Pictorial, ilustrita.
Picture, pentraĵo.
Picturesque, pentrinda.
Pie, pasteĉo.
Piebald, multkolora.
Piece (to patch), fliki.
Piece, peco.
Piecemeal, peco post peco.
Pier (pillar), pon-

Promoter, iniciatoro.
Prompt (quick), rapida.
Prompter, memorigisto.
Promptitude, rapideco.
Promptly, rapide, tuj.
Promulgate, publikigi.
Promulgation, publikigado, scigado.
Prone (inclined to), inklina, ema.
Prone (downward), terenkuŝa.
Proneness, emo, inklino.
Prong, forkego.
Pronominal, pronoma.
Pronoun, pronomo.
Pronounce, elparoli.
Pronunciation, elparolado.
Proof (for press), presprovaĵo.
Proof, pruvo, provo.
Prop, subtenaĵo, subteno.
Propaganda, propagando.
Propagandism, propagandismo.
Propagate, propagandi.
Propel, antaŭen puŝi, irigi.
Propensity, emo, inklino.
Proper (exact), ĝusta.
Proper, konvena.
Property, propreco, posedaĵo.
Prophecy, profetaĵo.
Prophesy, profetaĵi.

Prophet, profeto.
Propinquity, proksimeco.
Propitiate, favorigi, trankviligi.
Propitious, favora.
Proportional, proporcia.
Proposal, propono.
Propose, proponi.
Proposition, propono.
Proposition (gram.), propozicio.
Proprietor, posedanto.
Propriety, konveneco.
Pro rata, proporcie.
Prorogue, prokrasti.
Prosaic, proza.
Proscribe, ekzili.
Prose, prozo, prosaĵo.
Prosecute, persekuti.
Proselyte, prozelito.
Prospect, vidaĵo.
Prospective, antaŭvida, estonta.
Prospectus, prospekto.
Prosper, prosperi.
Prosperity, prospereco.
Prosperous, prospera.
Prostrate (one's self), terenkuŝiĝi.
Prosy, teda.
Protect, protekti.
Protection, protekto.
Protector, protektanto, zorganto.
Protectorate, protektorato.
Protégé, protektato.

tkolono.
Pier (landing place), enŝipigejo.
Pierce, trabori, penetri.
Piety, pieco.
Pig, porko.
Pigeon, kolombo.
Pigeon-hole (for papers, etc.), faketaro.
Pigeon-house, kolombejo.
Pigmy, pigmeo.
Pike (fish), ezoko.
Pike (tool), pikilego.
Pike (weapon), ponardego.
Pile up, amasigi.
Pile (logs), ŝtiparo. [Error in book: stiparo]
Pile (support), paliso, subteno.
Pile (heap), amaso—aĵo.
Pile (electric), elektra pilo.
Piles, hemorojdo.
Pilfer, ŝteleti.
Pilferer, ŝtelisto.
Pilgrim, pilgrimanto.
Pilgrimage, pilgrimo—ado.
Pill, pilolo.
Pillage, rabegi—ado.
Pillar, kolono.
Pillory, punejo.
Pillow, kapkuseno.
Pillow-case, kusentego.
Pilot, piloto, gvido.
Pimple, akno.
Pin, pinglo.
Pince-nez, nazumo.
Pincers, prenilo.
Pinch, pinĉi.
Pinch (of snuff, etc.), preneto.

Protest, protesti.
Protestation, protestado.
Protestant, protestanto.
Protocol, protokolo.
Protrude, elstari.
Protuberance, ŝvelaĵo.
Proud, to be, fieriĝi.
Proud, fiera, vanta.
Prove, pruvi, konstati.
Provender, bestnutraĵo.
Proverb, proverbo.
Provide, provizi.
Provided that, se nur.
Providence, antaŭzorgo, singardemo.
Provident, zorgema, ŝparema.
Province, provinco.
Provincial, provincano.
Provision, provizaĵo, manĝaĵo.
Provisional, provizora.
Provocation, incitego—ado.
Provoke, incitegi.
Prow, antaŭa parto.
Prowess, valoreco, kuraĝegeco.
Prowl, vagi.
Proximate, proksima, apuda.
Proximity, proksimeco, apudeco.
Proxy, anstataŭulo.
Prudence, singardemo.
Prudent, sin-

Pine (languish), konsumiĝi.
Pine away (plants, etc.), sensukiĝi.
Pining, sopiranta.
Pineapple, ananaso.
Pine tree, pinarbo.
Pinion (feather), plumaĵo, flugilo.
Pinion (to bind), ligi.
Pink (flower), dianto.
Pink (color), rozkolora.
Pinnacle, pinto, supro.
Pioneer, pioniro.
Pious, pia.
Pip (disease in birds), pipso.
Pip (of fruit), graĵno.
Pipe (tube), tubo, tubeto.
Pipe (for tobacco), pipo.
Piquancy, pikeco.
Piquant, pika.
Pique, ofendi.
Piracy, marrabo—ado.
Pirate, marrabisto.
Piscina, naĝejo.
Pistil (botany), pistilo.
Pistol, pafileto.
Piston, piŝto.
Pit (well, etc.), puto, fosaĵo, kavo.
Pit (theatre), partero.
Pitch (to smear with), kalfatri.
Pitch, peĉo.
Pitch (of ships), subakviĝi.
Pitcher, kruĉo.
Pitchfork, forkego.

gardema, prudenta.
Prune, ĉirkaŭhaki.
Prune, seka pruno.
Pruning shears, branĉotondilo.
Prussian, a, Pruso.
Prussic acid, ciana acido.
Pry, serĉi, rigardeti.
Psalm, psalmo.
Psalmody, psalmokantado.
Psalter, psalmaro.
Pseudonym, pseŭdonomo.
Psychology, psikologio.
Puberty, viriĝo.
Public, publika.
Publican, drinkejmastro.
Public-house, drinkejo.
Publicity, publikigo, publikigeco.
Publish, publikigi, eldoni.
Puerile, infana.
Puff, blovi.
Puff up, plenblovi.
Pug-dog, mopseto.
Pull, tiri.
Pull out, eltiri.
Pull together, kuntiri.
Pullet, kokidino.
Pulley, rulbloko.
Pulmonary, pulma.
Pulmonic person, ftizulo.
Pulp, molaĵo.
Pulpit, tribuno, predikseĝo.
Pulsation, pulsbatado.
Pulse, pulso.
Pulverize, pulvo-

Piteous, kompatinda.
Pitfall, enfalujo.
Pith, suko.
Pitiable, kompatinda.
Pitiful, kompatinda.
Pitiless, senkompata.
Pity, kompati, bedaŭri.
Pity, it is a, estas domaĝo.
Pivot, akso.
Placable, kvietebla, kvietema.
Placard, afiŝo, kartego.
Place (to put), meti.
Place, loko.
Place, a public, placo.
Place of abode, restadejo.
Placid, kvieta.
Plagiarist, verkoŝtelisto.
Plague, pesto—ego.
Plague-stricken (person), pestulo.
Plain, malbela.
Plain, senornama.
Plainly, simple, klare.
Plainness, simpleco.
Plaint, plendo.
Plaintive, plenda.
Plait (with straw), pajloplekti.
Plait, plekti.
Plait, plektaĵo.
Plait (hair), harligo.
Plan, plano.
Plan (geometrical), plato.
Plane, raboti.
Plane (tool), rabotilo.

rigi.
Pump, pumpi.
Pump, pumpilo.
Pumice-stone, pumiko.
Pumpkin, kukurbo.
Punch (drink), punĉo.
Punch and Judy, pulĉinelo.
Punctilious, precizema.
Punctual, ĝustatempa, akurata.
Punctuality, akurateco.
Punctuate, interpunkcii.
Punctuation, interpunkcio.
Puncture, trapiki.
Pungent, pika, morda.
Punish, puni.
Punishment, puno—ado.
Puny, malgranda, malfortika.
Pupil (scholar), lernanto.
Pupil (of eye), pupilo.
Puppet, pupo, marioneto.
Puppy, hundido.
Purchase, aĉeti.
Pure (clean), pura.
Pure (morals), virta.
Purée, pistaĵo.
Purgative, laksilo, laksigilo.
Purgatory, purgatorio.
Purge, laksigi.
Purify, purigi.
Puritan, Puritano.
Purity, pureco.
Purloin, ŝteli.
Purple, purpura.
Purpose, celi, intenci.
Purpose (end,

aim), celo.
Purr, bleketi, murmureti.
Purse, monujo.
Pursue, forpeladi, postesekvi.
Purveyor, liveranto.
Pus, puso—aĵo.
Push, puŝi.
Push through, trapuŝi.
Pusillanimous, timema.
Pustule, pustulo.
Put, meti.
Put aside, apartigi.
Put on airs, afekti.
Put away, formeti, forigi.
Put down, demeti.
Put instead of, anstataŭigi.
Put in order, reguligi, ordigi.
Put right, rektigi.
Put up with, suferi, toleri.
Putrefaction, putraĵo.
Putrescence, putro—eco.
Putrify, putrigi.
Putty, mastiko.
Puzzle, enigmo.
Pyramid, piramido.
Python, serpentego, pitono.

Q
Quack (duck), anasbleki.
Quack, ĉarlatano.
Quackery, ĉarlatanismo.
Quadrangle, kvarangulaĵo.
Quadrant, kvadranto.
Quadrate, kvadrato.
Quadrate, kvadrata.

Quadratic, kvadrata.
Quadrature, kvadrato.
Quadrille, kvadrilo.
Quadruped, kvarpieda.
Quadruple, kvarobla.
Quaff, glutegi.
Quaggy, marĉa.
Quagmire, marĉejo.
Quail (bird), koturno.
Quail, tremi.
Quaint, stranga.
Quake, tremi—egi.
Qualification, eco, kvaliteco.
Qualify, kvalitigi, ecigi.
Quality, eco, kvalito.
Qualm, konscidubo.
Quandary, embaraso.
Quantity, kvanto.
Quarrel, malpaco.
Quarrel, malpaci.
Quarry, ŝtonejo.
Quarter (1/4), kvarono.
Quarter (district), kvartalo.
Quarterly, trimonata.
Quartern, kvarono, kvaronujo.
Quartet, kvarteto.
Quartz, kvarco.
Quash (repress), premegi.
Quash (annul), senigi, nuligi.
Quaver, trilo.
Quay, surbordo, bordmarŝejo.
Queen, reĝino.
Queer, stranga.

Question, demandi.
Question (doubt), dubi.
Questionable, duba.
Quibble, ĉikani.
Quick (adj.), rapida.
Quick (adv.), rapide.
Quick (living), viva.
Quicken, vivigi.
Quicken, rapidigi.
Quicksilver, hidrargo.
Quiescence, ripozo, kvieteco.
Quiet, kvieta.
Quiet, kvietigi.
Quietude, trankvileco.
Quill, plumo.
Quilt, litkovrilo.
Quintal, centfunto.
Quip, sarkasmo.
Quit, lasi.
Quit, kvita.
Quite, tute.
Quittance, kvitanco.
Quiver, sagujo.
Quoin, kojno.
Quoit, disko, luddisko.
Quorum, kvorumo.
Quota, parto, porcio.
Quotation, cito.
Quote, citi.
Quoth, diras, diris.
Quotient, dividrezultato.

R

Rabbi, Rabbin, rabeno.
Rabbit, kuniklo.
Rabble, kanajlaro.
Rabid, rabia.
Rabies, rabio.
Raccoon, prociono.
Race (species), raso.
Race, to run a, far. kurson.
Racecourse, hipodromo.
Rack, hay, fojnujo.
Racket (noise), bruego.
Racy, sprita.
Radiant, radiluma.
Radiate, radii—igi.
Radical (grammar), radiko.
Radical, Radikalo.
Radicalism, radikalismo.
Radish, horse, raifano.
Radish, rafaneto.
Radius, radio.
Raffle, ludloto.
Raft, floso.
Rafter, tegmenttrabo.
Rag, ĉifono.
Rag-picker, ĉifonisto.
Ragamuffin, bubo.
Rage, to be in a, koleregi.
Rage, kolerego.
Ragged, ĉifona.
Ragout, spicaĵo.
Rail (to scoff), moki.
Rail off, bari.
Rail (railway), relo.
Raillery, mokado.
Railroad, fervojo.
Railway, fervojo.

Repletion, pleneco, sateco.
Reply, respondi.
Report, raporti.
Report, famo, raporto.
Report (official), protokolo.
Report (of gun, etc.), eksplodsono.
Repose, ripozo.
Repose, ripozi.
Repository, tenejo.
Reprehend, riproĉi.
Reprehensible, riproĉinda.
Represent, reprezenti.
Representation, reprezentado.
Representative, reprezentanto.
Repress, haltigi, subpremi.
Repression, subpremo—ado.
Repressive, subprema.
Reprieve, pardoni.
Reprimand, riproĉi, mallaŭdi.
Reprimand, riproĉo, mallaŭdo.
Reprisals, revenĝo.
Reproach, riproĉo.
Reproachful, riproĉa.
Reprobate, malaprobi, riproĉi.
Reproduce, reprodukti.
Reproduction, kopiaĵo, reproduktaĵo.
Reproof, riproĉo.
Reprove, malaprobi, riproĉi.
Reptile, rampaĵo.
Republic, respubliko.

Railway Station, stacidomo.
Raiment, vestaĵo.
Rain, pluvo.
Rainbow, ĉielarko.
Raise, levi, plialtigi.
Raise up, altlevi.
Raisin, sekvinbero.
Rake, rasti.
Rake (implement), rastilo.
Rake (a profligate), diboĉulo, malĉastulo.
Rally (gather together), kolekti.
Rally (to banter), moki.
Ram, ŝafoviro.
Ram (a gun), ŝtopi.
Ramble, vagi.
Ramble (in speech), paroli sensence.
Rampart, remparo, murego.
Rancid, ranca.
Rancour, malameco.
Random, at, hazarde.
Range (put in order), aranĝi.
Rank (a row), vico.
Rank (dignity), rango.
Ransom, reaĉeto.
Ransom, reaĉeti.
Rant, paroli sensence.
Ranunculus, ranunkolo.
Rap, frapeti.
Rap, frapo, frapeto.
Rapacious, rabema.
Rapacity, rabemeco.
Rape, forrabo.

Republican, respublikano.
Repudiate, nei.
Repugnance, antipatio—eco.
Repugnant, antipatia.
Repulse, repuŝi, repeli.
Repulsive, malbelega.
Reputable, estimebla, ŝatinda.
Reputation, famo, ŝato, reputacio.
Request, peti.
Require, postuli, bezoni.
Requirement, postulo, bezono, neceseco.
Requisite, necesa, bezona.
Requisition, rekvizicio.
Requite, rekompenci.
Rescind, eksigi, neniigi.
Rescue, savi.
Research, esploro, esplorado.
Resemblance, simileco.
Resemble, simili.
Resent, sentegi.
Resentment, kolero.
Reserve, rezervi.
Reserved (in speech), silentema.
Reservoir, akvujo, akvujego.
Reside, loĝi, restadi.
Residence, loĝejo, restadejo.
Resident, loĝanto.
Residue, restaĵo.
Resign, eksiĝi.
Resign one's self, submetiĝi.
Resignation, rezignacio.

Rapid, rapida.
Rapidity, rapideco.
Rapidly, rapide.
Rapier, rapiro.
Rapine, rabo.
Rapt, rava, entuziasma.
Rapture, ravo, entuziasmo.
Rare (seldom), malofta.
Rare (curious), kurioza.
Rare, antikva.
Rarely, malofte.
Rareness, malofteco.
Rarity, malofteco.
Rarity (dainty), frandaĵo.
Rascal, kanajlo.
Rase, disĵeti.
Rash, hazarda.
Rashness, hazardeco.
Rasp, raspi.
Rasp (a tool), raspilo.
Raspberry, frambo.
Rat, rato.
Rate, procento.
Rate of, at the, po.
Rate (estimate), taksi.
Rather, plivole.
Ratify, aprobi.
Ratio, proporcio.
Ration, porcio.
Rational, racionala.
Rationalism, racionalismo.
Rationalist, racionalisto.
Rattle (a toy), kraketilo.
Rattlesnake, sonserpento.
Raucous, raŭka.
Ravage (lay waste), ruinigi.
Rave, deliri, paroli sensence.

Resignation (giving up), eksiĝo.
Resin, rezino, kolofono.
Resin-wood, keno.
Resinous, rezina.
Resist, kontraŭbatali, kontraŭstari.
Re-sole (boots, etc.), replandumi.
Resolute, decida.
Resolution, decideco.
Resolve, decidi.
Resonant, resona.
Resort, kunvenejo.
Resound, resoni.
Resource, rimedo.
Respect, respekti.
Respect, respekto.
Respectable, respektinda.
Respectful, respekta.
Respecting (concerning), pri.
Respirable, spirebla.
Respiration, spirado.
Respire, spiri.
Resplendent, to become, briliĝi.
Respond, respondi.
Response, respondo.
Responsible for, to be, garantii, respondi pri.
Responsible, responda.
Responsibility, respondeco.
Resuscitate, revivigi.
Rest (pause), paŭzo.
Rest (remainder), restaĵo.
Rest (quietude), kvieteco, ripoze-

Ravel, maltordi.
Raven, korvo.
Ravenous, englutema.
Ravine, intermontaĵo.
Ravishing (delightful), rava.
Raw (chilly), freŝa, frosta.
Raw (uncooked), nekuirita.
Raw (without skin), senhaŭta.
Raw material, kruda.
Ray (of light), radio.
Razor, razilo.
Re, again (prefix), re.
Reach to, atingi.
React, kontraŭbatali—agi.
Read, legi.
Reader, leganto.
Reader (for press), preskorektisto.
Readily, volonte.
Reading, legado.
Ready, preta.
Ready money, kontanto.
Real, vera, reala.
Reality, realeco.
Reality, in, vere, efektive.
Really, vere, efektive.
Realise (finan.), efektivigi.
Realise (comprehend), kompreni.
Realm, reĝolando, reglando.
Ream (paper), rismo.
Re-animate, revivigi.
Re-arrange, rearanĝi.
Re-ascend, resupreniri.
Re-assure, reku-

co.
Rest (lean on), apogi.
Rest one's self, ripozi, kuŝi.
Restaurant, restoracio.
Restitution, redonado.
Restless, restive, maltrankvila.
Restoration, redoneco, ripareco.
Restorative, fortigilo, refortigilo.
Restore (give back), redoni.
Restore, refari, ripari.
Restrain, haltigi, deteni.
Restrict, malvastigi, malgrandigi.
Result, rezulti.
Result, sekvo, rezultato.
Resume (continue), daŭrigi.
Résumé (précis), resumo.
Resurrection, revivigo—iĝo.
Retail, to sell by, detale vendi.
Retail, by, pomalgrande, detale.
Retail (trade), detala.
Retailer, revendisto.
Retain, gardi, teni.
Retainer, vasalo.
Retaliate, revenĝi.
Retaliation, revenĝo.
Retard, prokrasti, malhelpi.
Retardation, prokrasto, malhelpo.
Retentive, persista, premorebla.
Retina, retino.
Retinue, sekvan-

ragigi.
Reap, rikolti.
Rear (bring up), elnutri.
Rear (hinder part), posta parto.
Rear-guard, postgvardio.
Reason (faculty), racio.
Reason (cause), kaŭzo.
Reason, rezoni.
Reason, for some, ial.
Reason, for any, ial.
Reasonable, rezona.
Reasoning, rezonado.
Rebate—ment, rabato.
Rebel, ribelanto.
Rebel, ribeli.
Rebellion, ribelo—ado.
Rebellious, ribela.
Rebound, resalti.
Rebuff, malprospero.
Rebuke, riproĉo.
Rebut, refuti.
Recall to mind, memorigi.
Recall (to dismiss), eksigi.
Recant, malkonfesi.
Recapitulate, resumi, ripeti.
Recede, malproksimiĝi.
Receipt, kvitanco.
Receipts, enspezoj.
Receive, ricevi.
Receiver (of taxes), kolektisto.
Receiver (recipient), adresato, ricevanto.
Recent, nova.
Recently, antaŭ ne longe.

taro.
Retire, reeniri.
Retirement, kvieteco.
Retort, respondi, reparoli.
Retort (chem. vessel), retorto.
Retouch (revise), korekti.
Retrace, reveni, repaŝi.
Retract, malkonfesi.
Retreat (place), rifuĝejo.
Retreat, foriri, remarŝi.
Retribution, repago.
Retrieve, trovi, gajni, re—.
Retrograde, malprogresi.
Retrospect, retrospekto.
Retrospective, retrospektiva.
Return (give back), redoni.
Return (come back), reveni.
Return, to make a, raporti.
Return (report), raporto.
Return, in, reciproke.
Reunion, rekuniĝo.
Re-unite, rekunigi.
Reveal, malkaŝi.
Revel, festenego.
Revenge, revenĝo.
Revenue, rento, enspezo.
Revere, respektegi.
Reverence, to make a, riverenci.
Reverence, respektegi.
Reverence (salutation), riverenco.

Reception, ricevo.
Recess (vacation), libertempo.
Recipe (medical), recepto.
Recipient (of income), rentulo.
Reciprocal, reciproka.
Reciprocity, reciprokeco.
Recital, rakonto.
Recitation, deklamo—ado.
Recite, deklami.
Reckless, senzorga.
Reckon, kalkuli.
Reckoner (book), kalkullibro.
Reckoning, kalkulo.
Reclaim (land), eltiri.
Reclaim, redemandi.
Recline, kuŝi, apogi.
Recluse, ermito.
Recognition, rekono.
Recognize, rekoni.
Recoil (of gun, etc.), repuŝo.
Recollect, memori.
Recommend, rekomendi.
Recommendation, rekomendo.
Recompense, rekompenci.
Reconcile, pacigi.
Reconciled, to be, paciĝi.
Reconciliation, pacigo.
Reconsider, rekonsideri.
Recopy, rekopii.
Record, registri, raporti.
Recount (relate), rakonti.

Reverie, revado.
Reverse, renversi.
Reverse (a loss), malprospero.
Reverse side, posta flanko.
Revert, reveni.
Review (journal), revuo.
Review (milit.), parado.
Revile, mallaŭdegi.
Revise, korekti, ekzameni.
Revival, revivigo.
Revive, revivigi.
Revocable, nuligebla.
Revocation, nuligo.
Revoke, nuligi.
Revolt, ribelo.
Revolution, revolucio.
Revolve, turniĝi, pivoti.
Revulsion, antipatio.
Reward, premio, rekompenco.
Rhapsodist, rapsodiisto.
Rhapsody, rapsodio.
Rhetoric, parolarto, retoriko.
Rhetorical, elokventa, retorika.
Rheumatic, reŭmatisma.
Rheumatism, reŭmatismo.
Rhinoceros, rinocero.
Rhomb, rombo.
Rhombus, rombo.
Rhubarb, rabarbo.
Rhyme, rimi.
Rhythm, ritmo.
Rib, ripo.
Ribald, malĉasta, diboĉa.
Ribaldry, di-

Recourse, to have, alkuri.
Recover (find), retrovi.
Recover (to get well), resaniĝi.
Recreant, timulo.
Recreate, rekrei.
Recreation, ludtempo.
Recriminate, kontraŭdiradi.
Recrimination, kontraŭdirado.
Recruit (health), resani, resanigi.
Recruit, varbi.
Recruit, varbito, rekruto.
Recruiting, varbo—ado.
Rectangle, rektangulo.
Rectify (make right), rektigi.
Rectify (purify), purigi.
Rectitude, rekteco, honesteco.
Rector, pastro, paroĥestro.
Rectory, pastrejo, pastra domo.
Recumbent, kuŝa.
Recur, reokazi.
Recurrence, reokazo.
Red, ruĝa.
Redbreast, ruĝgorĝo.
Redden, ruĝigi—iĝi.
Reddish, duberuĝa.
Redeem, reaĉeti, elaĉeti.
Redeemer, Elaĉetinto.
Redemption, elaĉeto.
Redness, ruĝeco.
Redouble, duobligi.
Redoubt (fortification), reduto.

boĉo—aĵo.
Ribbon, rubando.
Rice, rizo.
Rich, to grow, riĉiĝi.
Rich, riĉa.
Riches, riĉeco.
Rid, malembarasi, liberigi.
Riddle (sieve), kribrilo.
Riddle, enigmo, logogrifo.
Ride, rajdi.
Ridge, supro, pinto.
Ridge (agricul.), sulko.
Ridicule, moki.
Ridiculous, ridinda.
Riding-master, ĉevalestro, rajdmastro.
Riding-school, rajdejo.
Rife, ĝenerala.
Riff-raff, forĵetaĵo. [Error in book: foĵetaĵo]
Rifle, pafilo.
Rifle (plunder), rabi.
Rift, fendo.
Rig, ŝnurarmi.
Rigging, ŝnurarmilaro.
Right, dekstra.
Right (justice), rajto.
Right (straight), rekta.
Right (correct), prava.
Righteous, justa, pia.
Rightful, rajta.
Rightly, rajte, prave, juste.
Rigid, rigida, severa.
Rigid (exact), preciza.
Rigidity, rigideco.
Rigidly, severe.

Redoubtable, timinda.
Redress (amend), rebonigi, ripari.
Reduce (to powder), pisti.
Reduce (dissolve), solvi.
Reduce, malpliigi.
Redundance, sufiĉego.
Redundant, sufiĉega.
Reed, kano.
Reef (rocks), rifo.
Reel (stagger), ŝanceliĝi.
Re-enter, reeniri.
Re-establish, reigi.
Refection, manĝeto.
Refectory, manĝejo.
Refer to, turni sin.
Referring to, rilate al.
Refine, rafini.
Refined (manners), bonmaniera, ĝentila.
Refiner, rafinisto.
Refinery, rafinejo.
Reflect (light), rebrili.
Reflect (consider), pripensi.
Reflect (reproach), riproĉi.
Reflection (of light), rebrilo.
Reflection (thought), pripenso.
Reflector, rebrililo.
Reflection (censure), cenzuro, mallaŭdo.
Reflux, forfluo.
Refold, refaldi.
Reform, reformi, plibonigi.
Reformation, reformo, plibonigo.

Rigour, severeco.
Rigorous, severa, severega.
Rill, rivereto.
Rim, rando.
Rime, prujno.
Rind, ŝelo, ŝelaĵo.
Ring (intrans.), sonori.
Ring, ringo.
Ring (a circle), rondo.
Ringleader, instigulo, instiganto.
Ringlet, buklo, harleto.
Ringworm, favo.
Rinse, laveti, gargari.
Riot, tumulto, ribelo.
Riotous, tumulta, ribela.
Rip, ŝiri.
Ripe, matura.
Ripen (intrans.), maturiĝi.
Ripple, ondeto.
Rise (ascent), altaĵo.
Rise (origin), deveno.
Rise (in price), plikariĝo.
Rise (get up), leviĝi.
Risible, ridinda.
Risibility, ridindeco.
Rising (revolt), ribelo.
Risk, riski.
Rite, ceremoniaro.
Rival, konkuri.
Rival, konkuranto.
Rivalry, konkuro—eco.
River, rivero.
Rivulet, rivereto.
Roach, ploto.
Road, vojo, strato.
Road-labourer, stratlaboristo.
Roadstead, rodo.

Reformatory, reformejo, plibonigejo.
Refractory, ribela.
Refrain (song), rekantaĵo.
Refresh, refreŝigi.
Refreshment (food), refreŝigo.
Refreshment-room, bufedo, restoracio.
Refuge, to take, rifuĝi.
Refuge, a, rifuĝejo.
Refund, repagi, redoni.
Refusal, rifuzo.
Refuse, rifuzi.
Refuse (rubbish), forĵetaĵo, rubo.
Refutation, refuto.
Refute, refuti.
Regain, ricevi.
Regal, reĝa.
Regale, regali.
Regard (to look at), rigardi.
Regardful (careful), zorga.
Regarding, pri.
Regards (respects), respektoj.
Regatta, ŝipkurado.
Regency, regeco.
Regenerate, refari, renaski.
Regeneration, renasko.
Regent, reganto.
Regicide, reĝmortiginto.
Regiment, regimento.
Region, regiono.
Register (luggage, etc.), enskribi.
Register, registri.
Register (book), registrolibro.
Registrar, registristo.
Registration, reg-

Roam, vagi.
Roar (of wind), muĝi.
Roar (of animals), blekegi.
Roar (cry out), kriegi.
Roast, rosti.
Roast (meat), rostaĵo.
Rob, ŝteli, rabi.
Robber, ŝtelisto, rabisto.
Robbery, rabado.
Robe, vesti, robi.
Robe, robo.
Robing-room, vestejo, robĉambro.
Robust, fortika.
Robustness, fortikeco.
Rock, ŝtonego.
Rock (to move to and fro), luli.
Rock (reef), rifo.
Rocking, lulado.
Rocket, raketo.
Rock-oil, petrolo.
Rocky, ŝtonegplena.
Rod (switch), vergo.
Rod (for stairs, etc.), metalvergo.
Rod (fishing), hokfadeno.
Roebuck, kapreolo.
Rogue, fripono.
Roguish, fripona.
Rôle (play), rolo.
Roll (paper, etc.), kunvolvaĵo.
Roll, ruli.
Roll one's self, ruliĝi.
Roll (bread), bulko.
Roll (of drum), tamburado.
Roll (a list), registro.
Roller (caster), radeto.

istrado.
Regret, bedaŭri.
Regrettable, bedaŭrinda.
Regular, regula.
Regulate, reguligi.
Regulation, regulo.
Rehearse, ripeti.
Reign, regi.
Reimburse, repagi.
Rein, kondukilo.
Rein in, moderigi.
Reindeer, norda cervo.
Reinforce, plifortigi.
Reinstate, reenmeti—igi.
Reiterate, ripeti, ripetadi.
Reject, rifuzi.
Rejection, rifuzo.
Rejoice, ĝoji.
Rejoin (to reply), respondi.
Rejoin, rekunigi.
Rejoinder, respondo.
Rejuvenate, plijunigi.
Rekindle, rebruligi.
Relapse, refalo.
Relate, rakonti.
Related (to become), parenciĝi.
Relation (business), rilato.
Relation (mutual), interrilato.
Relation (a relative), parenco.
Relationship, parenceco.
Relatively to, rilate—al.
Relax, malpliigi.
Relax (speed), malakceli.
Relay (horses), ĉevalŝanĝo.
Release, liberigi.

Rolling (of ships), marrulado.
Roll-book, registrolibro.
Roman, a, Romano.
Roman, Roma.
Romance (a novel), romano.
Romance (music), romanco.
Romantic, sentimentala.
Romp, ludegi.
Romp, bubino, petolulo.
Rood (crucifix), krucifikso, kruco.
Roof, tegmento.
Roofing (material), tegmentaĵo.
Rook, frugilego.
Room, ĉambro.
Room (space), spaco.
Roomy, vasta.
Roost, stangiĝi.
Rooster, koko.
Root, to take, enradiki.
Root-word, radikvorto.
Root (of trees, etc.), radiko.
Root up, elradiki.
Rope, ŝnurego.
Rosary, rozario.
Rose, rozo.
Rosebush, rozarbeto.
Rose-coloured, rozkolora.
Rosette, banto.
Rosemary, rosmareno.
Rosewood, palisandro.
Rosin, kolofono.
Rostrum, tribuno.
Rosy, roza, ruĝa.
Rot, putri, putriĝi.
Rotate, turniĝi.
Rotation, turniĝado.
Rotation, in, laŭ

Relegate, apartigi.
Relent, dolĉiĝi, kvietiĝi.
Reliable, konfidinda.
Reliance, konfido.
Relic (sacred), sankta restaĵo.
Relic, memorigo.
Relict (widow), vidvino.
Relief (assistance), helpo.
Relief (raised out), reliefo.
Relieve, helpi.
Religion, religio.
Religious, religia.
Relinquish, forlasi.
Relish, ĝui, ŝati.
Relish (zest), gusto.
Reluctance, malbonvolo—onto.
Reluctant, malbonvola—onta.
Rely, konfidi.
Remain, resti.
Remainder, remains, restaĵo.
Remains (food), manĝrestaĵo.
Remake, refari.
Remand, reenmeti.
Remark, rimarki.
Remarkable, rimarkinda.
Remedy (medical), kuracilo.
Remedy, rimedo.
Remember, memori.
Remind, memorigi.
Reminder, memorigo.
Remiss, senzorga.
Remission, remeto, pardoni.
Remit, remeti, sendi.
Remnant, restaĵo.
Remodel, reformi.

vico, laŭvice.
Rottenness, putreco, putro—aĵo.
Rotunda, rotondo.
Rouble, rublo.
Rough (surface), malglata, malebena.
Rough (rugged), ŝtonplena.
Rough (manner), malafabla.
Rough, in the, krude.
Rough draft, malneto.
Roughen, malglatigi.
Roughness, malglateco.
Round, rondigi.
Round, to turn, turni, turnigi.
Round (form), ronda, rondforma.
Round (of ladder), ŝtupeto.
Round (sentry), patrolo.
Rouse, eksciti.
Rouse (waken), veki—iĝi.
Rout, malvenkego.
Route, vojo.
Routine, kutimo.
Rove, vagi.
Row (noise), bruego, tumulto.
Row (line, rank), vico.
Row (boat), remi.
Royal, reĝa.
Royalty, reĝeco.
Rub, froti—adi.
Rubbish, rubo, forĵetaĵo.
Rubric, rubriko.
Ruby, rubeno.
Ruby-color, ruĝa.
Rudder, direktilo.
Rude, malĝentila.
Rudeness, malrespekto.
Ruddiness, ruĝe-

Remonstrance, averto, kontraŭdiro.
Remonstrate, averti, kontraŭdiri.
Remorse, memriproĉo.
Remote, malproksima.
Remotely, malproksime.
Remove, transloki, formovi.
Remunerate, rekompenci.
Remunerative, gajniga, paga.
Rend, disŝiri.
Render, redoni.
Render possible, ebligi.
Render a service, fari servon.
Rendezvous, kunvenejo.
Rending, disŝiro.
Renew, renovigi.
Renewal, renovigo.
Renewable, renovigebla.
Renounce, forlasi, malpretendi.
Renovate, renovigi.
Renovation, renovigo.
Renown, famo.
Rent (payment), depago, lupreno.
Rent, disŝiro, disŝiraĵo.
Renunciation, forlaso, eksiĝo.
Repair, ripari.
Reparation, riparo.
Repartee, respondaĵo.
Repast, manĝado.
Repay, repagi.
Repeal, nuligi.
Repealable, nuligebla.

co.
Ruddy, ruĝa.
Rudiment (embryo), embrio.
Rudiment (elements), elementaĵo.
Rue (botan.), ruto.
Rue (to grieve), bedaŭregi.
Ruff, krispo.
Ruffian, malbonulo.
Ruffle (agitate), malkvietigi.
Rug, tapiŝeto.
Rugged, ŝtonplena, malebena.
Ruin (remains), restaĵo, ruinaĵo.
Ruin, ruino, ruinoj.
Ruin, ruinigi.
Ruinous, ruina.
Rule (to govern), regi.
Rule, or ruler, liniilo.
Rule (to regulate), reguligi.
Rule, regulo. [Error in book: reglo]
Ruler, regnestro.
Rum, rumo.
Rumble, bruegadi.
Ruminate (to chew the cud), remaĉadi.
Ruminate, pripensi.
Rumour, famo.
Rumple, ĉifi.
Run, kuri.
Run (flow), flui.
Run against, ektuŝegi.
Run away, forkuri.
Run to, alkuri.
Run off rails, elreliĝi.
Runaway, forkuranto.
Rung (of ladder), ŝtupeto.

Repeat, ripeti.
Repel, repeli, repuŝi.
Repent, penti.
Repentance, pento—ado.
Repetition, ripetado.
Repiece, fliki.
Repine, plendi, murmuri.
Replace, anstataŭi.
Replant, replanti.
Replenish, replenigi.
Replete, plena, sata.

S

Sabbath, dimanĉo.
Sable (animal), zibelo.
Sabot, ligna ŝuo.
Sabre, hakglavo, sabro.
Sacerdotal, pastra.
Sack, sako.
Sack (pillage), rabadi.
Sackcloth, ŝtofego.
Sacrament, sakramento.
Sacred, sankta.
Sacredness, sankteco.
Sacrifice, oferi.
Sacrilege, malpiaĵo.
Sad, malĝoja.
Sadden, malĝojigi.
Saddle, selo.
Sadness, malĝojeco.
Safe (money), monkesto.
Safe, sendanĝera.
Safety, sendanĝereco.
Saffron, safrano.
Sagacious, sagaca.

Rupture, rompo.
Rupture (med.), hernio.
Rural, kampa.
Ruse, ruzo.
Rush, ĵeti sin sur, kuregi.
Rush, junko.
Russet, flavruĝa.
Russia, Rusujo.
Russian, Ruso.
Rust, rusti, rustiĝi.
Rust, rustaĵo.
Rut, radkavo, radsigno.
Ruthless, kruelega.
Rye, sekalo.

Socket, ingo, tubeto.
Sod, bulo.
Soda, sodo.
Sofa, sofo.
Soft, mola.
Soft (mannered), dolĉa.
Soft (not loud), mallaŭta.
Soften, moligi.
Softly, mallaŭte.
Softly, kviete.
Softness, moleco.
Soil, tero.
Soil, malpurigi.
Soiled, malpura.
Soirée, vesperkunveno.
Sojourn, resti.
Sol (music), G.
Solace, komforti.
Solar, suna.
Solder, luti.
Soldier, soldato.
Sole, sola.
Sole (fish), soleo.
Sole (of the foot), plando.
Sole (of boot, etc.), ledplando.
Solecism, solicismo.
Solely, sole.
Solemn, solena.
Solemnity, soleno.
Solemnize, soleniĝi.
Solfa, notkanti.

Sagacity, sagaceco.
Sage, saĝa.
Sage (botany), salvio.
Sail (of a ship), velo.
Sail, surnaĝi.
Sailing-ship, velŝipo.
Sailor, maristo.
Sails, velaro.
Sainfoin, sanfojno.
Saint, sanktulo.
Saintly, sankta.
Sake of, for the, pro.
Salad, salato.
Salamander, salamandro.
Sal-ammoniac, salamoniako.
Salary, salajro.
Sale, vendo.
Saleable, vendebla.
Salesman, vendisto.
Saline, sala.
Saliva, kraĉaĵo.
Sally (of wit), spritaĵo.
Salmon, salmo.
Saloon, salono.
Salt, salo.
Salt-cellar, salujo.
Salt-meat, peklaĵo.
Saltpetre, salpetro.
Salubrious, saniga.
Salutation, saluto.
Salutary, sanplena.
Salute, saluti.
Salvage, savado.
Salvation, savo.
Salve, ŝmiraĵo.
Salver, pladeto.
Same, sama.
Same time, at

Solfeggio, notkanto.
Solicit, petegi.
Solicitor, advokato.
Solicitous, petega, zorga.
Solicitude, zorgeco.
Solid, fortika.
Solid, a, malfluido.
Solidarity, solidareco.
Solidity, fortikeco.
Solidify, malfluidiĝi
Soliloquy, monologo.
Solitary, sola.
Solitude, soleco.
Soluble, solvebla.
Solubility, solvebleco.
Solution, solvo.
Solvable, solvebla.
Solvable (payable), pagokapabla.
Solvability (solvency), pagokapableco.
Solvability, solvebleco.
Solve, solvi.
Solvency, pagokapableco.
Solvent, pagokapablo.
Sombre, malhela.
Sombre (manner), malgaja.
Some, kelkaj.
Some (indef.), ia.
Someone, iu.
Somebody, iu.
Somebody's, ies.
Somehow, iel.
Some (quantity), iom.
Something, io.
Sometime, iam.
Sometimes, kelkfoje
Sometimes—sometimes, jen—jen.
Some way, iel.
Somewhat, iom.
Somewhere, ie.
Son, filo.
Son-in-law, bofilo.
Sonata, sonato.
Song, kanto.

the, samtempe.
Sameness, sameco.
Sample, specimeno.
Sanctify, sanktigi.
Sanction, sankcii.
Sanctity, sankteco.
Sanctuary, sanktejo.
Sand, sablo.
Sand, a grain of, sablero.
Sandbank, sablaĵo.
Sandal, pantofleto.
Sandwich, vianda bulko.
Sane, racia.
Sanguinary, sangavida.
Sanguine, esperplena.
Sanhedrim, sinedrio.
Sanitary, higiena.
Sanity, racieco.
Sanscrit, Sanskrito.
Sap, suko.
Sap (undermine), subfosi.
Sapling, juna arbo.
Sapphire, safiro.
Sarcasm, sarkasmo.
Sarcastic, sarkasma.
Sardine, sardelo.
Sardinian, Sardo.
Sarsaparilla, smilako.
Sash, zono.
Satan, Satano.
Satanic, satana, diabla.
Satchel, saketo.
Sate, sati.
Satellite, sekvu-

Songster, kantisto.
Sonnet, soneto.
Sonorous, sonora.
Soon, baldaŭ.
Soon (early), frue.
Soot, fulgo.
Soothe, kvietigi.
Sop, trempaĵo.
Sophism, sofismo.
Soprano, soprano.
Sorb, sorpo.
Sorcerer, sorĉisto.
Sorcery, sorĉarto.
Sordid, malpurega.
Sore, ulcereto.
Sorrel, okzalo.
Sorrow, malĝojo.
Sorry, malĝoja—eta
Sort, speco.
Sort, dece kunmeti, disspecigi.
Sot, drinkulo.
Soul, animo.
Sound (try depth), sondi.
Sound (noise), sono.
Sound, soni.
Sound (trans.), sonigi.
Sound health, sana.
Soup, supo.
Sour, acida.
Sour (manner), malgaja.
Sourkrout, fermentita brasiko.
Source, fonto.
Source (origin), deveno.
Souse, trempegi.
South, Sudo.
Southern, Suda.
Southerly, suda.
Sovereign (pound), livro.
Sovereign, regnestro.
Sovereignty, regeco.
Sow, porkino.
Sow, semi.
Space, spaco.
Space (time), daŭro.
Spacious, vasta.
Spade, fosilo.
Spade (at cards),

lo, sekvanto.
Satiate, satigi.
Satiety, sato.
Satin, atlaso.
Satire, satiro.
Satisfaction, kontentigo.
Satisfactory, kontentiga.
Satisfied, to be, kontentiĝi.
Satisfied, kontenta.
Satisfy, kontentigi.
Satisfy (hunger), satigi.
Satrap, satrapo.
Saturate, saturi.
Saturday, Sabato.
Sauce, saŭco.
Saucer, subtaso, telereto.
Saucepan, kaserolo.
Saucy, insultema, petola.
Saunter, malrapidiri.
Sausage, kolbaseto.
Sausage, German, kolbaso.
Savage, sovaĝa.
Savage, a, sovaĝulo.
Savant, sciencul o.
Save (prep.), krom.
Save (rescue), savi.
Save (economise), ŝpari.
Saveloy, kolbaseto.
Saving, ŝparema.
Saviour, Savinto.
Savour, gusto.
Savoury, bongusta.
Saw, segi.
Saw, segilo.

piko.
Spain, Hispanujo.
Spangle, briletaĵo.
Spanish-fly, kantarido.
Spare (extra), ekstra
Spare, indulgi.
Sparing, to be, ŝpari
Sparing (saving), ŝparema.
Spark, fajrero.
Sparkle, brili.
Sparrow, pasero.
Sparrow-hawk, akcipitro.
Sparse, maldensa.
Spasm, spasmo.
Spatter, ŝprucigi (sur).
Spawn, fiŝsemo.
Speak, paroli.
Speak through the nose, nazparoli.
Speaker, parolanto.
Spear, lanco.
Special, speciala.
Specialise, specialigi.
Specialist, specialisto.
Speciality, specialo—eco.
Specie, monero.
Species, speco.
Specimen, modelo.
Specious, verŝajna.
Speck, makuleto.
Spectacle (a sight), vidaĵo.
Spectacles, okulvitroj.
Spectator, rigardanto.
Spectre, fantomo.
Spectrum, spektro.
Speculate, spekulacii.
Speculation, spekulacio.
Speculative, spekulativa.
Speculate (theorise), teoriigi.
Speculative (theoretic), teoria.

Saw (saying), proverbo, diro.
Sawdust, segaĵo.
Sawyer, segisto.
Say, diri.
Saying, a, proverbo, diro.
Scab, skabio.
Scabbard, glavingo.
Scaffold, eŝafodo.
Scaffold (for building), trabaĵo.
Scald, brogi.
Scale (music), skalo.
Scale (of fish), skvamo.
Scale of charges, tarifo.
Scale, surrampi.
Scales, pesilo.
Scamp, kanajlo.
Scan, elekzameni.
Scandal, skandalo.
Scandalise, skandali.
Scandinavian, Skandinavo.
Scantling, lignaĵo, trabetaĵo.
Scanty, malsufiĉega.
Scapegoat, propekulo.
Scapula, skapolo.
Scar, cikatro.
Scarabaeus, skarabo.
Scarce, malsufiĉa.
Scarcely, apenaŭ.
Scarcity, malsufiĉo.
Scare, timigi.
Scarecrow, timigilo.
Scarf, skarpo.
Scarlatina, skarlatino.

Speculum, spegulo.
Speech, parolado.
Speechless, muta.
Speed, rapido.
Speed, rapidigi.
Speedy, rapida.
Spell, silabi.
Spell, ĉarmo.
Spend, elspezi.
Spendthrift, malŝparulo.
Sphere, sfero.
Spherical, sfera.
Sphinx, sfinkso.
Spice, spico.
Spider, araneo.
Spider's web, araneaĵo.
Spike, najlego.
Spile, ligna najlo.
Spill (liquid), disverŝi.
Spill (corn, etc.), disŝuti.
Spin, ŝpini.
Spinage, spinaco.
Spinal, spina.
Spindle, akso.
Spine, spino.
Spinning-wheel, radŝpinilo.
Spinning-top, turnludilo.
Spinster, ŝpinistino (fraŭlino).
Spiral, helikforma.
Spire, preĝeja turo, sonorilejo.
Spirit (soul), spirito.
Spirit (energy), energio.
Spirit (ghost), fantomo.
Spirit, alkoholo.
Spiritual, spirita.
Spiritualism, spiritualismo.
Spiritualist, spiritualisto.
Spirituous, alkohola.
Spit, kraĉi.
Spit (spike), trapiko.
Spite, malamo.
Spite of, in, spite.
Spiteful, venĝema.

Scarlet, skarlato.
Scatter, disĵeti, dissemi.
Scene, scenejo.
Scene (painted), sceno.
Scenery, pejzaĝo.
Scent, odoro.
Scent, flari.
Sceptic, skeptikulo.
Sceptical, skeptika.
Sceptre, sceptro.
Schedule, katalogo.
Scheme, projekto.
Schism, disigo.
Schismatic, disiĝinta.
Scholar, lernanto.
Scholarship, klereco.
Scholastic, skolastika.
School, lernejo.
Schoolfellow, kunlernanto.
Schoolmaster, lernejestro, instruisto.
Science, scienco.
Scientific, scienca.
Scintillate, brileti.
Scissors, tondilo.
Scoff, moki.
Scold, riproĉegi.
Scoop, kulerego.
Scorbutic, skorbuta.
Scorch, bruleti.
Score, dudeko.
Scorn, malestimo.
Scorpion, skorpio.
Scotchman, Skoto.
Scoundrel, kanajlo.
Scour, frotlavi.

Spittle, kraĉaĵo.
Spittoon, kraĉujo.
Splash, ŝpruci.
Splash (with the hands), plaŭdi.
Spleen, lieno.
Spleen (ill-humour), ĉagreno.
Splendid, belega.
Splendour, belegeco.
Splice, kunigi.
Splinter, fendpeceto.
Split, fendi.
Spoil, difekti.
Spoil, malbonigi.
Spoil (booty), akiro.
Spoke (of wheel), radio.
Spokesman, parolanto.
Spoliation, ruinigo.
Sponge, spongo.
Sponsor, baptopatro—ino.
Spontaneous, propramova.
Spoon, kulero.
Spoonful, plenkulero.
Sport (joke), ŝerci.
Sport, sporto.
Sportsman, sportisto.
Spot (place), loko.
Spot (stain), makulo.
Spotless, senmakula.
Spouse, edzo—ino.
Spout, ŝpruci.
Sprain, elartikigi.
Sprawl, sterni.
Spray (sprinkle), surverŝi, ŝprucigi sur.
Spread (news), disvastigi.
Spread (extend), etendi.
Sprig, vergeto, branĉeto.
Sprightly, sprita, viva.
Sprightliness, viveco.
Spring, salti.

Scourge, skurĝi.
Scout, antaŭmarŝanto, antaŭrajdanto.
Scowl, sulkegiĝi.
Scramble up, suprenrampi.
Scrap, peceto.
Scrape, skrapi.
Scrapings, skrapaĵo.
Scratch, grati.
Scratch, grataĵo.
Scratch (claw), ungograti.
Scream, kriegi.
Screen, ŝirmilo.
Screw, ŝraŭbo.
Screw, ŝraŭbi.
Screw-driver, ŝraŭbturnilo.
Scribble, malbonskribi.
Scribe, skribisto.
Scripture, Sankta Skribo.
Scrofula, skrofolo.
Scroll, rulpapero.
Scrub, frotlavi.
Scruple, konsciencdubo.
Scrupulous, konscienca.
Scrutinize, esplori, serĉadi.
Scrutiny, serĉado.
Scuffle, interpuŝo.
Scull (oar), remilo.
Scullery, lavejo, potlavejo.
Sculptor, skulptisto.
Sculpture (art), skulptarto.
Sculpture (statuary), skulptaĵo.
Sculpture (to carve), skulpti.
Scum, ŝaŭmo.
Scurf, favo.
Scurrilous,

Spring (season), printempo.
Spring (of watch, etc.), risorto.
Springy, elasta.
Sprinkle, ŝprucigi sur.
Sprinkler, ŝprucigilo.
Sprite, feino, koboldo.
Sprout (bud), elkreski.
Spue, vomi.
Spume, ŝaŭmo.
Spur, sprono.
Spurious, falsa.
Spurn, elĵeti.
Spurt, elŝpruci.
Spy, spioni.
Spy, ekvidi, espori.
Spyglass, vidilo.
Squabble, malpaceti.
Squad, taĉmento, roto.
Squadron (milit.), skadro.
Squadron (naval), eskadro.
Squall, krieti.
Squall (wind), ventego.
Squander, malŝpari.
Square, kvadrato.
Square (tool), rektangulilo.
Square (adj.), kvadrata.
Square (make square), kvadratigi.
Square (math.), kvarobligi.
Squash, premegi.
Squat, dikkorpa.
Squeak, bleketi.
Squeamish, precizema.
Squeeze, premi.
Squib, raketo.
Squint, strabi.
Squint-eyed, straba.
Squirt, elŝprucigilo.
Squirt, elŝpruci.
Squirrel, sciuro.
Stab, vundi, pikegi.

maldeca, maldelikata.
Scurvy, skorbuto.
Scuttle, coal, karbujo—eto.
Scythe, falĉilo.
Sea, maro.
Seafaring, mara.
Sea-gull, mevo.
Sea-horse (walrus), rosmaro.
Seal, sigeli.
Seal, sigelo—ilo.
Seal (animal), foko.
Sealing-wax, sigelvakso.
Seam, kunkudro.
Seaman, maristo, marano.
Seamanship, marveturarto.
Seamstress, kudristino.
Sear, kaŭterizi, bruligi.
Search, serĉi.
Search-warrant, traserĉo.
Seaside, marbordo.
Seashore, marbordo.
Season (food, etc.), spici.
Season, sezono.
Seasonable, ĝustatempa.
Seasoning, spicaĵo.
Seaworthy, marirebla, martaŭga.
Seat, seĝo.
Seat, sidigi.
Seated, to be, sidi.
Sebaceous, sebeca.
Seclusion, soleco.
Second (order), dua.
Second (time), sekundo.

Stable, ĉevalejo.
Stable (firm), fortika.
Stability, fortikeco.
Stack (straw), garbaro.
Stadium, stadio.
Staff (pole), stango.
Staff, of officers, stabo.
Staff (managers), estraro.
Staff, flag, flagstango.
Stag, cervo.
Stag-beetle, cerva skarabo.
Stage, estrado.
Stage (theatre), scenejo.
Stagger, ŝanceliĝi.
Stagnant, senmova.
Stagnation, senmoveco.
Staid, deca, kvieta.
Stain, makuli.
Stain, makulo.
Stair, ŝtupo.
Staircase (stairs), ŝtuparo.
Stake, paliso, fosto.
Stake (wager), veto.
Stalactite, stalaktito.
Stalagmite, stalagmito.
Stale, malfreŝa.
Stalk (plant), trunketo.
Stall (at market, etc.), budo.
Stall (for beast), stalo.
Stallion, ĉevalviro.
Stamen (bot.), paliseto.
Stamin, stamino.
Stammer, balbuti.
Stamp (to mark), stampi.
Stamp (brand), stampaĵo.
Stamp, postage, poŝtmarko.
Stamp with foot, piedfrapadi.

Second offence, rekulpo.
Secondary school, duagrada lernejo.
Secrecy, sekreteco, kaŝeco.
Secret, sekreta.
Secretary, sekretario.
Secrete, kaŝi.
Sect, sekto.
Sectarian, sektano.
Section (group), sekcio.
Section (portion), parto.
Secular, monda.
Secure, sendanĝera.
Security, sendanĝereco.
Security (guarantee), garantiaĵo.
Sedan-chair, portilo.
Sedate, serioza.
Sedentary, hejmsida.
Sediment, feĉo.
Sedition, ribelo.
Seduce, delogi.
See, vidi.
See again, revidi.
See after, zorgi pri.
See to, zorgi pri.
See one's self, sin vidi.
Seesaw, balancilo.
Seed, semo.
Seedling, kreskaĵo.
Seek, serĉi.
Seem, ŝajni.
Seeming, ŝajna, verŝajna.
Seemly, deca.
Seer, profeto.
Seethe, boli.
Seize, ekkapti.
Seldom, malofte.
Select, elekti.

Stamper (marker), stampilo.
Stanch (firm), firma fortika.
Stanch (trusty), fidela, fervora.
Stanchion, subteno.
Stand, stari.
Stand, piedestalo.
Stand (trans.), starigi.
Standard (flag), standardo.
Standard (model), modelo.
Stanza, strofo.
Staple, komuna.
Star, stelo.
Starboard, dekstro.
Starch, amelo.
Stare, rigardegi.
Stark, rigida, tuta.
Stark (adv.), tute.
Starling, sturno.
Start (with fear), ektremi.
Start, ekiri.
Startle, ektremi.
Starve, malnutri.
State (social condition), etato.
State (condition), stato.
State, Ŝtato.
State (subject of a), Ŝtatano.
State, esprimi, diri.
Statement (report), raporto.
Statesman, politikisto.
Station (of life), situacio, stato.
Station, railway, stacidomo.
Stationary, senmova.
Stationary, senprogresa.
Stationer, papervendisto.
Stationery, paperaĵo
Statistics, statistiko.
Statue, statuo.
Stature, kresko.

Selection, elektaro.
Self, or selves, mem.
Self-conceit, tromemfido.
Self-denial, memforgeso.
Self-esteem, memestimo.
Self-evident, klarega.
Self-reproach, memriproĉo.
Self-taught, memlerninta.
Self-willed, obstina.
Selfish, egoista.
Selfishness, egoismo.
Sell, vendi.
Selvage, ŝtofrando.
Semaphore, semaforo, signalilo.
Semblance, ŝajneco.
Semibreve, plena noto.
Semicircle, duonrondo.
Semicolon, punktokomo.
Seminarist, seminariano.
Seminary, seminario.
Semolina, tritikaĵo.
Senate, senato.
Senate-house, senatejo, senatdomo.
Senator, senatano.
Send, sendi.
Send away, forsendi.
Send back, resendi.
Senile, maljuna.
Senility, maljuneco.

Statute, regulo.
Statutes, regularo.
Stave, in, krevi.
Stay (to remain), resti.
Stay (to stop), haltigi.
Stay (a support), subteno.
Steadfast, konstanta
Steady, neŝancelebla.
Steak, steko, bifsteko.
Steal, ŝteli.
Stealth, by, kaŝe, sekrete.
Stealthy, kaŝa, sekreta.
Steam, vaporo.
Steamboat, vaporŝipo.
Steam-engine, vapormaŝino.
Steed, ĉevalo.
Steel, ŝtalo.
Steelyard, pesilo, pesmaŝino.
Steep, kruta.
Steep, trempi.
Steeple, preĝejaturo.
Steer, juna bovviro.
Steer, direkti.
Steerage, antaŭparto.
Steersman, direktilisto.
Stem, trunketo.
Stem of a pipe, pipa tubo.
Stem (of ship), antaŭparto.
Stench, malbonodoro.
Stenographer, stenografisto.
Stenography, stenografio.
Step, ŝtupo.
Step, paŝi.
Step by step, paŝo post paŝo, paŝo paŝe
Step (relationship), duon.

Senior, plenaĝa, pliaĝa.
Sensation, sentado.
Sensational, sensacia.
Sense, sento.
Sense (meaning), senco.
Senseless, sensenta.
Senseless (unmeaning), sensenca.
Sensibility, sentemo.
Sensible (feelings), sentebla.
Sensible, saĝa.
Sensitive, sentema.
Sensual, voluptema.
Sensuality, volupteco.
Sentence (gram.), frazo.
Sentence (judgment), juĝo.
Sentence, juĝi, kondamni.
Sentient, sentema.
Sentiment (feeling), sento.
Sentiment, opinio.
Sentimental, sentimentala.
Sentinel, gardostaranto.
Sentry, gardostaranto.
Sentry-box, budeto.
Separate, apartigi, disigi.
Separate, aparta.
Separate, malkunigi, disigi.
Separately, malkune.
Separation, disigo.
September, Sep-

Stepfather, duonpatro.
Steppe, stepo.
Stereotype, stereotipo.
Stereotype plate, kliŝaĵo.
Stereometry, stereometrio.
Sterile, senfrukta.
Sterility, senfrukteco.
Sterling, vera.
Stern (of ship), posta parto.
Stern, severega.
Stertorous, stertora.
Stew, boleti.
Steward (of ship), ŝipintendanto.
Steward, intendanto.
Stick, bastono.
Stick, glui.
Stick bills, afiŝi.
Sticky, gluanta.
Stiff, rigida.
Stiff neck, koldoloro
Stifle, sufoki.
Stigma (bot.), rostreto.
Stigma, velkeco, malhonoreco.
Stigmata, vundpostsignoj.
Stigmatise, kalumnii, malhonori.
Still (distilling), distililo.
Still (calm), trankvila.
Still (adv.), tamen.
Still, senmova.
Stilts, iriloj.
Stimulant, stimulilo.
Stimulate, stimuli.
Sting, piki.
Sting, pikilo.
Stingy, avara, troŝpara.
Stink, malbonodori.
Stint, limigi.
Stipend, salajro.
Stipulate, kondiĉigi.
Stir, movi.
Stir up, eksciti, inci-

tembro.
Sepulchre, tombego.
Sequel, sekvo, sekveco.
Seraph, serafo.
Sere, velkinta.
Serenade, serenado.
Serene, trankvila.
Serenity, trankvileco.
Serf, servutulo.
Sergeant, serĝento.
Series, serio.
Serious, serioza.
Seriousness, seriozeco.
Sermon, prediko.
Serpent, serpento.
Serum, serumo.
Servant, servisto—ino.
Serve, servi.
Serve for, taŭgi.
Service, servo.
Service, table, manĝilaro.
Service, Divine, Diservo.
Serviceable, servema.
Serviette, buŝtuko.
Servile, sklava.
Servility, sklavemo.
Servitude, sklaveco.
Session, kunsido.
Set apart, apartigi.
Set free, liberigi.
Set out, foriri.
Set (a bone, etc.), enartikigi.
Set fire to, ekbruligi.
Set in order, ordigi.
Set (of the sun), subiri.
Set on edge,

ti.
Stir (the fire), inciti.
Stirrup, piedingo.
Stitch, stebi.
Stock, provizo.
Stock (of a wheel), aksingo.
Stockholder, rentulo
Stocking, ŝtrumpo.
Stoical, stoika.
Stoker, hejtisto.
Stomach, stomako.
Stomachic, stomaka
Stone, ŝtono.
Stone (of fruit), grajno.
Stone to death, ŝtonmortigi.
Stool, skabelo.
Stoop, kurbiĝi.
Stop (trans.), haltigi.
Stop (at a place), resti.
Stop (halt), halti.
Stop, full, punkto.
Stop (pause), paŭzo.
Stoppage, obstrukco.
Stopper, ŝtopilo.
Store (supply), provizo.
Store, magazeno.
Storehouse, tenejo.
Stork, cikonio.
Storm, ventego.
Storm, ataki.
Story (tale), fabelo.
Story (untruth), mensogeto.
Story (floor), etaĝo.
Stout, dika.
Stout (beer), nigra biero.
Stoutness, dikeco.
Stove, forno.
Strabism, strabeco.
Straight, rekta.
Straightforwardness sincereco.
Straightway, tuje.
Strain, streĉi.
Strain (filter), kribri
Strain after, celi.
Strainer, kribrilo.
Strait (geog.),

agaci.
Settle, loĝiĝi.
Settle an account, elpagi.
Settle, decidi.
Seven, sep.
Seventh (music), septimo.
Seventeen, deksep.
Seventy, sepdek.
Sever, disigi.
Several, diversa.
Several, multaj.
Severally, diverse.
Severe, severa.
Severity, severeco.
Sew, kudri.
Sewer, defluilejo.
Sewing machine, stebilo.
Sex, sekso.
Sexton, servisto de preĝejo.
Sexual, seksa.
Shabby (worn out), eluzita.
Shabby, malnobla.
Shackles, malhelpoj, baroj, katenoj.
Shade (screen), lumŝirmilo.
Shade, ombraĵo.
Shade (tint), nuanco.
Shade, nuanci.
Shadow, ombro.
Shadowy, ĥmera.
Shaft (of vehicle), timono.
Shaggy, harplena.
Shake, ŝanceli.
Shake (jolt), skui.
Shake (tremble), tremi.
Shaking (jolting), skuo.

markolo.
Strait (narrow), mallarĝa.
Strait (difficulty), embarasaĵo.
Straiten, mallarĝigi.
Strand, marbordo.
Strand (of rope, etc.), fadeno.
Strange, stranga.
Stranger, fremdulo, malkonulo.
Strangeness, strangeco.
Strangle, sufoki.
Strap, rimeno.
Stratagem, ruzo.
Strategy, militarto.
Stratify, tavoli.
Stratum, tavolo.
Straw, pajlo.
Strawberry, frago.
Stray, erariĝi.
Streak, streko.
Stream, rivereto.
Street, strato.
Strength, forteco.
Strengthen, plifortigi.
Strenuous, energia.
Stress, forto, premo—eco.
Stretch, streĉi.
Stretcher, portilo.
Strew, disĵeti.
Strict, severa.
Stride, paŝegi.
Strident, sibla sono.
Strife, malpaco, disputo.
Strike, frapi.
Strike (of workmen) striki.
Strike (coins), presi, monopresi.
Strike up singing, ekkanti.
Strike out (writing), surstreki.
Striking, surpriza, tuŝanta, solena.
String, ŝnureto.
Stringent, severa.
Strip, strio.
Strip off, senigi je

Shake hands, manpremi.
Shallow, malprofunda.
Sham, ŝajniĝi.
Sham, ŝajniĝo.
Shambles, buĉejo.
Shame, honto.
Shame, hontigi.
Shameful, hontinda.
Shameless, senhonta.
Shank, tibio.
Shape, formo.
Shape, formi.
Share, dividi.
Share (finance), akcio.
Share, parto, porcio.
Share, partopreni.
Shark, ŝarko.
Sharp (music), duontono supre.
Sharp (edge), akra.
Sharp (sour), acida.
Sharpen, akrigi.
Sharper (cheat), ŝtelisto.
Shatter, frakasi.
Shave, razi.
Shavings, rabotaĵo.
Shawl, ŝalo.
She, ŝi.
Sheaf, garbo.
Shear, tondi.
Shears, tondilo.
Sheath, ingo.
Shed, budo.
Shed tears, plori.
Sheep, ŝafo.
Sheepish, embarasita.
Sheepfold, ŝafejo.
Sheet, drapo.
Shelf, breto.
Shell, ŝelo.
Shell, senŝeligi.

Stripe, strio. [Error in book: streko]
Strive, penadi.
Stroke, streko. [Error in book: strio]
Stroke (a blow), bato.
Stroke (to touch), karesi, froti.
Stroll, promeni.
Strong, forta.
Stronghold, fortikaĵo.
Strophe, strofo.
Structure, strukturo.
Struggle, barakti.
Strut, paradi.
Strut (a stay), subtenaĵo.
Strychnine, striknino.
Stubborn, obstinega
Stubbornness, obstinegeco.
Stucco, stukaĵo.
Stud, butono.
Student, studento.
Studio, studĉambro.
Studious, lernema.
Study, lerni, studi.
Stuff (material), ŝtofo.
Stuff, plenigi.
Stumble, faleti.
Stump, trunkrestaĵo.
Stun, duonesveni gi.
Stupefy, malspritigi.
Stupefaction, mirego.
Stupendous, mireginda.
Stupid, malsprita.
Stupidity, malspriteco.
Stupor, letargio.
Sturdy, harda.
Sturgeon, sturgo, huzo.
Stutter, balbuti.
Stye (pig), porkejo.
Style, stilo.
Style (fashion), fasono.
Stylish, stila.
Subaltern, subulo.

Shell, bomb, bombo, kuglego.
Shelter (to screen), ŝirmi.
Shelter (refuge), rifuĝejo.
Shelve (slope), deklivo.
Shepherd, paŝtisto.
Shield, ŝildo.
Shield, ŝildi, ŝirmi.
Shift (garment), ĉemizo.
Shift, movi, transporti.
Shilling, ŝilingo.
Shin, tibio.
Shine, brili.
Shingle, ŝindo—eto.
Shining, brila.
Ship, ŝipo.
Ship, enŝipigi.
Shipwreck, ŝippereo.
Shipwright, ŝipfaristo.
Shire, graflando.
Shirk, eviti.
Shirt, ĉemizo.
Shiver, tremeti.
Shoal, fiŝaro.
Shock, frapo.
Shocking, terura.
Shoe, ŝuo.
Shoes, boots, etc., piedvesto.
Shoot (tree), branĉeto.
Shoot (to bud), ĝermi.
Shoot (a gun), pafi.
Shoot (to kill), mortpafi.
Shop, butiko.
Shore, marbordo.
Shore up, subteni.
Short, mallonga.
Shorten, mallongigi.
Shortly, frue.

Subcutaneous, subhaŭta.
Subdivide, redividi.
Subdue, submeti, venki.
Subject (gram.), subjekto.
Subject, regato, regnano.
Subject, objekto.
Subject (lit.), temo.
Subject, submeti, subigi.
Subjection, regateco submeteco.
Subjugate, submeti.
Subjunctive (gram.), relata modo.
Sublime, altega, belega.
Submarine, submara.
Submarine vessel, submarŝipo.
Submerge, subakvi.
Submission, submetiĝo.
Submissive, humila.
Submit (yield), cedi.
Submit, submetiĝi.
Subordinate, subulo
Subordinate, suba.
Suborn, subaĉeti.
Subpœna, asigno.
Subscribe (to a newspaper, etc.), aboni.
Subscribe (sign), subskribi.
Subscribe (money), monoferi.
Subscription, monoferado.
Subscription, abono
Subsequent, sekva.
Subside, mallevi.
Subsidy, helpa mono.
Substance, substanco.
Substantial, fortika.
Substantiate, pruvi.
Substantive, substantivo.
Substitute, anstataŭi.

Shortsighted, miopa.
Shortsightedness, miopeco.
Shot, pafo.
Should, devus.
Shoulder, ŝultro.
Shoulder-blade, skapolo.
Shout, kriegi.
Shove, puŝi.
Shovel, ŝoveli.
Shovel, ŝovelilo.
Show, montri.
Show, parado.
Show in, enigi.
Show goods, elmeti.
Shower, pluveto.
Shower-bath, pluvbano.
Showy, luksa.
Shred, peco, dispeco.
Shrewd, sagaca.
Shrewdness, sagaceco.
Shriek, kriegi.
Shriek (of the wind), muĝi.
Shrill, sibla.
Shrink, malpliiĝi.
Shrivel up, sulkiĝi.
Shrimp, markankreto.
Shroud, mortkitelo.
Shroud, kaŝi, protekti.
Shrub, arbeto.
Shrug, altigi.
Shudder, tremeti.
Shuffle (cards), miksi, enmiksi—igi.
Shuffle (prevaricate), ĉikani.
Shun, eviti.
Shut, fermi.
Shutter, window, fenestra kovrilo.
Shuttle, naveto.
Shy, timeta, hontema.

Subterfuge, artifiko.
Subterranean, subtera.
Subterraneous, subtera.
Subtile, maldika.
Subtle, ruza.
Subtract, elpreni.
Subtraction, elpreno.
Suburbs, ĉirkaŭurbo
Subvention, helpa mono.
Subversive, detruanta.
Succeed (order), postveni, sekvi.
Succeed, sukcesi.
Success, sukceso.
Successful, sukcesa.
Succession, in, vice.
Successive, intersekva.
Successor, posteulo.
Succinct, mallonga.
Succour, helpi.
Succulent, bongusta
Succumb, subfali.
Such a, tia.
Suck, suĉi.
Sucking-pig, porkido.
Suckle, mamnutri.
Suction, suĉado.
Sudden, subita.
Sue, procesi.
Suet, graso.
Suffer (endure), suferi.
Suffer (tolerate), toleri.
Suffering, sufero.
Suffice, sufiĉi.
Sufficiency, sufiĉeco.
Sufficient, sufiĉa.
Suffix, sufikso.
Suffocate, sufoki.
Suffrage (vote), voĉdono.
Sugar, sukero.
Sugar basin, sukerujo.
Suggest, proponi, inspiri.

Shyness, timeteco, honteco.
Si (music), B.
Si (flat), Bes.
Sibilant, sibla, sibla sono.
Sick (ill), malsana.
Sick, vomema.
Sicken, malsaniĝi.
Sickle, rikoltilo.
Sickly, malsanema.
Side, flanko.
Sideboard, telermeblo.
Side face, profilo.
Siege, sieĝo.
Sieve, kribrilo.
Sift, kribri.
Sigh, ekĝemi.
Sigh after—or for, sopiri pri.
Sight, vido.
Sight (view), vidaĵo.
Sign, signi—igi.
Sign, signo.
Sign (a document, etc.), subskribi.
Signboard, elpendaĵo.
Sign-manual, subskribo—aĵo.
Sign (noticeboard), surskribaĵo.
Signpost, signa fosto.
Signal, signalo.
Signal, signali.
Signal (milit.), signaldiro.
Signature, subskribo.
Signet, sigelilo.
Significant, signifa.
Signification, signifo.
Signify (to mean), signifi.

Suicide, memmortigo.
Suicide, to commit, sin memmortigi.
Suit, konveni.
Suitable, konvena, taŭga.
Suite, sekvantaro.
Suitor (lover), amanto.
Suitor, plendulo.
Sulk, kolereti.
Sullen, malgaja.
Sully, malpurigi.
Sulphur, sulfuro.
Sulphuric acid, vitriolo.
Sultan, sultano.
Sultry, varmega.
Sum, sumo.
Sum, sumi.
Sum up, resumi.
Summarise, resumi.
Summary, resumo.
Summary, mallonga.
Summer, somero.
Summerhouse, laŭbo.
Summit, supro.
Summon, asigni, citi.
Summon (a meeting), kunvoki.
Summons, citato.
Sumptuous, luksa.
Sun, suno.
Sunbeam, sunradio.
Sunday, dimanĉo.
Sundry, diversa.
Sunflower, sunfloro.
Sunshade, sunombrelo.
Sunstroke, sunfrapo.
Sup, noktomanĝi.
Superb, belega.
Superficial, supraĵa.
Superficies, supraĵo.
Superfluity, superfluo.
Superfluous, superflua.
Superhuman, superhoma.
Superintend, observi, zorgi pri.
Superior, supera.

Signify (to matter), esti grava.
Signify (to make known), sciigi.
Silence, silento.
Silence, silentigi.
Silence, to keep, silentigi.
Silent, silenta.
Silent, to be, silenti.
Silent, to become, silentiĝi.
Silex, siliko.
Silhouette, profilo.
Silk, silko.
Silkworm, silkvermo.
Silken, silka.
Silky, silkeca.
Sill, sojlo.
Silliness, malsaĝeco.
Silly, naivega.
Silver, arĝento.
Silver plate, arĝenti.
Silver-fir, pinio.
Similar, simila.
Similarity, simileco.
Similitude, komparaĵo.
Simile, simileco.
Simmer, boleti.
Simper, naivegrideti.
Simple, simpla.
Simple (foolish), naivega.
Simpleton, naivegulo.
Simpleness, simpleco.
Simplicity, simpleco.
Simplify, simpligi.
Simply (adv.), simple, nur.
Simultaneous, samtempa.
Sin, peko.
Sin, peki.

Superior, a, superulo.
Superiority, supereco.
Superlative (gram.), superlativo.
Supernatural, supernatura.
Supernumerary, ekstrulo.
Superscription, surskribo.
Supersede, anstataŭi.
Superstition, superstiĉo.
Superstitious, superstiĉa.
Supervise, observi.
Supper, noktomanĝo.
Supplant, anstataŭi, uzurpi.
Supple, fleksebla.
Supplement, aldono.
Supplement, aldoni.
Supplementary, aldona.
Supplicate, petegi.
Supply, provizi.
Support, subteni.
Support (prop), subportilo.
Supporter, partiano.
Suppose, supozi, konjekti.
Suppress, subpremi.
Supremacy, superegeco.
Supreme, superega, ĉefa.
Surcharge, supertakso.
Sure, certa.
Surely, certe, nepre.
Surety, garantiaĵo.
Surety, to be, garantii.
Surf, ŝaŭmo, mar—.
Surface, supraĵo.
Surfeit, supersati.
Surge, ondego.
Surgeon, ĥirurgiisto.
Surgery, ĥirurgio.
Surly, malgaja.

Sinapis, sinapo.
Sinapism, sinapa kataplasmo.
Since (conjunction), tial ke, ĉar.
Since then, de tiu tempo.
Since (adv.), antaŭ ne longe.
Sincere, sincera.
Sincerity, sincereco.
Sinecure, senlaborofico.
Sinew, tendeno.
Sinful, pekema.
Sing, kanti.
Singing (the art), kantarto.
Single (alone), sola.
Single, unuobla.
Singe, bruleti, flameti.
Singular (gram.), ununombro.
Singular, stranga.
Sinciput, verto.
Sinister, funebra.
Sink, ŝtonlavujo.
Sink, malflosi, iĝi.
Sinner, pekulo.
Sinovia (anat), sinovio.
Sip, trinketi.
Siphon, sifono.
Sir, sinjoro.
Sire, patro.
Sire, moŝto.
Siren, sireno.
Sister, fratino.
Sister-in-law, bofratino.
Sit, sidi.
Sit on eggs, sursidi.
Site, sido, situacio.
Sitting (of assembly), kunsido.
Situation, situacio, sido.

Surmise, konjekti.
Surmount, venki.
Surname, alnomo.
Surpass, superi.
Surprise, surprizi.
Surrender, kapitulaci.
Surreptitious, kaŝa.
Survey (land), termezuri.
Survey, vidadi, elvidi.
Surveyor, termezuristo.
Survive, postvivi.
Susceptible, sentebla—ema.
Susceptibility, sentemo.
Suspect, suspekti.
Suspend, pendigi.
Suspense (uncertainty), necerteco.
Suspicion, suspekto.
Suspicious, suspektema.
Sustain, subteni.
Sustenance, nutraĵo.
Swaddle, vindi.
Swaddling clothes, vindotuko.
Swagger, fanfaroni.
Swallow (bird), hirundo.
Swallow, gluti.
Swamp, marĉejo.
Swan, cigno.
Sward, herbejo.
Swarm, —aro.
Swarm of bees, abelaro.
Swarthy, nigraviza-ĝa, dube—nigra.
Swathe, envolvi, vindi.
Sway (swing), balanci.
Swear (jud.), ĵuri. [Error in book: juri]
Swear, blasfemi.
Sweat, ŝviti. [Error in book: sviti]
Sweater (garmen), trikoto.
Swede, a, Svedo.

Situation (post), oficio.
Six, ses.
Sixteen, dek-ses.
Sixty, sesdek.
Size, grandeco.
Size (of a book), formato.
Size, glueto.
Skate, gliti.
Skates, glitiloj.
Skein, fadenaro.
Skeleton, skeleto.
Sketch, skizi.
Sketch, skizo.
Skewer, trapikileto.
Skid, malakcelo.
Skiff, boateto.
Skilful, lerta.
Skill, lerteco.
Skilled, lerta.
Skim, senŝaŭmigi.
Skimmer, ŝaŭmkulero.
Skin, haŭto.
Skin (animal), felo.
Skin, senfeligi.
Skinner, felisto.
Skip, salteti.
Skirmish, bataleto.
Skirt, jupo.
Skittles, kegloj.
Skulk, kaŝiĝi. [Error in book: kasiĝi]
Skull, kranio.
Sky, ĉielo.
Skylight, fenestreto.
Slack, malstreĉa.
Slacken (speed), malakceli.
Slacken (loose), malstreĉi.
Slag, metala ŝaŭmo.
Slake, sensoifigi.
Slander, kalumnii.
Slang, vulgaresprimo.

Sweep, balai.
Sweepings, balaaĵo.
Sweet (mannered), dolĉa.
Sweet, a, sukeraĵo.
Sweet, malacida.
Sweetbriar, rozo sovaĝa.
Sweetheart (m.), amanto, fianĉo.
Sweetmeat, sukeraĵo.
Swell, ŝveli.
Swelling, ŝvelo.
Swerve, malrektiĝi.
Swift, rapida.
Swiftness, rapideco.
Swill, glutegi, drinkegi.
Swim, naĝi.
Swimming, naĝarto.
Swimming (in head) kapturno.
Swindle, ŝteli.
Swindler, ŝtelisto.
Swine, porko.
Swing, balanci.
Swing, a, balancilo.
Swiss, a, Sviso.
Switch, vergo.
Swivel, turnkruco.
Swoon, sveni.
Sword, glavo.
Syllable, silabo.
Syllogism, silogismo.
Symbol, simbolo.
Symmetry, simetrio.
Sympathetic, simpatia.
Sympathise, simpatii.
Sympathy, simpatio.
Symphony, simfonio.
Symptom, simptomo.
Synagogue, sinagogo.
Syncope, sveno.
Syndicate, sindikato.
Synod, sinodo.
Synonym, sinonimo, egalsenco.
Synonymous, sinonima, egalsenca.
Synopsis, resumo, sinopsiso.
Syntax, sintakso.
Synthesis, sintezo.
Syphilis, sifiliso.
Syringe, enŝprucigi.
Syrup, siropo.
System, sistemo.

Slanting, oblikva.
Slap in the face, survango.
Slash, tranĉadi, tranĉegi.
Slate, ardezo.
Slater, tegmentisto.
Slates (roofing), tegmentaĵo.
Slaughter (animals), buĉadi.
Slaughter, mortigi.
Slaughter-house, buĉejo.
Slave, sklavo.
Slavery, sklaveco.
Slavish, sklava.
Slavishness, sklavemo.
Slay, mortigi.
Sled, sledge, glitveturilo.
Sleek, glata.
Sleep, dormi.
Sleet, hajlneĝo.
Sleeve, maniko.
Sleigh, glitveturilo.
Slender, maldika.
Slender (graceful), gracia.
Slice, tranĉaĵo.
Slide, glitejo.
Slide, gliti.
Slight, maldika.
Slip, faleti.
Slip, let, preterlasi.
Slipper, pantoflo.
Slippery, glata.
Slim, gracia.
Slime, ŝlimo.
Slimy, ŝlima.
Sling (stones), ŝtonĵetilo.
Slit, fendo.
Sloe, prunelo.
Slop, verŝeti.
Slope, deklivo.
Slope (cut out), eltranĉi.

Sloth, mallaboremo.
Slothful, mallaborema.
Slough, ŝlimejo.
Sloven, negliĝulo.
Slow, malrapida.
Slowness, malrapideco.
Slug, limako.
Sluggard, mallaborulo.
Slumber, dormeti.
Slut, negliĝulino.
Sly, ruza, kaŝema.
Small, malgranda.
Smallness, malgrandeco.
Small-pox, variolo.
Smart (to suffer), doloreti.
Smart, eleganta.
Smash, disrompi.
Smear, ŝmiri.
Smell (trans.), flari.
Smell (intrans.), odori.
Smell, odoro.
Smell (sense), flaro—ado.
Smelt, fandi.
Smile, rideto.
Smile, rideti.
Smite, frapi.
Smithy, forĝejo.
Smock, kitelo.
Smoke, fumi.
Smoke, fumo.
Smoke (fish, etc.), fumaĵi.
Smoker, fumamanto.
Smooth, glata.
Smooth (level), ebena.
Smother, sufoki.
Smoulder, bruleti.
Smuggle, kontra-

bandi.
Smut, nigrigi, makuli.
Snail, limako.
Snake, serpenteto.
Snap (noise), kraki.
Snap, ataketi.
Snappish, atakema.
Snare, kaptilo.
Snatch, ekpreni.
Sneak, rampi.
Sneer, ridmoki.
Sneeze, terni.
Sniff, enflari.
Snip, tondeti.
Snivel, ploreti.
Snore, ronki.
Snort, ekronki.
Snout, nazego.
Snow, neĝi.
Snow, neĝo.
Snowflake, neĝero.
Snuff, flartabako.
Snuffle, nazparoli.
Snug, komforta.
So (adv.), tiel, tiamaniere.
So, tia.
So many, much, tiom da.
Soak, trempi.
Soap, sapo.
Soap, sapumi.
Soar, alte flugi.
Sob, ploregi.
Sober, sobra.
Sober (serious), serioza.
Sobriety, sobreco.
Sobriquet, moknomo.
Sociable, societama.
Social, sociala.
Socialism, socialismo.
Socialist, socialisto.
Society, societo.

Sock, ŝtrumpeto.
T
Tabernacle, sanktejo, tendo.
Table, tablo.
Table (index), tabelo.
Table cloth, tablotuko.
Table requisites, teleraro, manĝelaro.
Tacit, neesprimita, silenta.
Taciturn, silentema.
Tack, najleto.
Tack, najleti.
Tackle (apparatus), ilaro.
Tact, delikateco.
Tactics, taktiko.
Tadpole, ranido.
Taffeta, tafto.
Tail, vosto.
Tailor, tajloro.
Taint, difekti.
Take, preni.
Take away, forpreni.
Take away (by force), rabi.
Take care! atentu!
Take care of, zorgi pri.
Take care (of a child), varti.
Take from, depreni.
Take notice of, observi.
Take off (undress), senvestigi, senvestiĝi.
Take part, partopreni.
Take place (happen), okazi.
Take refuge, rifuĝi.
Take snuff, flari tabakon.
Take supper, noktomanĝi.
Taking (attrac-

tive), ĉarmeta, beleta.
Tale, rakonto, fabelo.
Talent, talento.
Talented, lerta, klera.
Talisman, talismano.
Talk, paroli.
Talk foolishly, paroli sensence.
Tall, granda.
Tallow, sebo.
Tally, egali, kunegali.
Tal'mud, Talmudo.
Tal'on, ungego.
Tame, malsovaĝigi, kvietigi. [Error in book: kiretigi]
Tame, malsovaĝa.
Tamely, kviete.
Tamper, intrigi, enmiksiĝi pri.
Tan, tani.
Tan, tanilo.
Tan (the skin), brunigi.
Tangent, tangento.
Tangible, palpebla.
Tangle (entangle), enmiksigi.
Tank, akvujo.
Tankard, pokalo, kaliko.
Tanner, tanisto.
Tannin, tanino.
Tantamount to, egalvalora al.
Tap, bateti, frapeti.
Tap, krano.
Tape, kotonrubando.
Tape worm, solitero.
Taper, kandeleto.
Taper, maldikigi.
Tapestry, to hang with, tapeti.
Tapestry, tapeto.
Tar, gudri.
Tar, gudro.

Tocsin, tumultsonorilo.
To-day, hodiaŭ.
Toe, great, piedfingrego.
Toe, piedfingro.
Together, kune.
Toil, laboro, penado.
Toilet, tualeto.
Toilsome, labora.
Token, signo.
Tolerable, tolerebla.
Tolerably, tolereble.
Tolerance, toleration, tolereco, toleremo.
Tolerant, tolerema.
Tolerate, toleri.
Toll, takso, depago.
Toll (bell), sonoradi.
Tomato, tomato.
Tomb, tombo.
Tom cat, katviro.
Tome, volumo.
To-morrow, morgaŭ.
To-morrow, the day after, postmorgaŭ.
Tone (music), tono.
Tongs, prenilo.
Tongs, fire, fajrprenilo.
Tongue, lango.
Tonic, fortigilo.
Tonic accent, tonakcento.
Tonnage, enhavebleco.
Tonsure, tonsuro.
Too (much), tro.
Tool, ilo.
Tooth, dento.
Toothless, sendenta.
Top (summit),

supro.
Top (peak), pinto.
Top (of head), verto.
Topaz, topazo.
Topic, subjekto.
Topmost, plejsupra.
Topography, topografio.
Topple, fali.
Topsy-turvy, to turn, renversi.
Topsy-turvy, renversita—ite.
Toque, ĉapo.
Torch, torĉo.
Toreador, toreadoro.
Torment, turmenti.
Torment, turmento—ado.
Torpedo, torpedo.
Torpedo boat, torpedoboato.
Torpid, sensenta.
Torpidity, sensenteco.
Torpor, sensento.
Torrent, torento.
Torrid, varmega.
Torsion, tordo.
Torso, torso.
Tortoise, testudo.
Tortuous, torda.
Torture, turmentego.
Torture, turmentegi.
Tory, konservativulo.
Toss, skui.
Toss (throw), ĵeti.
Total, tuto, a.
Totality, tuteco.
Totter, ŝanceli.
Touch, tuŝi.
Touch (feel), palpi.
Touch lightly, tuŝeti.
Touch up (improve), korekti.
Touch, palpo.

Tardy, malfrua, malrapida.
Target, celtabulo.
Tariff, tarifo.
Tarnish, malheligo.
Tarnish, malheligi.
Tarry, malfrui.
Tarry (to stay in a place), resti.
Tart (pastry), torto.
Tart, acida.
Task, tasko.
Taskwork, tasklaboro.
Tassel, drappendaĵo.
Taste, gustumi.
Taste, gusto.
Tasty (palatable), bongusta.
Tatter, ĉifonaĵo.
Tattle, babilaĵo, babilado.
Tattoo, tatui.
Taunt, sarkasmo.
Taut, streĉa.
Tautology, ripetado, taŭtologio.
Tavern, drinkejo.
Taw, felpreparadi.
Tawdry, falsluksa.
Tawny, dubeflava.
Tax, taksi.
Tax, takso, imposto.
Tea, teo.
Tea canister, teujo.
Tea caddy, teujo.
Tea plant, tearbeto.
Teapot, tekruĉo.
Teach, instrui.
Teacher, instruisto.
Teaching, instruo—ado.
Tear, ŝiri.
Tear in pieces, dispecigi, disŝiri.
Tear (a rent), deŝiraĵo.

Touchiness, ofendsenteco.
Touching, tuŝanta.
Touching (emotion), kortuŝanta.
Touchy, ofendsentema.
Tough, malmola.
Tour, vojaĝo.
Tourism, turismo.
Tourist, turisto.
Touring club, turisma klubo. [Error in book: turing klubo]
Tow, posttreni.
Tow, stupo.
Toward, al.
Towel, viŝilo.
Tower, turo.
Towing-vessel, trenŝipo.
Town, urbo.
Township, urbeto.
Toy, ludilo.
Trace (plan), desegni.
Trace, postsigno.
Track (path), vojo, vojeto.
Tract (of land), regiono.
Tract (pamphlet), traktato.
Traction, tiro—ado.
Trade, negoci, komerci.
Trade (business, etc.), negoco, komerco.
Trade (profession, etc.), metio.
Trade, free, libera interŝanĝado.
Tradesman, butikisto, komercisto.
Tradition, tradicio.
Traduce, mallaŭdegi.
Traffic (commerce, etc.), negoco, komerco.
Tragedian,

Tear, larmo.
Tease, inciteti, tedi.
Teat, mampinto.
Technical, teknika.
Tedious, teda.
Tediousness, tedeco.
Teem, sufiĉegi.
Teeth, dentoj.
Telegram, telegramo.
Telegraph, telegrafi.
Telegraph (instrument), telegrafilo.
Telegraphic, telegrafa.
Telegraphist, telegrafisto.
Telegraphy, telegrafo.
Telephone, telefoni.
Telephonic, telefona.
Telescope, teleskopo.
Tell (to relate), rakonti.
Tell, diri.
Temerity, bravegeco.
Temper, karaktero, humoro. [Error in book: humro]
Temperance, sobreco.
Temperate, sobra.
Temperate, modera.
Temperature, temperaturo.
Tempest, ventego, uragano.
Temple (forehead), tempio.
Temple (edifice), templo.
Temporal, monda.
Temporary, kelkatempa, provizora.

tragediisto.
Tragedy, tragedio.
Tragic, tragical, tragedia.
Trail (to draw along), treni.
Train, instrui, dresi.
Train (railway), vagonaro.
Train (retinue), sekvantaro.
Train (of carriages), veturilaro.
Train (of a dress), trenaĵo.
Train (to drag), treni.
Trait, trajto.
Traitor, perfidulo.
Traitorous, perfida.
Tramcar, tramveturilo.
Tramway, tramvojo.
Trammel, malhelpi, embarasi.
Tramp, vagisto.
Trample, trabati per la piedoj.
Trance, katalepsio, svenadego.
Tranquil, trankvila.
Tranquilise, trankviligi.
Tranquility, trankvileco.
Transaction, interkonsento.
Transcribe, transskribi.
Transfer, transloki, transporti.
Transfigure, aliformigi.
Transfix, trabori, trapiki.
Transform, aliformigi—iĝo.
Transformed, to be, aliformiĝi.
Transformation, aliformigo.

Temporize, prokrasti.
Tempt, tenti.
Temptation, tento—ado.
Tempter, tentanto.
Ten, dek.
Tenacity, persisteco.
Tenant, luanto.
Tench, tinko.
Tendency, emo, inklino.
Tender (to become), kortuŝiĝi.
Tender (offer), proponi, prezenti.
Tender (affectionate), amema.
Tenderness, ameco.
Tendon, tendeno.
Tenement, loĝejo, apartamento.
Tenet, dogmo, kredo.
Tenor, tenoro.
Tension, streĉo.
Tent, tendo.
Tentative, prova.
Tepid, varmeta.
Term (time), templimo.
Term (expression), termino.
Termagant, kriegulino.
Terminate, fini.
Terminology, terminaro.
Termite, termito.
Terrace, teraso.
Terrestrial, tera.
Terrible, terrific, terura.
Terrify, timegigi.
Territory, teritorio.
Terror, teruro.
Terrorise, terurigi.
Test, provi.
Testament, testamento.
Testator, testamentanto.

Transfuse, transverŝi.
Transgress, peki, ofendi.
Transgression, ofendo, transpaŝo.
Transgressor, ofendanto, pekanto.
Transit, pasado.
Transition, transiro.
Transitory, rapida.
Translate, traduki.
Translation, traduko.
Translator, tradukisto.
Transmarine, transmara.
Transmission, transigo.
Transmit, transigi.
Transmitter, transiganto.
Transmute, aliformigi.
Transparent, travidebla, diafana.
Transparency, diafaneco.
Transpire, konigi, okazi.
Transplant, transloki.
Transport (to delight), ravi.
Transport (by vehicle), veturigi.
Transport, transporti.
Transportation, transportado.
Transpose, transloki.
Transverse, laŭlarĝa, diagonala.
Trap (snare), kaptilo, enfalujo.
Trap, kapti.
Trapdoor, plankpordo.

Testify, atesti.
Testimonial, atesto, rekomendo.
Testy, kolerema.
Tetanus, tetano.
Tether, ligilo.
Text, teksto.
Textile, teksa.
Textual, laŭteksta.
Texture, teksaĵo.
Thaler, talero.
Than, ol.
Thank, danki.
Thankfully, danke.
Thankfulness, dankeco.
Thankless, sendanka.
Thanks, dankon.
That, tio.
That (demon. adj.), tiu.
That (rel. pron.), kiu.
That (conj.), ke.
Thatch, pajla tegmento.
Thaw, degeli.
Thaw, degelado.
The, la.
The more, the more, ju pli, des pli.
Theatre, teatro.
Theatrical, teatra.
Theft, ŝtelo.
Their, theirs, ilia, sia.
Them, ilin.
Theme, temo.
Then, tiam.
Then (after that), poste.
Then (therefore), do.
Theologian, teologisto.
Theology, teologio.
Theorem, teoremo.
Theory, teorio.
Theoretic, teoria.

Trapezium, trapezo.
Trash (rubbish), forĵetaĵo.
Travail, nasklaboro, naskdoloro.
Travel (by car), veturi.
Travel, vojiri, vojaĝi.
Traveller, vojaĝanto.
Traverse, trapasi, trairi.
Travesty, maskaĵo.
Tray, pleto.
Treacherous, perfida—ema.
Treachery, perfideco.
Treacle, mielsiropo.
Tread, premi, subpremi, marŝi, paŝi.
Treadle, pedalo.
Treason, perfido.
Treasure, trezoro.
Treasurer, kasisto.
Treat (to feast), regali.
Treat (medicinally), kuraci.
Treat (to discuss), trakti.
Treatise, traktato.
Treatment (medical), kuracado.
Treaty, kontrakto, traktaĵo.
Tree, arbo.
Trefoil, trifolio.
Trellis, palisplektaĵo.
Tremble, tremi.
Trembling, tremo—ado.
Tremendous, grandega.
Tremor, tremeto, skueto.
Tremulous, trema,

Therapeutics, kuracarto.
There (adverb), tie.
There is, jen estas, estas.
There are, jen estas, estas.
Therefore, tial
Thermometer, termometro.
Thesis, tezo.
They, ili.
Thick, dika.
Thick (dense), densa.
Thicket, arbetaĵo, arbetaro.
Thickness, dikeco.
Thickset, dikkorpa.
Thickskinned, dikhaŭta.
Thief, ŝtelisto.
Thieve, ŝteli.
Thievish, ŝtelema.
Thigh, femuro
Thigh bone, femurosto.
Thimble, fingringo.
Thin (slender), maldika.
Thine, cia, via.
Thing (matter), afero.
Thing, some, io.
Thing, any, io
Think, pensi.
Thinker, pensulo.
Think over, pripensi.
Thirst, soifo.
Thirsty, to be, soifi.
This, tio ĉi.
This (demon. pron.), tiu ĉi.
Thistle, kardo.
Thong, ledrimeno.
Thorax, brustkesto.
Thorn, dorno
Thorough, plenega.

skueta.
Trench, fosaĵo.
Trenchant, akra.
Trencher, lignotelero.
Trepidation, tremeco, tremado.
Trespass, transpaŝo, ofendo.
Tress (hair), harligo.
Tress, plektaĵo.
Trestle (bench), stablo.
Trial (an attempt), provo—aĵo—ado.
Triangle, triangulo.
Tribe, gento.
Tribulation, doloro, malĝojo, suferado.
Tribunal (place), juĝejo.
Tribunal (judges), juĝistaro.
Tributary, depaganta.
Tribute, depago.
Trice, in a, momente.
Trick, friponi.
Trick, malbonfaraĵo.
Trick (at cards), preno.
Trickle, guteti.
Tri-coloured, trikolora.
Tricycle, triciklo.
Trident, tridento.
Triennial, trijara.
Trifle, bagatelo, trivialaĵo.
Trifling, triviala.
Trigger, tirilo.
Trigonometry, trigonometrio.
Trill (mus.), trili.
Trinity, the, Triunuo.
Trinket, juveloeto.
Trio, trio.
Trip, faleti.

Thoroughfare, trairejo.
Thou, ci, vi.
Though, kvankam.
Thought, penso, pensado.
Thoughtful, pripensa.
Thoughtless, senpripensa.
Thraldom, servuto.
Thrash, draŝi, bategi.
Thread, fadeno.
Threadbare, eluza, eluzita.
Threat, minaco.
Threatening, minaca.
Three, tri.
Threshold, sojlo.
Thrift, ŝpareco.
Thrifty, ŝparema.
Thrill, vibri, eksciti.
Thrive, prosperi.
Throat, gorĝo.
Throb, bati, palpiti.
Throbbing, bato—ado, ekbato.
Throe, agonio.
Throne, trono.
Throng (crowd), amaso.
Throttle, sufoki.
Through, tra.
Throw, ĵeti.
Throw across, transĵeti.
Throw out, elĵeti.
Thrush, turdo.
Thrust, puŝegi, enpuŝi.
Thumb, dika fingro.
Thump, frapegi, bategi.
Thunder, tondri.
Thunderstorm, fulmotondro.
Thunderstruck, fulmofrapa.

Trip, vojaĝo—eto.
Tripe, tripo.
Triple, triobla.
Tripod, tripiedo.
Trisyllable, trisilabo.
Trite, komuna, eluzita.
Triturate, pisti.
Triumph, triumfi.
Triumphal, triumfa.
Trivial, triviala.
Triviality, trivialaĵo.
Trombone, trombone.
Troop (people), bando, amaso.
Trooper, rajdistarano.
Trophy, venksigno.
Tropics, tropiko.
Tropical, tropika.
Trot, troti.
Trot, troto—ado.
Trouble, konfuzi, ĉagreni.
Troublesome, malfacila.
Trough, trogo.
Trousers, pantalono.
Trousseau, vestaro.
Trout, truto.
Trowel, trulo.
Truant, kuŝemulo, forkuranteto.
Truce, interpaco.
Truck, manveturilo.
Truculent, kruelega.
True, vera.
Truffle, trufo.
Truly, vere.
Trump (cards), atuto.
Trumpery, ĉifaĵo senvalora.
Trumpet, trumpetadi.
Trumpet, trum-

Thursday, ĵaŭdo. [Error in book: jaŭdo]
Thus, tiel, tiamaniere.
Thwart, malhelpi.
Thy, cia, via.
Thyme, timiano.
Tibia, tibio.
Tick, bateti, frapeti.
Ticket, bileto.
Tickle, tikli.
Ticklish, tiklosentema.
Tidal, marmova.
Tide, incoming, alfluo.
Tide, receding, forfluo.
Tidings, sciigo.
Tidiness, malnegliĝeco.
Tidy, malnegliĝa.
Tie, ligi.
Tie together (unite), kunligi.
Tie (cravat), kravato.
Tier (row), vico.
Tier (string, etc.), ligilo.
Tiger, tigro.
Tight, prema, troprema.
Tile, tegmenta briko.
Till (money-box), monujo, monokesteto.
Till, until, ĝis.
Till (cultivate), kulturi.
Tillage, kulturaĵo, terkulturo.
Tiller (of boat), direktilo.
Tilt, klini—igi, duonlevi.
Tilt (an awning), kovrilego.
Timber, ligno, lignaĵo.
Time, tempo.
Timely, ĝustatempeto.
Trumpeter, trumpetisto.
Trunk (animal or insect), rostro.
Trunk (tree), trunko.
Trunk (box), kesto, vojaĝkesto.
Trunk (of body), torso.
Truss (bandage), bandaĝo.
Truss (a pack), pakaĵo, ilaro.
Trust, konfidi.
Trustful, konfidema.
Trustworthy, fidinda.
Trusty, fidinda.
Truth, vero—eco.
Truthful, verema.
Truth, in, vere.
Try (attempt), peni.
Try (test), provi.
Tsar, Caro.
Tub, kuvo—eto.
Tube, tubo.
Tuber, tubero.
Tubercle (med.), tuberkulo.
Tuberosity, tubero.
Tubular, tubforma.
Tuck up, alfaldi.
Tuesday, mardo.
Tuft, tufo.
Tuft (hair), hartufo.
Tug, posttreni.
Tug boat, trenŝipo.
Tulip, tulipo.
Tulle, tulo.
Tumble, elrenversi.
Tumbler, glaso.
Tumbrel, ŝarĝoveturilo.
Tumour, ŝvelabsceso.
Tumult, tumulto.
pa.
Timepiece, horloĝo.
Timid, timema.
Timidity, timeco.
Timorous, timema.
Tin, stani.
Tin, stano.
Tinder, fajrfungo.
Tinfoil, hidrargaĵo.
Tinge, koloretigi.
Tingle, vibreti, soneti.
Tinkle, tinti.
Tint, koloretigi.
Tiny, malgrandeta.
Tip, pinto.
Tip (gratuity), trinkmono.
Tippet, manteleto.
Tipple, drinki.
Tippler, drinkemulo.
Tipsy, ebria.
Tirade, denuncado, mallaŭdegado.
Tire, lacigi.
Tire (bore), tedi, enui.
Tired, laca.
Tiresome, teda, enua.
Tissue, teksaĵo.
Tithe (a tenth part), dekono.
Tithing, dekoneco.
Title, titolo.
Titmouse, paruo.
Titter, rideti, ekrideti.
To, al.
Toad, bufo.
Toast (a health), toasto.
Tobacco, tabako.
Tobacco box, tabakujo, tabakskatolo.
Tobacco pouch, tabakujo.
Tobacco shop,
Tumultuous, tumulta.
Tun, barelego.
Tune, agordi.
Tuneful, belsona.
Tunic, ĵako.
Tuning-fork, tonforketo.
Tunnel, subtervojo.
Turban, turbano.
Turbid, ŝlima.
Turbot, rombfiŝo.
Turbulent, tumulta.
Tureen, supujo.
Turf, torfo.
Turk, Turko.
Turkey, Turkujo.
Turkey (bird), meleagro.
Turmoil, bruego, tumulto.
Turn, turni.
Turn (on a lathe), torni.
Turn, vico.
Turner, tornisto.
Turnip, napo.
Turnscrew, ŝraŭbturnilo.
Turnspit, turnrostilo.
Turnstile, turnkruco.
Turpentine, terebinto.
Turpitude, hontindaĵo.
Turquoise, turkiso.
Turret, tureto.
Turtle-dove, turto.
Tusk, dentego.
Tutor, guvernisto.
Twain, du.
Tweezers, preniletto.
Twelve, dekdu.
Twig, branĉeto.
Twilight, vespera krepusko.
Twin, dunaskito.
Twine, ŝnureto.
Twinkle, brileti.
tabakbutiko.
Toboggan, glitveturilo.

U
Ubiquity, ĉieesto.
Udder, mamo.
Ugliness, malbeleco.
Ugly, malbela.
Ukase, ukazo.
Ulcer, ulcero.
Ulterior, posta, nekonata.
Ultimate, lasta, ultimata.
Ultimately, laste, ultimate.
Ultimatum, ultimatumo.
Ultramarine, ultramarino.
Umbra, ombro.
Umbrage, ombraĵo.
Umbrella, ombrelo.
Umpire, juĝanto—isto.
Unaccountable, neklarigebla.
Unadorned, senornama.
Unadvisedly, malprudente.
Unadulterated, nefalsita, pura.
Twist, tordi.
Twitter, pepi.
Two, du.
Tympanum, oreltamburo.
Type (model), modelo.
Type, tipo, preslitero.
Typhoid (fever), tifa febro.
Typhus, tifo.
Typical, modela.
Typographist, preslaboristo.
Typography, tipografio.
Tyrannical, tirana—ema.
Tyranny, tiraneco.
Tyrant, tirano.
Tyro, novico.

Uniformity, simileco, unuformeco.
Unify, unuigi.
Uninhabited, senhoma.
Union, unuigo, kunigo.
Unique, sola, senegala.
Unison, in (mus.), agorde.
Unit, unuo.
Unite, unuigi, kunigi.
Universal, universala.
Universe, universo.
University, universitato.
Unjust, maljusta.
Unknown, nekonata—ita.
Unlawful, malpermesita, nelaŭleĝa.
Unless, esceptinte ke.
Unlikely, neverŝajna.
Unlimited, senlima.

Unaffected, neafekta, naiva, simpla.
Unalloyed, nemiksita.
Unalterable, neŝanĝebla.
Unanimity, ununanimeco.
Unanimous, ununuvoĉa, ununanima.
Unanimously, ununuvoĉe, ununanime.
Unassuming, neafektema, modesta.
Unavailing, malutila.
Unawares, senatente.
Unbar, malbari, malfermi.
Unbearable, netolerebla.
Unbecoming, malkonvena.
Unbelief, malkredeco.
Unbeliever, malkredulo.
Unbend (relax), distri, amuzi, cedi.
Unbending (resolute), decidega, neceda.
Unbiased, senpartia.
Unblushing (shameless), senhonta.
Unbosom (to disclose), malkaŝi.
Unbound (of books, etc.), nebindita.
Unbounded, senlima.
Unbridle, senbridigi.
Unbroken, senintermanka.
Unburden (reveal, tell), malkovri.
Unbutton, debutonumi.

Unload, senŝarĝi.
Unman, malkuraĝigi.
Unmask, senmaskigi.
Unnatural, kontraŭnatura.
Unnerve, malkuraĝigi.
Unoccupied, neokupata, senokupa.
Unpack, elpaki.
Unpardonable, nepardonebla.
Unpleasant, malplaĉa.
Unpolished (surface), malglata.
Unpretending, neafektema, simpla.
Unprincipled, malhonesta, senprincipa.
Unproductive, senfrukta.
Unpublished, neeldonita.
Unquiet, malkvieta.
Unravel, maltordi.
Unrecognisable, nerekonebla.
Unremitting, senĉesa.
Unreserved, nerezerva.
Unrestrained, nedetena, libera.
Unroll, malruli, malfaldi.
Unroof, maltegmenti.
Unruffled, trankvila, nemaltrankvila.
Unruly, malĝentila.
Unsaddle, senseligi.
Unsafe, danĝerhava.
Unsalable,

Unceremonious, senceremonia.
Uncertain, necerta.
Unchain, elĉenigi.
Unchangeable, neŝanĝebla.
Uncivil, malĝentila.
Uncivilized, necivilizita.
Uncle, onklo.
Unclean, malpura.
Uncleanness, malpureco.
Uncomfortable, to make, ĝeni.
Uncommon, nekomuna.
Uncommunicative, nekomunikema, silentema.
Unconcerned, nezorgema.
Unconditional, nekondiĉa, absoluta.
Unconnected, nekunigita.
Unconscious, nekonscia.
Uncork, malŝtopi.
Uncorrupted (phys.), neputrigita.
Uncorrupted (moral), neaĉetita.
Uncouth, malĝentila.
Uncover, malkovri.
Unction, ŝmiraĵo.
Unctous, grasa.
Uncultivated, senkultura.
Undaunted, neintimigita.
Under (prep.), sub.
Under (adv.), sube.
Underbred (rude), vulgara.
Undergo, suferi.
Underground,

subtera.
Unseal, sensigeligi.
Unsearchable, neserĉebla.
Unseemly, malkonvena.
Unsettle (disturb), malordigi, konfuzi.
Unshaken, firma, neŝanceliĝa.
Unsightly, malbelega.
Unskilful, mallerta.
Unsociableness, nesocietamo—emo.
Unspotted (stainless), senmakula.
Unstable, ŝanĝema.
Untamed, sovaĝa.
Untidy (dress), negliĝa.
Untie, malligi.
Until, ĝis.
Untimely, antaŭtempa, trofrua.
Untiring, senlaciĝa.
Untoward, kontraŭa.
Unto (prep.), al.
Untrammeled, libera.
Untrue, malvera.
Unused, neuzita.
Unusual, neordinara, malofta.
Unvarnished (plain), simpla, neafektema.
Unveil, malkovri.
Unwary, malsingardema.
Unwavering, neŝanceliĝa.
Unwell, malsana.
Unwholesome, malsana, malsaniga.
Unwieldy, multepeza, nemanrege-

bla.
Underhand, sekreta, kaŝema.
Underlie, subtavoli, subteni.
Underline, substreki.
Undermaster, submajstro.
Undermine (to dig), subfosi.
Undermost (adv.), la plej sube.
Underneath (prep.), sub.
Underneath (adv.), sube.
Underrate, malestimi.
Underscore, substreki.
Understand, kompreni.
Understanding, intelekto.
Understanding, to have an, interkonsenti pri.
Undertake, entrepreni.
Undertaking, entrepreno.
Underwrite, garantii.
Undesigned, senvola, senintenca.
Undignified, malinda.
Undisciplined, malobeema.
Undo, malfari.
Undo (the hair), malligi.
Undress (one's self), malvesti, senvestigi.
Undulate, ondolinii.
Undulating, ondolinia.
Undulation, ondolinio.
Unearthly, supernatura.
Uneasiness, mal-

bla.
Unwillingly, kontraŭvole, malbonvole.
Unwise, malsaĝa.
Unwittingly, senintenca.
Unwonted, nekutima.
Unworthy, malinda.
Unyoke, maljungi.
Up (adv.), supre.
Upbraid, mallaŭdi, riproĉi.
Uphill (fig.), malfacila.
Uphill, to go, supreniri.
Uphold, subteni.
Upholsterer, meblisto, meblofaristo.
Uplift, altlevi.
Upon (prep.), sur.
Upper (adj.), plisupra.
Uppermost (adj.), la plej supra.
Upright (erect), vertikala, rekta.
Upright (honest), honesta.
Upright (post), fosto.
Uprightly, rekte, honeste.
Uprightness, rekteco, honesteco.
Uproar, bruego, tumulto.
Uproot, elradikigi.
Upset, renversi, renversiĝi.
Upshot, rezultato.
Upside down, renversite.
Upstairs, supre.
Upstart, elsaltulo.
Up to (until), ĝis.
Up to now, ĝis nun.
Urban, urba.

trankvileco.
Uneasy, maltrankvila.
Unemployed, senokupa.
Unendurable, nesuferebla.
Unequal, neegala.
Unerring, neerara, certa.
Uneven, neebena, malglata.
Unexpected, neatendita.
Unexpectedly, neatendite.
Unexpressed, neesprimita.
Unfair (dishonest), malhonesta, malrajta.
Unfaithful, malfidela.
Unfasten, malligi.
Unfavourable, malfavora.
Unfeeling, sensenta.
Unfeigned, sincera.
Unfilial, nefila.
Unfold (open), malfaldi, malvolvi.
Unfold (disclose), malkovri, malkaŝi.
Unfold (relate, tell), rakontadi.
Unforeseen, neantaŭvidita.
Unfortunate, malfeliĉa.
Unfrequently, malofte.
Unfruitful, senfrukta.
Unfurl, malfaldi, malvolvi.
Unfurnish, senmebligi.
Ungainly, mallerta.
Ungodly, malpia.
Ungrateful, nedanka, nedankema.

Urbane, ĝentila.
Urchin, bubo.
Urge, urĝi.
Urgent, urĝa.
Urine, urino.
Urinal, urinejo.
Urn, urno.
Us, nin.
Usage, uzo—ado.
Use, uzi.
Use (employment), uzo.
Use (custom), kutimo.
Use, to be of, utili.
Use up (wear out), eluzi.
Useful, utila.
Useless, senutila.
Uselessness, senutileco.
Usher (school), submajstro.
Usher (beadle), pedelo.
Usual, ordinara, kutima.
Usually, kutime.
Usufruct, ĝuado.
Usurer, procentegisto.
Usurp, uzurpi.
Usurpation, uzurpo—ado.
Usurper, uzurpulo.
Usury, procentego.
Utensil, uzaĵo, ilo, ujo.
Utilise, utiligi.
Utility, utilo—eco.
Utmost, ekstrema.
Utopia, utopio.
Utopian, utopia.
Utter, ekparoli.
Utterance, ekparolo.
Utterly, tute.
Uttermost, ekstrema, la plej.

ma.
Unguent, ŝmiraĵo.
Unhandy, mallerta.
Unhappy, malfeliĉa.
Unhappiness, malfeliĉeco.
Unhealthy, malsana.
Unheeded, nezorgita.
Unhook, malkroĉi.
Unhurt, sendifekta.
Unicorn, unukornulo.
Unification, unuigo.
Uniform (dress), uniformo.
Uniform, unuforma.

V
Vacancy, malplenaĵo.
Vacant, neokupata.
Vacate, forlasi.
Vacation, libertempo.
Vaccinate, inokuli.
Vacillate, ŝanceliĝi.
Vacillating, ŝanceliĝa.
Vacuous, malplena.
Vacuum, malplenaĵo.
Vagabond, sentaŭgulo, vagisto.
Vagary, kaprico.
Vagrant, vagisto.
Vague, malpreciza.
Vain (fruitless), vana.
Vain (conceited), vanta.
Vain, in, vane.
Vainly, vane.
Vale, valeto.
Valet, lakeo,

servisto.
Valiant, brava.
Valid, leĝa.
Valise, valizo.
Valley, valo.
Valorous, brava.
Valour, braveco.
Valse, valso.
Value (appraise), taksi.
Value (esteem), ŝati.
Value, valoro.
Valuable, multekosta.
Valuation, takso, taksado.
Valueless, senvalora.
Valve, klapo.
Van, veturilego.
Van (of army), antaŭgvardio.
Vane, ventoflago.
Vanguard, antaŭgvardio.
Vanilla, vanilo.
Vanish, neniiĝi.
Vanity, vaneco.
Vanquish, venki.
Vanquisher, venkanto.
Vapid, sengusta.
Vaporisation, vaporigo.
Vaporise, vaporigi.
Vapour, vaporo.
Vapour-bath (place), ŝvitbanejo.
Vapourous, vapora.
Variable, ŝanĝebla.
Variance, to set at, malpacigi.
Variation, diverseco, ŝanĝo.
Varicose vein, vejnego.
Variegate, multkolorigi.
Variegated, multkolora.

Vestibule, vestiblo.
Vestige, postsigno.
Vestment, vestaĵo.
Vestry, preĝejoĉambro.
Veteran, malnovulo.
Veterinary surgeon, bestokuracisto.
Veto, vetoo, malpermeso.
Vex, ĉagreni.
Vexation, ĉagreno.
Viaduct, vojponto.
Vial, boteleto.
Viands, viando, manĝaĵo.
Vibrant, multesona.
Vibrate, vibri.
Viburnum, viburno.
Vicar, paroĥestro.
Vicarage, paroĥestrejo.
Vice, malvirto.
Vice (screw press), prenilego.

Viceroy, vicreĝo.
Vice versa, kontraŭe, male. [Error in book: *versâ*, kontraue]
Vicinity, proksimeco, najbareco.
Vicious, malvirta.
Vicissitude, sortovico.
Victim, suferanto.
Victimise, suferigi.
Victor, venkanto.
Victorious, venkinta.
Victory, venko.
Victuals, manĝaĵo, provizaĵo.
Vie, konkuri.
View, vidi.
Vigil (watch), viglo, gardo.
Vigilant, vigla.
Vignette, vinjeto.
Vigorous, fortega.
Vigour, fortegeco.
Vile, malnobla.
Vileness, hontindaĵo.
Villa, domo, kampodometo.
Village, vilaĝo.
Villager, vilaĝano.
Villain, kanajlo.
Villainous, malbonega.
Vindicate, pravigi.
Vindication, pravigeco.
Vindictive, venĝema.
Vine, vinberujo—arbo.
Vine-culture, vinberkulturo.
Vinegar, vinagro.
Vinery, vinberejo.
Vine-branch, vinberbranĉo.
Vine-stock, vinbertrunko.

Variety, diverseco.
Variola, variolo.
Various, diversa.
Varnish, laki.
Varnish, lakoaĵo.
Vary, diversi.
Vase, vazo.
Vaseline, vazelino.
Vassal, vasalo.
Vassalage, vasaleco.
Vast, vasta.
Vat, kuvego.
Vault (leap), salti.
Vault, arkaĵo.
Vaunt, fanfaroni.
Veal, bovidviando, bovidaĵo.
Veer, turni, iĝi.
Vegetable, legomo.
Vegetable-garden, legoma ĝardeno.
Vegetate, vegeti.
Vegetation, kreskaĵado.
Vehemence, perforteco.
Vehement, perforta.
Vehicle, veturilo.
Veil (for face), vualo.
Veil, vuali, kovri.
Veil (conceal), kaŝi.
Vein, vejno.
Veined, vejna.
Vellum, veleno.
Velocipede, velocipedo.
Velocity, rapideco.
Velvet, veluro.
Venal, aĉetebla.
Vend, vendi.
Venerable, respektinda.
Venerable (aged), maljuna.
Venerate, respektegi.
Veneration, re-

Vineyard, vinberejo.
Vintage, vinrikolto.
Vintner, vinvendisto.
Violate, malrespekti.
Violation, malrespekto.
Violence, perforto.
Violent, perforta.
Violet, violo.
Violet color, violkoloro.
Violin, violono.
Violinist, violonisto.
Violoncello, violonĉelo.
Violoncellist, violonĉelisto.
Viper, vipero.
Virago (fig.), drakino.
Virgin, virgulino.
Virginal, virga.
Virginity, virgeco.
Virgin, The Blessed, La Sankta Virgulino, Dipatrino.
Virile, vira.
Virility, vireco.
Virtue, virto.
Virtuous, virta.
Virtuoso, virtuozo.
Virulent, venena, malboniga.
Virus, veneno.
Visage, vizaĝo.
Vis-a-vis, kontraŭulo.
Viscera, internaĵo.
Viscuous, gluanta.
Visible, videbla.
Visibly, videble.
Vision (sense), vido.
Vision (apparition), aperaĵo.
Visit, viziti.
Visiting-card, viz-

spektego.
Vengeance, venĝo.
Venial, pardonebla.
Venison, ĉasaĵo.
Venom, veneno.
Venomous, venena.
Vent, ellaso.
Vent-hole, ellastruo.
Ventilate, ventoli.
Ventilator, ventolilo.
Ventriloquist, ventroparolisto.
Venture, riski.
Venture, risko
Venturous, riska.
Veracious, verema.
Veracity, vereco.
Verandah, balkono.
Verb, verbo.
Verbal, parola.
Verbena, verbeno.
Verbatim (adv.), laŭvorte.
Verbiage, babilaĵo
Verbose, parolegema.
Verbosity, parolegeco.
Verdant, verdanta.
Verdict, juĝo.
Verdigris, verdigro.
Verdure, verdaĵo.
Verger, pedelo
Verify, verigi, ekzameni.
Verily, vere.
Veritable, vera.
Verity, vereco.
Vermicelli, vermiĉelo.
Vermifuge, kontraŭvermaĵo.
Vermilion, cinabro.
Vermin, insektoj.
Vermouth, vermu-

itkarto.
Visitor, vizitanto.
Visor, viziero.
Visual, vida.
Vital, vivema.
Vital, necesega.
Vitality, vivemo.
Vitiate, difekti.
Vitreous, vitreca.
Vitrify, vitrigi.
Vitriol, vitriolo.
Vivacity, viveco.
Vivid (color), hela.
Vivifying, viviga.
Vixen, vulpino.
Viz, nome, tio estas, t.e.
Vizier, veziro.
Vocabulary, vortareto.
Vocal, voĉa.
Vocalist, kantisto.
Vocation, profesio, inklino, emo.
Voice, voĉo.
Voice (vote), voĉdono.
Void (empty), malplena.
Void (null), nuliga.
Void (emptiness), malplenaĵo.
Volatile (fickle), flirtema.
Volatilise, vaporigi.
Vol-au-vent, pasteĉo.
Volcano, vulkano.
Volcanic, vulkana.
Volley (gun firing), pafilado.
Voluble, babilema, fluantparola.
Volume (book), volumo.
Volume (size), dikeco.
Voluminous, multdika.
Voluntary, memvola, propramova.

to
Verse, verso.
Verses, to make, versi.
Versed (learned), klera.
Versifier, versisto.
Version, traduko.
Verst, versto.
Vertebra, vertebro.
Vertebral, vertebra.
Vertex, supro, pinto
Vertical, vertikala.
Vertigo, kapturno.
Very, tre.
Vesicle, veziketo.
Vespers, Vespera Diservo.
Vessel (ship), ŝipo, boato.
Vessel, vazo, ujo.
Vest, veŝto, jaketo.

W
Wobble, ŝanceliĝi.
Wadding, vato, vataĵo.
Waddle, balanciĝi, ŝanceliĝi.
Wade, akvotrairi.
Wafer, oblato.
Waft, flugporti.
Wag, ŝerculo.
Wage (make, carry on), fari.
Wager, veto.
Wages, salajro.

Volunteer, memvolulo.
Voluptuous, voluptema.
Voluptuousness, volupteco.
Vomit, vomi.
Vomiting, vomado.
Vomitory, vomilo.
Voracious, englutema.
Voracity, englutceco.
Vortex, turnakvo, turniĝado.
Vote, voĉdoni, baloti.
Vouch, garantii, atesti.
Voucher, garantio, garantianto, atesto.
Vow, dediĉi, promesi.
Vow (religious), religia promeso.
Vowel, vokalo.
Voyage, vojaĝo, vojiro.
Vulgar, vulgara.
Vulgarise, vulgarigi.
Vulgarity, vulgareco.
Vulgate, Latina Biblio.
Vulnerable, vundebla.
Vulture, vulturo.

Whim, kaprico.
Whimper, ploreti.
Whimsical, kaprica.
Whine, ploreti, bleketi.
Whinny, ĉevalbleketo.
Whip, vipi.
Whip, vipo.
Whip, riding, vipeto.
Whir, turniĝadi.
Whirl, turniĝadi.

Waggish, ŝerca.
Waggon (cart), ŝarĝveturilo.
Waggon (of train), vagono.
Waggoner, veturigisto, veturisto.
Wail, ploregi, ĝemegi.
Wain, ŝarĝveturilo.
Waist, talio.
Waistcoat, veŝto.
Wait, atendi.
Wait on (serve), servi.
Waiter, kelnero.
Waive (abandon), forlasi.
Wake, veki.
Wake of ship, ŝippostsigno.
Waking time (reveille), vekiĝo.
Walk, marŝi, promeni.
Walk (path), aleo.
Walking stick, bastono.
Wall, muro.
Wallet, sako, tornistro.
Wallow, ruliĝi, enŝlimiĝi.
Walnut, juglando.
Walrus, rosmaro.
Waltz, valso.
Wan, pala, palega.
Wand, vergo, vergego.
Wander, erari, vagi.
Wander (be delirious), deliri.
Wanderer, nomadulo, vagisto.
Wandering, nomada, eraranta.
Wane, ekfiniĝi.
Wanness, paleco.
Want, seneco, mizerego.
Want (need, require), bezoni.
Wanton, malica.

Whirlpool, turnakvo.
Whirlwind, turnovento.
Whisk, fojnbalao.
Whiskers, vangharoj.
Whisper, paroleti, murmuri.
Whisper, murmuro.
Whistle (of wind), sibli.
Whistle, fajfilo.
Whistle, fajfi.
Whist, visto.
Whit, porcieto.
White, blanka.
White of egg, albumeno.
Whiten, blankigi.
Whiting, merlango.
Whitish, dubeblanka.
Whither, kien.
Whitsuntide, Pentekosto.
Whizz, sibli.
Who, kiu.
Whoever, kiu ajn.
Whole, tuta.
Whole, tuto.
Wholesale, pogrande.
Wholesome, saniga.
Whom, kiun.
Whooping cough, kokluŝo.
Whosoever, kiu ajn.
Whose, kies.
Why, kial.
Wick, meĉo—aĵo.
Wicked, malvirta, malbona.
Wickedness, malvirteco, malboneco.
Wicket, pordeto.
Wicker, salikaĵo.
Wide, larĝa.
Widen, plilarĝigi.
Widow, vidvino.

War, milito—ado.
Warble, pepi.
Warbler, pepulo, silvio.
Ward (guard), gardi, prizorgi.
Ward (turn aside), deklinigi, evitigi.
Ward (a person), zorgatulo.
Ward (care), gardeco, zorgateco.
Ward (district), kvartalo.
Ward off, deturni.
Warder, gardanto.
Wardrobe, vestotenejo.
Warehouse, provizejo, tenejo.
Wares (merchandise), komercaĵo.
Warfare, bataladó.
Warlike, militama.
Warm, varmigi.
Warm, varma.
Warm (zealous), fervora.
Warm bath, varmbano.
Warm up, revarmigi.
Warmth, varmeco.
Warn, averti.
Warning, averto.
Warp (twist), tordi.
Warrant (money), mandato, monmandato.
Warrant (justify), pravigi.
Warrant (assure), certigi.
Warrantable, pravigebla.
Warren, kuniklejo.
Warrior, militisto.
Wart, veruko.
Wary, atenta, singardema.
Wash, lavi.
Wash one's self,

Widower, vidvo.
Widowhood, vidveco.
Width, larĝeco.
Width, in, laŭlarĝe.
Wield, manpreni, manregi.
Wife, edzino.
Wig, peruko.
Wild, sovaĝa.
Wilderness, dezerto.
Wile, ruzo.
Wilful, obstina.
Will, to make, testamenti.
Will (bequeath), testamenti.
Will, testamento.
Will-o'-the-wisp, erarlumo.
Willing, to be, voli.
Willingly, volonte.
Willow, saliko.
Willy-nilly, volenevole.
Wily, ruza.
Win, gajni.
Wince, ektremi.
Winch, turnilo.
Wind (air), vento.
Wind (coil), vindi.
Wind (twist), tordi.
Wind (on spool), bobenumi.
Wind up (watch, etc.), streĉi.
Winding sheet, morttuko, mortkitelo.
Windlass, turnilo.
Window, fenestro.
Window blind, rulkurteno.
Windpipe, traĥeo.
Windy, venta.
Wine, vino.
Wine making, vinfarado.
Wine merchant, vinvendisto.
Wing, flugilo.

sin lavi.
Washerwoman, lavistino.
Wash-house, lavejo.
Washstand, lavtablo.
Wasp, vespo.
Wasp's nest, vespejo.
Waspish, malĝentila, ekkolerema.
Waste (squander), malŝpari.
Waste (grow thin), konsumiĝi, malgrasiĝi.
Waste (rubbish), forĵetaĵo, difektaĵo.
Waste (untilled), senkultura.
Wasteful, malŝparema.
Watch, observi, spioni.
Watch (guard), gardi.
Watch (timepiece), poŝhorloĝo.
Watch (a look out), observisto.
Watchful, atentema, zorgema, vigla.
Watchman, observisto.
Watchword, signaldiro.
Water, akvo.
Water (plants, etc.), surverŝi.
Watery, akva.
Water-closet, necesejo.
Water-colour, akvopentraĵo.
Waterfall, akvofalo.
Water-spout, trombo.
Water-tank, akvujo.
Watering-pot,

Wing (building), flankaĵo.
Wink, palpebrumi.
Winning (pleasing), ĉarma, plaĉa.
Winnow, ventoli.
Winter, travintri.
Winter, vintro.
Wintry, vintra.
Wipe, viŝi.
Wire, metalfadeno.
Wisdom, saĝo, saĝeco.
Wise, saĝa, saĝema.
Wish, want, deziri, voli.
Wish, volo, deziro.
Wistful, pensanta.
Wit, sprito.
Wit, spritulo.
Witch, sorĉistino.
Witchcraft, sorĉo—arto.
With, kun, per, je, de.
With reference to, rilate al.
With regard to, rilate al.
With respect to, rilate al.
Withdraw, eliĝi.
Withdrawal, reenpaŝo.
Wither, velki, sensukiĝi.
Withhold, fortiri.
Within, en, interne (adv.).
Without, sen.
Withstand, kontraŭstari, kontraŭbatali.
Witness, atesti.
Witness, atestanto.
Witness, eye, okulvidanto.
Witticism, spritaĵo.
Wittiness, spriteco.

verŝilo.
Waterproof, nepenetrebla.
Wave, ondo.
Wave, agiti, svingeti.
Wavelet, ondeto.
Waver, ŝanceliĝi, ŝanceli.
Wax (bees), vakso.
Wax (shoemaker's), peĉo.
Wax, sealing, sigelvakso.
Wax candle, vakskandelo.
Way (road), vojo.
Way (sea), marrodo.
Way (manner), kutimo, maniero.
Way, Milky, lakta vojo.
Way, in that, tiel, tiamaniere.
Way out (exit), eliro.
Wayfarer, vojiranto.
Waylay, inside ataki.
Wayward, memvola.
We, ni.
Weak, malforta.
Weak (to become), malfortiĝi.
Weaken, malfortigi.
Weakness, malforteco.
Weal, feliĉeco.
Wealth, riĉeco.
Wealthy, riĉega.
Wean (a child), debrustigi.
Wean (alienate), forigi, foriĝi.
Weapon, batalilo.
Wear (use as clothes), porti.
Wear away (decay by use), eluzi.
Wear away (to de-

Witty, sprita, spritema.
Wizard, sorĉisto.
Woe, ve.
Woful, ĉagrenega, malĝoja.
Wolf, lupo.
Woman, virino.
Womb, utero.
Wonder, miri.
Wonder, mirego, miro.
Wonder, a, mirindaĵo.
Wonderful, mirinda—ega.
Wonted, kutima.
Woo, amindumi.
Wood (material), ligno.
Wood, arbareto.
Woodcock, skolopo.
Woodcutter, arbohakisto.
Wood flooring (parquetry), pargeto.
Woodhouse, lignejo.
Woodpecker, pego.
Wooer, amisto, amindumisto.
Woof, teksaĵo.
Wool, lano.
Woollen stuff, lanaĵo, drapo.
Woolly, laneca.
Word (spoken), parolo.
Word (written), vorto.
Wordiness, babilaĵo.
Word for word, laŭvorte.
Work, labori.
Work (physical), laboro—ado.
Work (literary), verko.
Worker, laboristo.
Worker (literary), verkisto.

cline), konsumiĝi.
Weariness, enuo, laceco.
Wearisome, enua, enuiga.
Weary, to, enui.
Weary, laca, enua.
Weather, vetero.
Weather, to, kontraŭstari.
Weathercock, ventoflago.
Weave, teksi, plekti.
Weaver, teksisto, plektisto.
Web (tissue), teksaĵo.
Wed (cf. marry), edziĝi.
Wedding (cf. marry), edziĝo.
Wedge, kojno.
Wedlock, edzeco.
Wednesday, merkredo.
Weed, malbonherbo.
Weed, sarki.
Weeding hook, sarkilo.
Week, semajno.
Weekly (adj.), semajna, ĉiusemajna.
Weep, plori.
Weft, teksaĵo.
Weigh, pezi.
Weigh (trans.), pesi.
Weigh (ponder), pripensi.
Weight, pezo.
Weight, pezilo.
Weight (importance), graveco.
Weighty, peza.
Weigh-bridge, pesilego.
Weir, akvoŝtopilo. [Error in book: akvostopilo]
Welcome, to, bonveni, bonvoli.
Welcome, bon-

Workman, laboristo, metiisto.
Works (place), fabrikejo.
Workbox, necesujo.
Working day, simpla tago.
Workshop, metiejo, laborejo.
Workmanlike, lerta.
Workmanship, metiistarto.
World, mondo.
Worldly, monda.
Worm, vermo.
Worm-shaped, vermoforma.
Wormwood, absinto.
Worn out, eluzita.
Worry (vex), inciteti, enuigi.
Worry (importune), trudpeti.
Worry, enuo, ĉagreno.
Worse (adj.), plimalbona.
Worse (adv.), plimalbone.
Worship, adori.
Worship, adoro—ado.
Worst (adj.), plejmalbona.
Worst (adv.), plejmalbone.
Worsted, malvenkita.
Wort, mosto.
Worth, to be, valori.
Worth (value), valoro.
Worth (esteem), indo.
Worthless (morals), malnobla.
Worthless, senvalora.
Worthy (of), inda (je).

veno.
Welcome! bonvenu!
Welcome, bonvena.
Weld, kunforĝi.
Welfare, bonstato.
Well, nu.
Well (pit), puto.
Well, to be, sani.
Well (adv.), bone.
Well-mannered, bonmaniera.
Well-nigh, preskaŭ.
Well-spring, fonto, akvoputo.
Well-wishing, bonvola, bonvolanta.
Welter, enŝlimiĝi.
Wen, tubero.
Wench, knabulino.
West, okcidento.
Westerly, okcidenta.
Westward (adv.), okcidente.
Wet, malsekigi.
Wet, malseka.
Whale, baleno.
Whalebone, balenosto.
Wharf, enŝipigejo.
What, what a? kia?
What? kio, kion?
Whatever, kia ajn.
Whatsoever, kia ajn.
Wheat, tritiko.
Wheedle, karesi, delogi.
Wheedling, karesa, deloga.
Wheedler, delogisto.
Wheel (turn), turnigi.
Wheel, rado.
Wheelbarrow, puŝveturilo.
Wheelwork, radaro.
Wheelwright, rad-

Wound, vundi.
Wrack, fuko.
Wrangle, disputi, malpaci.
Wrangle, disputado, malpacado.
Wrap, faldi, kovri
Wrapper, kovrilo.
Wrath, kolerego.
Wrathful, kolerega.
Wreath, garlando.
Wreathe, plekti, girlandi.
Wreck (ship), ŝippereo.
Wreckage, derompaĵo.
Wren, regolo.
Wrench, ektiregi.
Wrest, tiregi.
Wrestle, barakti.
Wrestler, baraktisto.
Wretch, malbonulo, krimulo.
Wretched, mizera.
Wriggle, tordi, tordeti.
Wring (twist), tordi, premegi.
Wring (the hand), premi.
Wrinkle, sulkigi.
Wrinkle (facial), sulko.
Wrist, manradiko.
Write, skribi.
Writer (author), verkisto.
Writer, skribisto.
Writing, skribaĵo.
Writing-table, skribotablo.
Wrong, malpraveco.
Wrong, malprava.
Wrongfully, malrajte.
Wrongly, malrajte, malprave.
Wroth, kolerega.
Wry, torda.

faristo.
Whelp, ido, hundido, bestido.
When, kiam.
Whenever, kiam ajn.
Where, kie.
Wherefore, kial.
Wherever, kie ajn.
Wherry, barketo.
Whet, akrigi.
Whether, ĉu.
Whey, selakto.
Which (rel. pron.), kiu, kiun.
Which, kio, kion, kiu, kiun.
Whiff, subitventeto.
While, dum.

Y

Yacht, ŝipeto.
Yard, korto.
Yard (of ship), velstango.
Yarn, lanfadenaĵo.
Yawn, oscedi.
Yawn, oscedo—ado.
Ye, vi.
Yea, jes, vere.
Year, jaro.
Yearly, ĉiujara.
Yearn, deziregi.
Yearning, dezirego—ado.
Yeast, panfermentilo.
Yell, kriegi.
Yell, kriego.
Yellow, flava.
Yellowish, dubeflava.
Yelp, hundbleki.
Yet, tamen.
Yet (adv.), ankoraŭ.
Yew, taksuso.
Yield (surrender), kapitulaci, cedi.
Yield (produce), produktaĵo.
Yoke, jugo.
Yolk of egg, ovoflavo.
Yonder, tie, tien.
You, vi, vin.
Young, juna.
Young (offspring), ido, idaro.
Young lady (unmarried), fraŭlino.
Young man (unmarried), fraŭlo.
Younger, plijuna.
Youngest, la plej juna.
Yeoman (farmer), farmisto.
Yes, jes.
Yes, truly, jes, vere.
Yesterday, hieraŭ.
Yesterday, the day before, antaŭhieraŭ.

Z

Zany, ŝercemulo.
Zeal, fervoro.
Zealot, fervorulo.
Zealous, fervora.
Zebra, zebro.
Zenith, zenito.
Zephyr, venteto.
Zero, nulo.
Zest, gusto.
Youngster, junulo—ino.
Your, yours, via.
Youth, junulo.
Youth (collectively), junularo.
Youth (state of), juneco.
Youthful, juna.
Youthfulness, juneco.
Yule, kristnasko.
Zigzag, zigzago.
Zinc, zinko.
Zinc-worker, zinkisto.
Zodiac, zodiako.
Zone, terzono.
Zoology, zoologio.
Zoophyte, zoofito.
Zouave, zuavo.

NOTE BY THE PUBLISHER.

The larger English-Esperanto Dictionary, to which reference is made in the Authors' Preface to this volume, and for which Continental Experts have kindly promised collaboration and counsel, is being prepared by Mr. Joseph Rhodes, President, and Mr. John Ellis, the Hon. Sec. of the Esperanto Society at Keighley, Yorkshire. Due notice will be given of the publication of this work.

CHATHAM:
W. & J. MACKAY & CO., LTD.

ESPERANTO:
THE STUDENT'S COMPLETE TEXT-BOOK.

Containing Full Grammar, with Exercises, Conversations Commercial Letters, and two Vocabularies

Edited by J. C. O'CONNOR, Ph.Dr., M.A.

Price One Shilling and Sixpence. By Post 1/7.

THE
English=Esperanto Dictionary.
By J. C. O'CONNOR and C. F. HAYES.

Revised and approved by Dr. Zamenhof

Price 1s 6d net. By Post, 1s. 8d
Foolscap 8vo, 216 pages

THE
Esperanto=English Dictionary.
By A. MOTTEAU.

Foolscap 8vo, 138 pages.
Price, 2s. 6d. net. By Post, 2s. 8d.

FIRST LESSONS IN ESPERANTO.
By TH. CART.

Done into English by JOSEPH RHODES
(President of the Esperanto Society),
And Approved by Dr ZAMENHOF

PRICE SIXPENCE By Post, 6-1/2d
"Review of Reviews" Office Mowbray House, Norfolk Street,
London WC

"The British Esperantist."

A Monthly Gazette in English and Esperanto containing
reading for beginners and those more advanced

It has an International Circulation.

Annual Subscription, 1s 6d, should be sent to the Hon Sec,
British Esperanto Association, 14, Norfolk Street, London, WC